BAAL
The TESHUVA
Survival Guide

Dedication

This book is dedicated to three men who changed my life and the lives of thousands of other Jews: Rabbi Pinchas Stolper's vision created NCSY (formerly the National Conference of Synagogue Youth), without which I wouldn't be who I am today. He and Rabbi Yitzchak Rosenberg, who ran the Orthodox Union's Synagogue Services, made it possible for me to share my knowledge and love of being Jewish with many other Jews.

Rabbi Mat Hoffman convinced me 30 years ago that I could speak in front of an audience. I will forever be grateful that he saw my potential as a public speaker to the Jewish world when no one else did. I thank him for his encouragement and for making it possible for me to develop my ability to share Judaism with others.

To the countless other rabbis and teachers whose love, concern, wisdom, and teaching have influenced thousands of Jews to become observant and knowledgeable—we all thank you from the bottom of our hearts. May the Almighty repay you many times over for your priceless gifts.

BAAL

The TESHUVA

Survival Guide

Lisa Aiken PhD

With Foreword By Rabbi Abraham J. Twerski, MD

ROSSI PUBLICATIONS

Approbation

Dear Friends,

I have read most of the manuscript of The Baal Teshuva Survival Guide by Dr. Lisa Aiken and have found it informative, interesting, and thought provoking. Dr. Aiken has established her credentials as a serious thinker and writer in the Torah community through her previous works on topics of Torah interest. She deals with the complex issues of the "Baal Teshuva" phenomenon of recent time, with the return of many estranged Jews back to their roots. This movement of return was given a surge after the Six Day War. Many organizations have given baal teshuvas an important place on their agendas. Other organizations have been created with this as their sole agenda.

Over the years many statistics have been gathered, methods of kiruv discussed, and the successes and failures analyzed.

Dr. Aiken presents a handbook for both those making the return and those who have to guide and mentor them. Since we are dealing with human beings and not machines, there is no one monolithic model for the baal teshuva. Hence, the plethora of varied and different organizations with different approaches and methods. Dr. Aiken offers advice and guidance that takes this fact of diversity into account.

The points she makes are presented in a lucid manner and will provoke thought and discussion. Although I may not agree with every point made, the presentation is within an acceptable halachic and hashkafic framework. In the final analysis, how to utilize the information given, in a practical sense, will depend on seeking the guidance of a bona fide rabbinic guide who will apply the information halachically and hashkafically to that specific person's situation and circumstances. Dr. Aiken emphasizes this point many times throughout the book.

I recommend this book as an informative guide to this complex issue, from which kiruv workers, baal teshuvas, and the public at large will be able to gain insight and inspiration.

May Hashem grant the author and her family long life and health to continue to benefit the community with further Torah works.

Sincerely,
With Torah blessings,

Rabbi Zev Leff
Rav of Moshav Matityahu
Rosh Yeshivah
Yeshiva Gedolah Matityahu

Acknowledgements

This book is a compilation and distillation of many people's experiences in becoming *baal teshuvas*. I am indebted to the hundreds of *baal teshuvas* who have shared their stories of the good, the bad, and the ugly aspects of becoming religious Jews. I want to thank the many therapists, rabbis, teachers, and outreach professionals who have discussed with me the struggles that *baal teshuvas* face, and how they can best overcome those challenges. Most of all, I would like to thank Rebbetzin Lynn Finson, whose constant concern for the psychological well-being of students in Midreshet Rachel V'Chaya was the impetus for this book.

In addition, I would like to express my gratitude to the outside readers of this book—Rabbis Zev Leff, Nota Schiller, Yaacov Haber, Mordechai Sherr, Ivan Lerner, Abraham Twerski, MD, and Yisrael Levitz, PhD, as well as Rebbetzins Arleeta Lerner and Tzippora Heller—for their helpful comments. I would also like to express special appreciation to Sara Malka Laderman and to Adam Simon and his staff at Rossi Publications for bringing this book to fruition.

First Edition MMIX

Copyright © MMIX by Rossi Publications

Editing and Layout by Rossi Pub.
General Editor: Sara Malka Laderman
Editorial Consultant: Shoshi Kreitenberg
Cover Design: Adam Simon
Production Manager: Adam Simon

ISBN 0-9779629-3-8
ISBN13 978-0-9779629-3-8

ROSSI PUBLICATIONS

269 South Beverly Drive Suite 296
Beverly Hills, CA 90212
310-867-6328

www.RossiPublications.com

10 9 8 7 6 5 4 3 2 1

Contents

Foreword

The Baal Teshuva Survival Guide is a comprehensive handbook for people who wish to become observant of Torah, for their families and friends, for people who are mekarev (seek to encourage others to become Torah observant), for rabbis, and for anyone else who relates in any way to a person making this change in lifestyle.

The term *baal teshuva* is generally applied to a person who wishes to embrace Torah observance. But the words *baal teshuva* may have yet another meaning.

The word *baal* means "owner," and the word *teshuva* means "response" or "answer." Thus a *baal teshuva* is someone *who owns the answer.*

Owns the answer? To what question? Why, to the first question ever posed in the world, when God asked Adam, *"Ayekah*—Where are you?" Rabbi Shneur Zalman of Liadi says that the question posed to Adam, the first human, is an eternal question posed to every human being on earth. "Where are you in your life? What have you done with your life? What do you intend to do with it?"

Unfortunately, Adam's *teshuva*, or answer, was unwise. "I heard Your voice, and I feared because I am naked, so I hid." The *baal teshuva* has the correct answer. "I heard Your voice within me, calling me to You. I am *not* naked, because I am endowed with the Divine spirit You instilled within me, and therefore, I have no need to hide, not from You and not from myself. " The *baal teshuva* is indeed one who owns the answer.

So many, many people try to hide from themselves. Haunted by a delusion of emptiness and unworthiness, they feel naked, and seek to escape this shame in any one of a myriad ways, some manifestly destructive like the various addictions, others by indulging in a lifestyle that does not befit the dignity of man.

Modern society is unprecedently hedonistic, living a perhaps more sophisticated lifestyle than the primitive "eat, drink, and be merry, for tomorrow we die." This is a lifestyle based on the assumption that the world was not created for a purpose, but is the product of a freak accident that occurred many billions of years ago. In a pointless, purposeless world, seeking the maximum of pleasure makes sense.

Those who do not believe in Creation nevertheless have great respect for the wisdom of nature. Every serious scientist will tell you that nature is not stupid; nature does not make mistakes. If all there is to life is to indulge in pleasure, nature made a grave error in providing man with a brain of one hundred billion cells, capable of producing the philosophy of Aristotle, the plays of Shakespeare and the music of Beethoven. Man's miseries, individual and collective, are ultimately due to his anxieties and insecurities. Man would have been much happier with a brain that was closer to the bovine.

If you see a child wearing trousers that drag two feet behind him, a jacket whose sleeves reach the floor and a hat that comes down beneath his nose, you know immediately that he is wearing his father's clothes. These clothes were certainly not designed for him. Similarly, if you consider the enormous capacity of the human brain, it is clear that it was not designed simply to enjoy mundane pleasures.

Just as a body that is deprived of essential nutrients will develop deficiency diseases if these are lacking, so will the human spirit develop a deficiency syndrome if it is not provided with its nutrients. Medicine has identified the symptoms of physical deficiency conditions, and effective treatment can be only by providing the missing nutrients. The primary symptom of the spiritual deficiency syndrome is a pervasive feeling of discontent, unhappiness with life, which can be relieved only by providing the spirit with its essential nutrients.

People experiencing chronic discontent may seek relief by drinking, using drugs, gambling, overeating, seeking acclaim, hoarding money, or sexual indulgence. These can give only fleeting relief, following which the unhappiness may return in an even more intense form. The pursuit of relief requires more of the diversion, often leading to serious addictive behavior.

The Designer of man knows which nutrients are essential for proper functioning of the whole person, spiritual and physical. These are described and prescribed in the Torah.

The epidemic of mind-altering drugs is just one manifestation of spiritual bankruptcy. When the "Just Say 'No' to Drugs" campaign was launched, researchers interviewed people for their reaction. When one 14-year-old girl was asked for her opinion, she answered, "Why? What else is there?" This, too, is the question to which there is a proper *teshuva* (answer), and the *baal teshuva* is one who has the answer.

Dr. Lisa Aiken elucidates the many issues involving the change of the lifestyle to one of Torah observance and provides sagacious guidance. It is a painstaking process, requiring much understanding, consideration, and patience on the part of everyone, but it is the only satisfactory and enduring answer to the challenging question every human faces:

Ayekah—Where are you?

Rabbi Abraham J. Twerski, MD
Founder and Medical Director Emeritus
Gateway Rehabilitation Center, Pittsburgh
Author of more than 50 books

Introduction

"Light bulb" jokes in vogue in the 1980s included the following:

Q: "How many psychiatrists does it take to change a light bulb?"

A: "Only one. But the light bulb has to really want to change."

Q: "How many Israelis does it take to change a light bulb?"

A: "One. But it takes the entire Security Council of the United Nations to denounce it as an act of aggression."

Q: "How many *baal teshuvas* (non-observant Jews who became observant) does it take to change a light bulb?"

A: "One. But it takes two parents to ask where they went wrong, most of their friends to ask if this is just a stage he or she is going through, and a reporter from the *New York Times* to ask if this is the beginning of a national phenomenon."

Since the *baal teshuva* movement began in the 1960s, tens of thousands of Jews have become observant. The movement's effects were so noticeable by the 1980s that the *New York Times*, *New York Magazine*, the *Baltimore Jewish Times*, and even *Rolling Stone* magazine all ran feature articles about this phenomenon. David's story is indicative of why some *baal teshuvas* have made this life-altering change:

Had It All   David is a formerly secular Jew who is now observant. Before becoming a baal teshuva, he thought he had it all. He
had a wife, two great kids, an MBA, a great job, a beautiful mansion
with a swimming pool in Beverly Hills, and two fancy cars in the
driveway. He took vacations all over the world, bought everything
he wanted, and had the best that money could buy. And yet, David
felt that something wasn't quite right—that something was missing
in his life. He had no idea what it was until his father passed away
when David was 35 years old.

Despite having no formal religious background, David knew he
should say *kaddish* (a mourner's prayer) for his deceased father. So,
David walked into a nearby Orthodox synagogue and was surprised
to find that the rabbi there was friendly and warm. The congregants
were a cross-section of ages, backgrounds, and professions—warm
and welcoming, very intelligent professionals well ensconced in
American secular life. It was not the kind of cold, staid synagogue
that his father had left as a boy in Germany.

It didn't take David long to feel comfortable in that synagogue.
He soon had many questions to ask the rabbi, such as: "What is the
purpose of life? Why do we say kaddish for someone who passes
away? What is required to be a good Jew—isn't it enough just to
feel like a good Jew in one's heart? Why do modern people observe
archaic Jewish rituals?"

Not only did the rabbi answer David's questions with intelligence
and sensitivity, he also invited David, his wife Judy, and their children to join him at his Shabbos (Jewish day of rest from Friday night
to Saturday night) table for the special meals of the holy day.

David was eager, but Judy wasn't interested.

David continued going to that synagogue by himself for the year.
He finally convinced Judy to go once. She was so taken by the rabbi's
sterling character, his wonderful explanations of Judaism, and his
warm personality that she became excited about taking a journey
with her husband to discover their religion. Together, they learned
about and started living observant Judaism. They attended beginners' services regularly on Saturday mornings and were soon inviting
their own guests to their Shabbos meals. Within a year, David and

Judy became pillars of their Jewish community and sent their children to a Jewish school. They felt fulfilled becoming givers rather than takers. They enjoyed giving their tithe money to less-fortunate Jews, and they supported Jewish education. They loved sharing their Shabbos table with strangers. They found meaning in comforting those who were troubled or bereaved. They discovered that the "restrictions" of Jewish law actually allowed them to sanctify the most mundane acts and thereby give meaning to every part of their lives. Eating became an act of worship, dressing became an act of holiness, refraining from creative activity on Shabbos became an act of testimony to God's greatness. They realized, slowly but surely, that the nebulous void they had felt prior to becoming religious was the lack of holiness and meaning. When they returned to traditional Judaism, they became acquainted with the souls that they didn't know they had. Their souls had been starving for spiritual health food.

When David was 50 years old, he, Judy, and their four children immigrated to a religious community in Israel.

Jewish Revival Through the combined efforts of outreach individuals and organizations since the 1960s, many formerly non-observant Jews now keep kosher (eating only foods that Jewish law deems spiritually fit), observe Shabbos, and embrace the laws of family holiness. Ephraim Buchwald, director of National Jewish Outreach Program, once estimated that at least 40,000 Jews returned to *Torah* (the Jewish canon) observance between 1970-1990.

The large-scale return of non-observant Jews to Judaism has changed the face of the religious Jewish world. Fifty years ago, it wasn't unusual to see observant Jewish men wearing *yarmulkas* (skullcaps) in the diamond district, in the Lower East Side of Manhattan, or in parts of Brooklyn, but it was rare to see them elsewhere in America. Today, men dressed in the garb of religious Jews don't even occasion a second glance throughout New York—nor on the streets of Miami, Chicago, Detroit, Baltimore, Los Angeles, and elsewhere.

Thirty years ago, kosher food was mostly available in neighborhoods with a significant number of traditional Jews. Today, gourmet and healthy kosher foods and fine kosher wines are available (as we will note later) throughout the Western world, including far-flung places such as the Cayman Islands, Hawaii, and Alaska.

Jewish Learning in Demand   Jewish day schools and *yeshivas* (institutions where males learn about Judaism or study Jewish texts) that once went begging for students are now bursting at the seams. Many even have waiting lists. Judaism and crash Hebrew classes, Shabbos services for beginners, and *Shabbatons* (retreats where Jews get together to celebrate Shabbos) are now standard in many American cities. It seems that all a Jew has to do today to learn about observant Judaism is to access the Internet or pick up a telephone and dial a toll-free number. Waiting in the wings are rabbis, partners with whom to learn Torah, and taped classes on a wide variety of interesting Jewish topics. The plethora of English Judaica publications, Jewish Internet sites, and Jewish outreach activities are all due to the changes brought about by the *baal teshuva* movement and have, in turn, created the resources to successfully attract and assist many more *baal teshuvas* in coming years.

Guiding Baal Teshuvas

With the passage of time, we have begun to understand why non-observant Jews become observant, what helps and hinders them in this process, and how they and their families can best adjust to their myriad changes. To date, the handful of books that were supposed to help *baal teshuvas* have been limited to *halachic* (Jewish legal) questions or specific issues, such as keeping kosher in one's parents' non-kosher home. None so far have addressed the psychological and practical upheaval that *baal teshuvas* go through and none have offered tools to make their transitions as painless as possible. The *Baal Teshuva Survival Guide* is the first book to address these issues in a comprehensive way.

Lone Journey   When I became observant in a process that spanned years, no one advised me about how to deal with relatives who were antagonistic to my religious practices. No one told me how to navigate the day-to-day social challenges of being an observant adolescent in a public high school. No resource people prepared me for the tug-of-war of trying to balance my desire to spend Shabbos and Jewish holidays in a religious neighborhood with the wishes of my not-yet-observant parents that I stay home with them, where I would have to observe the holy days in a less-than-optimal religious environment.

Today, there are many such advisors, but *baal teshuvas* do not always know where to find them (see "Choosing an Advisor" and Appendixes A & B).

This book will discuss how and why Jews become *baal teshuvas*, how to deal with some of the challenges, and how to integrate Judaism into one's life. It will recommend ways of bridging the secular and religious worlds and suggest support systems that can help cushion the inevitable road bumps. It will help *baal teshuvas* to develop themselves spiritually while continuing to interact with others who do not share their religious path.

Indeed, many *baal teshuvas* have discovered a Judaism that their parents and friends knew little about and, in many cases, were anxious to distance themselves from. Consequently, many *baal teshuvas* have to tread a delicate tightrope between observing God's will and dealing with a world that is sometimes hostile to, and ignorant of, Torah values.

Too, there are many parents (and other relatives) of *baal teshuvas* who struggle to understand what has happened to the person they loved. These relatives would like to stay part of that person's life. This book will shed light on how non-observant Jews can live harmoniously with those who are (in the process of becoming more) observant, and vice versa. By respecting and being patient with one another, many bridges can be built.

Guiding the Guide

Yet, this book is not only for people who are becoming, or who have already become, *baal teshuvas*. As I was writing this book, a number of people asked me, "Who will your audience be—*baal teshuvas*, outreach workers, rabbis, teachers, or parents of *baal teshuvas*?"

My answer is "Yes." I hope that *baal teshuvas* will gain valuable insights and practical information to make their journeys and relationships easier and more rewarding. They may also find comfort knowing that they are not the only ones struggling with their issues and to learn that there are many approaches to becoming an observant Jew.

I also hope that this book will help outreach workers, rabbis, teachers, and family members to better understand what *baal teshuvas* go through and to use the insights given here to make those paths easier for all concerned.

Sensitivity to Individual Needs   There are some well-meaning "helpers" whose good intentions do not enable baal teshuvas to resolve their issues in healthy ways. Educators, rabbis, and outreach workers can learn from this book about the emotional and practical challenges that baal teshuvas face and how to guide them in ways that respond to those complexities. This book identifies how to be sensitive to individual needs and how to anticipate when approaches that seem good in the short term are likely to backfire in the long term.

Among other challenges, advisors and educators need to be careful to teach in a way that identifies what are customs, stringencies, and basic Jewish laws. In addition, they must be psychologically aware, sensitive, broad-minded, and experienced in working with a variety of *baal teshuvas* and their issues. Since no one can be an expert in all fields, it is recommended that those who do outreach with *baal teshuvas* not give advice about areas that are not their forte and that they consult experts before they assume that they know how to respond to sensitive topics.

When teachers are sensitive to these issues, the kind of family upheaval illustrated in the following story can be avoided:

Torah at Starbucks   A rabbi went into a Starbucks coffee store, bought a coffee, and sat down to drink it. As he was putting milk into his coffee, a middle-aged man walked over to him and asked, "Are you an Orthodox rabbi?"

"Yes, I am," replied the rabbi.

The man looked bewildered.

"How can you put non-kosher milk into your coffee?"

"What makes you assume that this milk isn't kosher?" responded the rabbi.

"Our daughter went to Israel last year, got involved with a religious group, and is now studying in a seminary," answered the man. "She came home for a week and told us that everything in our home was treif (non-kosher)—the meat, the milk, the dishes, the pots, the pans—the works!!"

The rabbi proceeded to teach the man the difference between stringencies in how Jews keep kosher versus basic Jewish law. While some Jews eat only dairy products that are chalav yisrael (milk that was supervised by a Jew from the time of milking), Jewish law allows drinking chalav akum (milk that comes from kosher animals milked by a gentile) when the government ensures that no non-kosher products were added to that milk. He then explained that some Jews are stringent in eating only pas yisrael (kosher bread that was baked by a Jew) while basic Jewish law allows eating pas akum (kosher bread baked without a Jew's involvement).

The man was both appreciative and relieved to hear this.

Before the conversation ended, the rabbi took the man to the candy counter and showed him the ⓤ, on a bar of Hershey's chocolate. The ⓤ emblem shows that a product is kosher and under the rabbinical supervision of the Union of Orthodox Jewish Congregations of America. The ₀ following the ⓤ means that the item contains dairy. ⓤ, products are normally made from kosher milk that wasn't supervised from the time of milking (chalav akum) and are not from chalav yisrael.

The man immediately reacted, "My daughter told us that the ONLY acceptable ⓤ certification is the plain one, and that ⓤ, means NOT COMPLETELY KOSHER!

Clearly the girl had completely misunderstood what the ּ is for, presumably because her teacher misrepresented its meaning.

This book is an outgrowth of 35 years of *baal teshuvas'* journeys to serve God authentically. I hope that my observations and ideas will help to prevent many of the misunderstandings that cause so much unnecessary divisiveness between parents and children, between observant and non-observant Jews. It is also my wish that this book will help other Jews to connect more closely with God, to their families and friends, and to themselves.

Lisa Aiken
Jerusalem, Israel
Cheshvan 5769 (November 2008)

Part One:
The Path Of The Baal Teshuva

ONE

Why Jews Become Baal Teshuvas: The Case for Judaism

What was it about traditional Judaism that attracted, and still attracts, so many returnees to observant Judaism?

Part of the answer lies in the inherent makeup of the Jewish soul, and part is related to the social changes that occurred during the 1960s and subsequently.

Pintele Yid   Many Jews experience their soul's pilot light (in Yiddish, this is called the "pintele yid") burning at some point in their lives. This soul seeks to (1) improve the world and (2) pursue meaning and spirituality.

Improving the World   Jews have tried to change the world through communism, socialism, and other social movements. Such activism is often based on the soul's yearning to make the world the place that the Almighty wants it to be. Yet, when such desires are manifested in ways that are antithetical to Judaism, the soul really wants to come back to the most important and overriding "ism" there is—Judaism.

Seeking Meaning   When people feel their Jewish soul screaming out in loneliness and pain, those disconnected from their true Source may try to silence it by adopting other religions in their quest for a spiritual connection to God. By the late 1960s, many Jews sought greater meaning and spirituality in life by turning to Far Eastern religions, not realizing that Judaism has its own sensible, authentic, and meaningful spiritual teachings. Other Jews at the time used this wake-up call to find their way back to their roots.

Social Changes of the '60s Revolution   In the 1960s, the Western world saw a social revolution in which many rebelled against authority, traditional religious and sexual norms, and conventional morality and replaced them with their own ideas of right and wrong. The social order in the United States changed drastically, and its effects were felt around the world.

Man-Made Morality   These social changes had far-reaching ramifications. Human emotions and logic can only go so far in designing judicial and ethical systems that make the world a positive, healthy place. The advice of secular leaders is only as good as the gurus of the day. One decade, marriage and chastity are good; the next decade they are primitive. One decade, money is the root of all evil; another decade it is the source of much good. Sometimes, infanticide, euthanasia, and eugenics are despicable; at other times, they are as valued as they were when the Greeks or modern Germans killed undesirables as an important component of their society's development.[1]

When people create their own laws and ethics, societies can become violent, lawless, and exploit others. When people strive to amass money and attain immediate pleasures and comfort, they often lose a sense of transcendent meaning and often get restless or depressed. They expend their energies in activities that aren't healthy and, at worst, damage themselves or the people around them.

Crime   Among the consequences of these social changes were that crime spiraled out of control. As violence affected more and more Americans, even public schools and public transportation in many cities became unsafe. In addition to the usual concerns about crime, many American began to worry about carjackings and kidnappings in the late 1990s. In 1993, nearly 25,000 Americans were murdered, as compared with 9,110 in 1960.[2] Law enforcement officials considered it a triumph that just under 17,000 Americans were murdered in 2006.[3]

More than 13 million Americans are victims of violent crimes every year,[4] and the Bureau of Justice projects the following crime statistics:[5]

One of every 133 Americans will be murdered and one of every 12 women will be raped or be the victim of an attempted rape.

Nearly every American will be the victim of a personal theft at least once, and 87 percent will be personal theft victims three or more times.

Eighty-nine percent of 12-year-old boys and 73 percent of 12-year-old girls can expect to become victims of violent crimes during their lifetimes.

Almost three out of four households will be burglarized at least once in a 20-year period, and nine out of 10 homes will be robbed without forcible entry.

Decline in Marriage   In addition to the post-1960 surge in violence, the change in social mores was paralleled by, and contributed to, the disintegration of the family. Between 1970-2005, the number of marriages per 1,000 women declined by half.[6] Whereas only 5.3 percent of American children were born out-of-wedlock in 1960, that number had soared to 37% by 2005.[7]

Divorce   Sixty years ago, divorce was fairly rare, and most children grew up in two-parent homes. Only 6.3 children per thousand under the age of 18 had divorced parents in 1950. That number doubled to 12.5 by 1970, and nearly tripled to 17.3 by 1980.[8] The traditional nuclear family of a married couple with children made up only 26

percent of households in 1998, down from 45 percent in 1972.[9] Many
singles don't even want to get married, sometimes because they don't
want to fall victim to unhealthy marriages and divorce. It is well
known that first marriages have at least a 40-60% chance of ending
in divorce.[10]

By 1996, only two-thirds of American children lived with their
biological, married parents,[11] and every year since 1997, 1 million
American children have had parents who got divorced.[12] Currently,
nearly half of American children will have parents who divorce,[13]
and almost half of these children will grow up in homes where their
parents divorce, remarry, and divorce a second time before the children are 18 years old.[14]

Erosion of Parental Guidance   Technological and scientific ad-
vances have brought unimaginable wealth and knowledge to Americans, but those gains have sometimes brought other problems in
their wake. Only 63 percent of people in households with children
under age 18 eat dinner together five or more nights a week.[15] Seven
percent of families eat no meals together each week.[16] Due to work
involvements and broken families, fathers are largely absent from
many children's lives. To add insult to injury, use of the Internet,
text messaging, video games, watching DVDs, movies, and television, have replaced meaningful conversation, doing kind deeds for
others, and developing empathy, communication, and real connection.

Drugs & Alcohol   Contemporary lists of societal and emotional
ills go on and on. At least 10-20 percent of Americans have serious
drug and alcohol problems.[17] That is an inevitable consequence of
living in a society where people are taught that pain and discomfort
should be avoided whenever possible, and that life's goals are short-
term—often mindless—pleasures.

Sex   The striving for personal pleasure is also reflected in the
sexual mores of Americans. Ninety-five percent of them have had
premarital sex. For the past 30 years, the median age for a child first
having sex has been before age 18.[18] By comparison, around 75 percent

of unmarried, 19-year-old white women were still virgins in 1960; that percentage had plummeted to 25 percent by 1991.[19] Forty-three percent of white American women who married between 1960-1965 were virgins;[20] by the 1990s, only 14% of such women were virgins when they married.[21] In the 1950s, only one in ten women lived with a partner before marrying him.[22] When cohabitation became legal in the United States around 1970, 523,000 couples cohabited. By 1998, 4.2 million unmarried couples were living together, representing a jump from 0.2% of all couples in 1960 to 7.1% in 1998.[23]

Backlash   There has been a backlash for decades against the changes in Western society. Many people today want to live in a safe world where they can grow and find meaning. They want a fulfilling and lasting marriage. They want something to believe in that is bigger than themselves or the fads of the decade. They want stable moral and ethical standards that have stood the test of time and that have built strong societal foundations. They want to make sure that their lives, and those of their children, revolve around truth and goodness rather than around sex, violence, materialism, and/or mind-numbing substances.

Questioning the status quo, people began to wonder why life itself had become so meaningless and violence and disrespect for social rules and traditions so pervasive. Were people learning values that were causing such negative consequences in their homes, in school, on television, or in the movies? Wasn't there some way to encourage people to become more wholesome and to pass that way of thinking and living on to their children?

The Jewish Response

The Jewish response to seeking healthy structure and rituals is to learn, and live by, the religion that gave the world ethical monotheism and that has continually changed the world for the better. This religion has stood the test of time for more than 3,300 years. Many Jews have decided to embrace a system of absolute morality, self-development, and spiritual striving that requires adhering to a way of life that in many ways is the antithesis of the values that led to the moral breakdown of western society. Some *baal teshuvas* start their journey because they want something more than what secular mores can provide. Many of them are touched when they see the harmony and intactness of observant Jewish marriages and families. Some meet truly observant Jews in the workplace and admire their honesty and integrity. Others see how observant Jews do their best to live Godly lives. Yet others read about God's plan for living and appreciate what such a world based on Torah could be like. Every *baal teshuva* has a unique combination of reasons that he or she was motivated to adopt observant Judaism.

Emotional and Communal Support

In addition to teaching morality that is practiced, not just professed, observant Judaism offers healthy emotional and practical support that the secular world often does not. Its moral teachings promote healthy attitudes and its rituals promote family cohesion and community support.

Healthy Attitudes   A central tenet of Judaism is that it is a great mitzvah (Divine commandment) always to be happy by living in a way that fulfills God's will and feeling a resulting closeness to Him. We are also bidden to be givers more than takers. The Torah stresses how to appreciate, and be grateful for, what one has instead of always wanting more and more materially.

Community Support   The observant community looks after its members from cradle to grave. When someone is ill, members visit the sick person, bringing whatever is needed—a hot meal, a supportive listener, prayers for the person's recovery, even household help. In many communities, families cook and bring new mothers weeks' worth of meals to tide over their families until the woman regains her strength.

At least 10 observant families must live within walking distance of a synagogue or place to pray. They are bonded by praying and studying together, as well as by celebrating holidays and life-cycle events together. When a child is born, has a ritual circumcision, becomes *bar* or *bat mitzvah* (reaches Jewish adulthood), or gets married, the community shares in the joy. They invite one another to their homes for Shabbos and holiday meals. Families invite strangers, those who have no families of their own, relatives, and friends to eat with them. One can travel around the observant Jewish world and always have a place to stay and enjoy kosher, home-cooked meals. The observant Jewish world is, in many ways, a large, global village.

Children who grow up in observant neighborhoods often attend the same schools and summer camps and vacation together. Their families share similar values, Jewish lifestyles, and mutual support.

Jews in financial need are provided charity from communal funds and can get interest-free loans when needed.

When a Jew passes away, people in the observant community provide food and comfort the mourners for at least a week, and often longer. The awesome networking in observant communities typically includes social services, medical care, practical information, job contacts, and help finding marriage partners.

Family Cohesion   A great deal of Jewish observance requires involvement with one's family. Parents are minimally required to teach their children how to live according to the Torah. Mothering is still valued. Often there is a great emphasis on women having children and raising them rather than spending most of their time elsewhere and having maids or nannies raise their kids. There are also social/chessed (charitable) organizations that support mothers with convalescence and housekeeping when necessary. At least once a week, family members sit down together and share Friday night and Saturday meals. They have 25 hours every week when computers, telephones, television, and radio are mercifully silent. Instead of spending Friday nights partying, visiting clubs and bars, or watching movies—or spending Saturdays shopping at the mall, or otherwise being passively entertained—most observant Jews spend Shabbos learning Torah, eating with family and friends, praying, and focusing on the spiritual aspects of life.

Some believe that there is far less drinking and drug use among observant Jews than among the population at large,[24] and the family unit is often very strong. Their sense of purpose and meaning gives them tools to cope with adversity and tragedy. Due to Jews' historical upheavals, many have learned that home and security is not in a physical structure or geographic location—it is a connection with their Creator, with their family, and with a people whose roots go back thousands of years.

Yeshivas and Seminaries   Apart from the nurturing and support by families and communities, observant Jews enjoy social and emotional support in their schools of higher learning—yeshivas for men and seminaries for women. These schools offer peer support as well as nurturing relationships with a rav or rebbe (male religious mentor), rebbetzin (a rabbi's wife, often a religious mentor), or with teachers who provide direction, support, and help with problems.

While secular American families have generally become more fragmented and dysfunctional, many Jews spend time with religious Jewish families and appreciate the latter's relative normalcy and cohesiveness. Many non-observant Jews admire, and are beneficiaries of, the communal caring by observant Jews in a world where people care mostly about themselves. Jews who have been exposed to these positive aspects of religious Judaism often want to know more about a God-centered philosophy and how to bring His vision to reality.

A Personal Journey

Although the above reasons have motivated many Jews to become observant, we each have our unique journeys and story. I was typical of many *baal teshuvas* in the 1960s and 1970s whose journeys to full observance spanned many years. The catalyst for my becoming observant actually started with my secular father's decision to say Kaddish when his mother passed away. That led to his being influenced by an Orthodox rabbi who taught a class between afternoon and evening services at the synagogue where my father went to pray. As my father, who was formerly hostile to observant Judaism and observant Jews, appreciated the ideas that the rabbi taught, he decided that he wanted to keep a kosher home. My mother, however, was not initially prepared for such a major upheaval in the way she lived.

Thankfully, the rabbi's wife taught my mother about the benefits of keeping kosher and becoming more traditional. She also taught my mother how to modify her gourmet, non-kosher recipes so that living in a kosher home would not significantly compromise anyone's enjoyment. Thanks to the individual attention of the rabbi and rebbetzin, my parents decided to send their children to Orthodox Jewish schools. Later, we attended a Conservadox Jewish day school where my fourth grade Hebrew studies teacher taught that God gave the Torah to the Jews and that we were Jewish so that we would observe its laws. I wanted to become observant, but it would be another six years before I met observant Jews who taught me what to do! Until my teens, my sole education about how to observe Shabbos consisted of being told activities not to do on Shabbos. I learned first-hand how unpleasant being observant is when it isn't practiced joyfully, with a family, and as part of a religious community.

None of my classmates in public high school had sought spirituality or religion in their lives as I did. Thus, it surprised me years later to hear that some of them had become *baal teshuvas* in college. These *baal teshuvas* had encountered a wonderful rabbi who ran the Chabad house at the University of Maryland. He helped these college students discover that Torah-observant Jews had the values, direction, and meaning that they sought. They started wondering in college, "What is life all about? Why do bad things happen to people? What difference does it make if I'm Jewish or not? Why shouldn't I intermarry?" Their parents and professors could not give them satisfying answers. Traditional Judaism did.

Finding Stability and Logic in Judaism   Some Jews are initially motivated to become baal teshuvas due to gnawing emotional voids or feelings of meaninglessness. Such catalysts are sometimes necessary to impel Jews such as Daniel to search for meaning in Judaism.

Premium on Study   Daniel became a baal teshuva while in college. He grew up in a small, working class town with an alcoholic gentile father and Jewish mother. The family spent most evenings enduring their father verbally or physically fighting with Daniel's mother. In high school, Daniel investigated various religions, including several varieties of Christianity and Buddhism, but found them all wanting. He couldn't wait to leave his hometown immediately after graduating to go to college in New York. At least there, he knew that he would be intellectually stimulated even if he didn't find answers to any of his existential questions.

In the Big Apple, he encountered many observant Jews. He had never met groups of non-Jews who valued education as much as Jews did. He was always impressed by the Jews' intelligence and began to wonder why, as a group, they placed such a premium on study. He studied Judaism intensively for the next few years. The more he studied, the more sense it made to him. He gradually became observant because he believed in the truth of Judaism, and the Orthodox community gave him the support, acceptance, and love that his own family had never provided.

Sometimes, Jews embrace observance due to an existential, not personal, emotional void. Such voids may surface when a person gets philosophical about life or experiences a tragedy, such as the death of a loved one.

Confronting Tragedy and Loss   Every Jew's soul continually burns with a desire to have a passionate relationship with God. Some Jews only feel their soul's yearning to connect to their Creator when they are faced with a crisis or tragedy. For example, most American parents whose child passes away become more religious. They want to find meaning in such tragedies and develop the tools to cope with their terrible loss. Traditional Judaism can give them both.

If someone offers Torah wisdom at such a time, it can help bereaved people understand why tragedies occur, why death exists, why good people suffer, and how to find meaning in all of life's experiences. Judaism teaches that everything in the world has a purpose, and that the purpose of this world is to spiritually refine our souls. Our job is to spiritually rectify the world, not to get immediate pleasure. Contrary to what many non-observant Jews learn, our souls will go to an eternal spiritual afterlife when our bodies die. There, God will mete out perfect justice and allow us to feel His infinite love.

Many a Jew, including my father, found his or her way back to Judaism due to the death of a loved one. A bereaved Jew who sits *shiva* (mourning at home for a week) and says Kaddish after the death of a close relative not only learns the wisdom of traditional Judaism, but may also experience the compassion of those who live it. That combination may impel the person to continue learning about traditional Judaism and to become observant. It is up to observant Jews to let other Jews know that we needn't flounder in a world without direction, meaning, or constructive goals. Traditional Judaism has had the answers to life's big questions for thousands of years. Unbeknownst to the majority of the world, we gave them a great gift by sharing with others the basics of those answers. Jews need only look in their own backyard to find what so many others have adopted as their own.

Summary

The social revolution in the US of the 1960s and 1970s had many repercussions. These included a breakdown of the family and former social structure, a massive increase in violence, drug use, disregard for authority, a breaking away from belief in God and formal religion, and a questioning of traditional values. As Western society became more morally disconnected, many Jews were raised without any knowledge of—or belief in—traditional Judaism. As a result of these changes, many Jews began searching for greater spirituality, structure, emotional connection, and/or meaning in life. Jewish outreach organizations, classes, and schools were created to respond to this need. Today, many thousands of Jews have found their way back to Torah Judaism. It offers them a more fulfilling spiritual, religious, emotional, and communal life than they had before.

TWO

How Life Stages Affect Religious Change

People come to observance for different reasons, in different ways, and via different channels. The paths to observance that people travel often vary according to age.

Teens & Young Adults

Adolescents want to carve out an identity and role that is different from the way that they were raised. Teens and young adults who were raised with few rules and boundaries may welcome the rules, guidance, and structure of Torah. As they try to make sense of the world, some appreciate how observant Judaism makes life into a coherent whole and fills a spiritual void. It gives direction to their passions, focus for their idealism, and a channel for energy that seeks positive expression. It helps them sort out inner turmoil and chaos and gives form to their present and future lives.

When parents are ashamed of being Jewish, and their children have spiritual yearnings, the parents may discourage their children from learning about Judaism. That keeps the children away from the very source that could give them what they seek, as happened with Pia.

Coming Home   Pia was raised as a Methodist. Until she was a teenager, she and her father attended church together every Sunday, and the whole family celebrated Easter and Christmas. When she was 14, she tried out Presbyterian churches but found them dry and lifeless. She felt an intense desire for spiritual connection but didn't know where to find it.

One day, she was shocked to find out that her mother was Jewish, which meant that according to Judaism, Pia was, too. She felt betrayed that her mother had been so ashamed of being Jewish that she had deprived Pia of her heritage. She decided then and there that she would do everything possible to make up for lost time and live in a way that would actualize her deepest self.

It wasn't easy. She tried going to a Reform temple, but it was not a good fit. It didn't fill her spiritual void. She tried going to Israel on a youth group tour. Unfortunately, it was big on socializing and had little spiritual content. She came back to America feeling no more Jewishly connected than before she left. When she was in college, she took a course in Judaism but the professor lectured in such a sterile and academic way that she felt no affinity for the religion that he presented.

It wasn't until she was 24 years old that Pia finally stumbled upon a Judaism class given by an observant teacher. Instead of being a cold academician, this teacher taught with enthusiasm, emotion and love for the subject. Pia felt for the first time that this woman embodied what Judaism was meant to be. Her teacher invited Pia to spend Shabbos at her house, and Pia enjoyed it immensely. Pia was so excited that she finally had a way to address the great responsibility that she felt to uphold the covenant that God had made with the Jewish people.

Over the next few years, Pia attended a variety of classes taught by observant Jews, and experienced Shabbos and Jewish holidays with a number of observant families. She slowly became observant and moved to a traditional community.

Reparenting   As mentioned above, the shift in the American family life that began in the 1960s has left many teens and young adults yearning for nurturing parental figures, healthy role models, and cohesive families. Some are privileged to find Torah teachers and observant families who can give them what they are looking for. They become baal teshuvas in part because of the warmth they see in intact, emotionally healthy, religious families. The baal teshuvas admire how kind and caring religious parents are and how they give their children meaningful direction, love, and limits. The "solidness" of religious families, and the normalcy that commitment to God and His Torah creates, is a powerful motivation to become religious.

A psychologist once discussed the theoretical approach he used when treating patients. "One of the biggest problems I see is that parents haven't done their job. My job as a therapist is to 'reparent' the people I treat," he explained. While some Jews become observant because they believe in Judaism's theological system, many come to learn about the religion because of Torah Judaism's emotional benefits. Many *baal teshuvas* in their teens and 20s are "reparented" by a nurturing religious mentor or are welcomed into religious families who make them feel part of a healthy family. There, some get more attention and unconditional love than they did from parents, who were too busy to spend quality time with them, who were emotionally unable to make their children feel loved, or who never gave them a meaningful set of values to live by.

Only Tuesday   A baal teshuva once interviewed for a job at a busy law firm. In the middle of the interview, the senior partner's telephone rang. She pressed the speakerphone button and her secretary announced, "There's a call for you on line one. It's your son."

The lawyer pressed line one and asked, "What is it?"

The sad and worried voice of a six-year old came over the speaker, "Mommy, will I see you this week?"

The lawyer curtly responded, "I don't know yet, it's only Tuesday. It's too early to tell."

With more than sixty percent of American mothers working outside the home, many children come home to an empty house after school. Other parents are physically there but are emotionally detached. It is easy to be perpetually distracted by television, the Internet, telephone calls, and working while at home. Adolescents who can't confide in their parents find good listeners in rabbis, rebbetzins, Torah teachers, and Shabbos hosts.

A student once asked the principal of a *baal teshuva* seminary, "Do you know how we teenagers spell 'love?'"

The reply was, "T-i-m-e."

This idea was illustrated by a conversation between a high school student and a Torah teacher:

Randy:	*Guess what, Mrs. Gold, tomorrow's my birthday!*
Mrs. Gold:	*That's great, Randy, what are you going to do to celebrate?*
Randy:	*I told my mother that I want her to give me a present.*
Mrs. Gold:	*What did you ask her for?*
Randy:	*I told her that I want to spend an evening alone with her, just the two of us, without her answering the phone or going on the Internet, and without her getting involved with anything else. I just want some uninterrupted time with her.*

Parents of *baal teshuvas* may feel hurt, betrayed, resentful and angry when their children prefer to spend time with, and get advice from, observant Jews, rather than from the parents. The parents feel that they have invested so much in raising their child and now the child has spurned them in favor of religious fanatics who are enjoying, and brainwashing, their children. There are times when parents are justified in feeling that their children lack sensitivity to their feelings, and *baal teshuvas* need to be more appreciative of their parents' emotions and efforts to be good parents. Yet there are also times when parenting by outsiders saves children emotionally and fills a huge void that the parents—with all of their good intentions—never addressed.

Religious Camps & Youth Groups   Two other avenues by which some teens become observant are religious camps and youth groups such as the National Conference of Synagogue Youth (NCSY). There, the excitement of learning Torah is combined with positive social interactions, and the two forces often draw participants toward observance. Adolescents can find peers who are striving for the same spiritual and moral goals that they are and are provided a wholesome, enjoyable environment where they can socialize with one another.

Challenges Unique to Teens & Young Adults   Whatever their reasons for becoming *baal teshuvas*, adolescents and young adults may have unique challenges because they aren't independent. Most teens either live at home and/or depend on their parents' financial support. When parents disapprove of a child's religious commitment, they can exert great emotional and financial pressure to force the child to give it up instead of respecting their child's choices. A major source of tension occurs around keeping kosher in a non-kosher home. Parents who don't believe in Torah observance may not want to be inconvenienced by making their house kosher, and some parents don't even allow the child to buy kosher food and keep separate kosher dishes, pots, and pans.

It takes tremendous fortitude to observe Shabbos and Jewish holidays when someone lives in a community without observant people or a synagogue. Staying home on holy days when the television is on, music is blaring, people are watching videos in front of you, and the refrigerator light is left on is no picnic. When the rest of the family doesn't respect the *baal teshuva*'s religious choices, and parents won't allow the *baal teshuva* to spend Shabbos elsewhere, observance becomes a misery. Most adolescents need and appreciate support from parents, peers, members of a religious community, teachers and rabbis. People who do Jewish outreach should try to facilitate this kind of support on all levels. The less support one gets in some areas, the more important it is to try to find it in other areas.

Supermarket Shabbos   Jason exemplified the challenges that many adolescents face if they attempt to become baal teshuva. He was so excited to be bar mitzvah (13-year-old Jewish male who attains the status of a Jewish adult) because he wanted to take on the responsibilities of being a Jewish adult. Unfortunately, his father insisted that Jason work at the local supermarket as soon as synagogue services ended every Saturday. Neither Jason nor his parents needed his meager salary. The father forced Jason to work to make sure that Jason would never be observant. The father was especially worried that Jason would enjoy the activities of the synagogue's religious youth group on Saturday afternoons and be influenced by the wonderful rabbi and rebbetzin to become observant.

People doing outreach with such teens can stress to them that even if they can't observe Judaism now, they should observe whatever they can and appreciate that God values whatever they can do. When they become more independent in a few years, they will be free to do more.

College Students

College is the first time that many Jewish students are formally exposed to a variety of religions and religious people. They may connect with a religious Jewish professor or classmate who prompts them to learn more about Torah Judaism or who invites them to experience Shabbos at their home. Debbie and Jay came to Jewish observance in this way.

Influential Professor   Debbie and Jay met in college. She majored in English literature, he in philosophy. One of the courses that he attended was taught by an observant Jew. The professor stayed an hour after teaching his university classes in order to teach a group of interested students about Shabbos observance. Jay was so fascinated by the philosophy lectures that he stayed for the class about Shabbos. He invited Debbie to join him, and she did. They both enjoyed the class so much that they questioned the professor about Judaism. He not only answered their questions, but he also invited them to spend Shabbos with his family. Within the year, Debbie and Jay were attending the professor's synagogue, spent Shabbos with other families in his community, and had attended an observant Jewish wedding. By the time they graduated college, both had become baal teshuvas.

During college years, students sometimes sit around discussing philosophy, the purpose of life, and various religions. A campus Chabad or Hillel House, or kosher dining hall, encourage Jewish students to have these kinds of socializing and discussions in a Jewish framework. It was via an encounter with a fellow college student that Rina and Steven were introduced to observant Judaism.

College Travels Rina and Steven were both from secular Jewish backgrounds. They met at Tel Aviv University. Rina had enrolled there, erroneously thinking it would be a good place to learn about Judaism. When she realized that this was not the case, she tried to read more about Judaism on her own.

One day, she and Steven went on a university-sponsored trip where she met Leah, one of the half-dozen observant students in the school. She invited Rina to spend Shabbos with her on a religious *moshav* (collective settlement, similar in some ways to a kibbutz) while the rest of the trip participants spent Friday night driving back to Tel Aviv. Rina and Steven agreed to join Leah.

When Rina and Steven saw for the first time how religious Jews observed Shabbos, they found it beautiful, yet overwhelming. There were so many seemingly picayune restrictions! You could carry, but only if you were inside a building or an *eruv* (a wire or structure that encases the perimeter of an area). You couldn't floss your teeth or comb your hair. You couldn't flick a switch to turn appliances or lights on and off. If your parents called, you couldn't even answer the telephone. Rina and Steven returned to the university thinking

that they would like more spirituality in their lives, but they didn't
know what form it should take. They certainly didn't think that they
wanted to become observant Jews.

A few weeks later, Leah suggested that Rina spend the holiday of
Purim in a Chabad-Lubavitch community where there would be a
great deal of merry-making. Rina and Steven decided to go. They
stayed not only for Purim, but also for the rest of that week. Their
baal teshuva Chabad hosts spent hours talking with them about their
way of life, Jewish rituals, meaning, and spirituality. The couple
agreed with almost everything their hosts said. Rina and Steven
decided to learn more and enrolled in a yeshiva and seminary when
the university year ended. By the time they got married, Rina and
Steven (now Yechezkel) were fully observant.

Birthright   In recent years, more than 150,000 young Jewish
adults have visited Israel on Birthright programs. Birthright offers
any Jew between the ages of 18-26, who has never been on a group
tour of Israel, the opportunity to go on one for free. While most
Birthright programs do not expose the participants to Torah observance, some do, and some young adults who don't come on a religious program seek traditional Judaism after the ten-day program
ends. They extend their stay in Israel and take Judaism classes or
meet people who influence them to become observant. It is doubtful
that many of these young adults would have become baal teshuvas
without this trip.

Meaningless Pursuits   Yet another impetus for college students
to become observant is the meaninglessness with which many of
them live. The main pleasures on many campuses are drinking and
partying on weekends, using drugs, watching sport events, and having sex. Some students think that there must be more to life than
this. Some are fortunate enough to meet a religious Jew, go to a
Jewish event, or be intrigued by books, Internet sites, or outreach
videos that help them to explore Judaism more intensely. That may
eventually lead to their becoming observant.

Adulthood

In the 1980s, outreach organizations such as Arachim (for Israelis) and Aish HaTorah developed weekend crash courses in Judaism. These kinds of seminars, taught by rabbis and scientists, were soon offered all over the world. In the space of a few hours, Discovery seminars teach what the Torah is, why Jews should observe it, how it was transmitted from Sinai, and the basics of Jewish history. Attendees leave with a much better understanding of what Torah and observant Judaism are and why they are relevant to us. This inspires many Jews to continue learning and become more observant. Some even become observant despite themselves, as happened with Sean.

Discovery About-Face   Sean's parents got divorced when he was 12, and he moved in with his father. They had many serious discussions, including about the meaning of life. Sean's father convinced Sean that the world is so messed up that it's unlikely that God exists. Sean had it drummed into his head that people only believe in God as a crutch.

One day, Sean asked his father why they were Jewish. His father couldn't give him any good reason. Instead, he explained that believing in Judaism was not making a leap of faith, it was jumping into an abyss. His father convinced Sean that Judaism is an archaic religion whose only virtues were that it preached some humanistic ethics.

When Sean graduated college, his father got him a good sales job in a friend's business. One day, Sean spent several hours with an Orthodox Jewish customer. Before leaving, the man asked Sean if he would be interested in spending Shabbos with his wife and him some time. Sean said that he might, but never bothered to call.

Some months later, the man invited Sean to a weekend Discovery retreat. Sean decided to attend with his girlfriend, Julie. The man thought that Sean wanted to learn more about his Jewish roots. In fact, Sean wanted to set the rabbis straight about the fact that there is no God and that Judaism is total foolishness.

Sean was not prepared for what he heard that weekend. From his perspective the rabbi proved, beyond a shadow of a doubt, that

Judaism was an authentic religion that God Himself gave the Jewish people, and that it was incumbent on Jews to follow its laws forever. The rabbi was not simply saying what he felt in his heart. He was using historical and logical proofs that Sean found incontrovertible.

Sean had initially tried to convince the rabbi of the folly of the rabbi's beliefs. During the course of the weekend, Sean began to see the folly of his own beliefs. He knew that to be intellectually honest with himself, he would need to practice that which he now knew was true.

Although it was an extremely difficult process for him, and one that his family vehemently opposed, Sean studied how to be an observant Jew. He first learned how to keep kosher so that he could begin observing a commandment that affected him frequently. He slowly started to observe the dietary laws. Next, he tackled the basics of Shabbos observance. When he was ready to stop driving on Shabbos, though, he had a dilemma. He had recently bought a beautiful house far away from an Orthodox synagogue. Instead of spending Shabbos and Jewish holidays in his house, over the next six months Sean and Julie spent those times with observant families. Before they got married, he was courageous enough to sell his house and move to an observant community.

Today, thanks to outreach professionals, English books, tapes, classes, and websites, hundreds of thousands of Jewish adults who don't live close to observant communities can learn about Torah Judaism in a relevant and interesting way. Stories abound about people who became observant listening to Torah tapes—some while they jogged or drove to work every day!

Seeking God's Will Jews who don't live near a large Jewish community may come to Torah observance in yet other ways, as happened with Rob and Sharon. They got married in a civil ceremony and moved to a small city in the mid-West. They both felt that they wanted a God-centered life, but they didn't know how to do this. So, they attended a local Reconstructionist synagogue where they got turned off by what they felt was a "do-it-yourself religion." Rob and

Sharon believed that if religion was about truth, God and His will had to be in the center, and there had to be some absolute rights and wrongs. They were annoyed that Reconstructionists made people's ideas center stage and that its humanistic values changed year after year.

Next, they tried a Reform synagogue. They got turned off by the rabbi's liberal politics and rejection of traditional morality.

A year later, they tried again. This time they went to a Conservative synagogue, but its rabbi and his teachings were too wishy-washy. People there seemed to be guided by what felt good, not by how God wanted them to live.

Finally, they sought out an Orthodox outreach website and learned about basic Torah Judaism. At long last, they felt something click. This felt to them like a stable God-centered religion. The observant rabbis they met via the Internet put God and His will in the center of their world, and they lived with that focus in their daily lives.

The truth of Torah made sense to Rob and Sharon and they learned as fast as they could how to make life holy. A year later, they moved to a different city with an observant Jewish community and joined a *baal teshuva* synagogue there. Two years later, they were fully observant.

Some adults (and occasionally children) become observant in the process of coming to terms with tragedy and loss or with disability and illness. They are comforted by discovering that what is most important is our souls, not our bodies, and that every experience in life can allow us to create an intimate closeness with the Almighty. An observant Jew can have a meaningful life even if his or her circumstances don't turn out as he or she had hoped. Our greatest opportunities for growth are often through adversity and challenge.

The Test   Sid was an example of how the death of a loved one can be a catalyst for religious change. He was raised to be all-American. His parents emigrated in 1910 from Eastern Europe to America, the land of opportunity. Most immigrant Jews of that era wanted their children to be successful, to have good secular educations, and to have families. They didn't want their children to be religious. The Judaism that they had experienced in Europe was one in which the rituals of Torah observance were burdensome and meaningless. The immigrants didn't want their children to be stifled by the kind of intense and sometimes oppressive Jewish education that they had endured.

It was not surprising that Sid disdained observant Jews and Orthodox rabbis. He thought that they were all mindless people who couldn't think for themselves and who lived in the Dark Ages. He had never heard any intelligent rationales for their outdated customs and laws.

The European Jews who moved to America were right in feeling that the Judaism they knew lacked vibrancy and meaning. That had been their unfortunate experience. However, it was not Judaism that was at fault—their parents and teachers weren't able to transmit the joy and fulfillment of authentic Jewish living and Torah study. It's not so easy to serve God happily when you're trying to survive pogroms, or to find meaning in Judaism when the authorities are confiscating your business, your house, and your land. A thousand years of being forced to choose baptism or death, and being barred from professions and universities, didn't convince many modern Jews that they wanted to stay observant when they had a choice.

After the Enlightenment, when Jews questioned their religion, they rarely got satisfying explanations as to why Jews should observe the Torah. Until the *baal teshuva* movement took off, many Jewish American children had religious teachers who were also ill-equipped to deal with their students' questions.

Sid had a deficient Jewish education, yet in those days it was still important to marry a Jew, to give charity to Jewish cultural organizations like Bnai Brith or the Jewish National Fund, and to say Kaddish for a deceased parent. When his mother passed away, although he didn't like Orthodoxy, he had no choice but to attend a daily Orthodox *minyan* (prayer quorum) if he wanted to say Kaddish for her. No other Jewish denomination could guarantee that 10 men would show up for daily prayer services.

In the process of attending services, Sid began asking the rabbi questions. He also started attending classes. In time, Sid and his wife decided to keep kosher and send their children to Jewish religious schools. Over many years, the couple and their children became observant Jews.

The Influence of Children   Some parents want to transmit Jewish values, but not many rituals, to their children. They also want to keep their children away from the problems that are rife in public schools. Their solution is to send the children to a Jewish day school. The only catch is that once the children want to observe the Jewish rituals and holidays that they learn about in school, some parents decide, "They are taking this Jewish stuff too seriously. Now it's time to take our child out and put him in regular classes." Sadly, the negative moral environments in many public schools are not nearly as fearsome to some Jewish parents as a child's becoming observant. Thankfully, some parents do the heroic thing. They learn and observe more about Judaism to keep pace with their child's Jewish education and ensure that the family isn't fragmented.

"Why Don't We Keep Kosher?"   That was the case with Jerry and Suzanne. They were from Conservative Jewish homes. When they got married, they largely left Jewish observances behind. After completing graduate school, they moved to Detroit and started a family. They refused to enroll their children in public schools because of the amorality and violence there. They decided that it would be best to enroll their children in a traditional Jewish school.

A month later, their fourth-grader came home from school and confronted them, "In school, we learn that Jews are supposed to keep kosher. Why don't we keep kosher?"

Needless to say, the parents didn't have a good answer. Now it was soul-searching time.

Many other Jewish parents would have transferred their children to a different school. Instead, Jerry and Suzanne had a heart-to-heart talk about what Judaism really meant to them. If its values were good enough to admire, why weren't its rituals good enough to observe?

Due to their daughter's prompting, they made their home kosher. Over time, as she grew up, they became increasingly observant because they realized that it was the best way for them to live and to raise their children.

When a child becomes observant, some parents become more observant to keep peace in the family. Not infrequently, the parents later see the truth and value in staying observant for its own sake.

Middle Age and Older

Older, Wiser Many people who attend Discovery or Judaism seminars may agree with everything that they learn there, yet go home and never change their lives. Their emotional contentment with the status quo overrides their belief in a system that requires change and growth. Some may even enroll in Judaism classes, but draw the line at changing.

Older adults sometimes come to Torah Judaism having "been there and done that." Without the passion for money or sensual pleasure that sometimes blinds people to truth and good ethics, older people may be more objective about Torah's sensibility and relevance in today's world. Their intellectual honesty may make them unwilling to stagnate spiritually to stay comfortable as they are. Some are willing to make the sacrifices necessary to live in concert with a Divine plan for their lives—even if it means selling a business, moving to a religious community, studying in a yeshiva, or immigrating to Israel.

Middle-Age Crises Some Jews are jolted by the threatened or impending intermarriage of a child or by an economic or medical crisis that leads them to question the life that they had. Some are brought back to Judaism by their baal teshuva child's modeling a way of life that seems full and meaningful. Others start by kashering (making kosher) their home so that their children can feel comfortable eating there and spending holidays together with them. No matter what the impetus, the parents realize that their lives are not as rich as they could be and they decide that life is too precious to waste any more golden opportunities for growth.

Child-Led Return   A mid-life crisis, combined with a child's becoming a baal teshuva, motivated Al and Paula to become observant. After ten years of marriage, they were living a comfortable life, thanks to his working 60 hours a week while she raised their three children. Life seemed ideal, until the economy collapsed a few years later and he lost his business. Al sunk into depression while his wife held the family together.

Their son Barry was close with his mother, but he wasn't close with Al, who had been a workaholic and a not-very-involved father. On Saturdays, Barry felt envious as he watched observant families stream past his house as they went to and from a nearby synagogue. One day, he decided to go there himself. He didn't understand the Hebrew prayers, but the boys there were friendly and welcoming. One invited him to his house for lunch and Barry accepted. For the next two years, Barry kept going to shul every Shabbos, and he spent afternoons and Jewish holidays at his friend's house.

One day, Barry's parents accepted an invitation to join Barry's friend's family for a Shabbos meal. As Al and Paula spent time with this observant family, they realized that there was great value in the way these people lived. They had good relationships, spent quality time together, and put money and work into a proper perspective. They even had interesting ideas about life issues, such as why people get depressed and how to cope with crises.

That summer, Barry and his friend went to Israel to study in a yeshiva. Around the same time, Al got back on his feet financially. He realized that he had missed having a relationship with all of his children because he had been so busy working—and for what? He could have worked much less hard and had a wonderful family life, too.

Instead of re-entering a business where he would have resumed his workaholism, Al became an employee, making less money but gaining more free time. While Barry studied in yeshiva, Al and Paula made time to learn about Judaism. Once they started observing Shabbos, Al was pleased that he finally had a real day of rest, and Paula was pleased that she had a wonderful husband. He now had a healthy perspective about God's role in providing for their family. Al's job was to work normally five days a week and leave the rest up to the Almighty.

It says in the book of Prophets that before the Messiah comes, the hearts of the children will be turned toward the parents and the hearts of the parents will turn toward their children. We see how this prophecy has been fulfilled by the thousands of Jewish families who are observant today, thanks to children who brought their parents home.

Summary

Jews of all ages can potentially become *baal teshuvas*, but the challenges and motivations may vary depending upon one's stage in life. Adolescents are often fueled by an idealism to live with greater meaning. Their greatest challenges can be living in a home where they are dependent on parents who don't want to accommodate their religiosity or who don't want them to be observant.

College students are often exposed to other cultures and religions, including Torah-observant Jews and Judaism, at a time when they are trying to solidify their identities. They may have the freedom to study Judaism full time in a yeshiva or seminary. Their greatest struggles may be with parents who object to supporting them financially or emotionally if the children eschew secular career and educational goals.

Young adults may become Torah observant to create a stable family with lasting values for their children. Their challenges may involve the need to change their job and/or relocate to a religious community. There may also be intra-familial conflicts when some family members become observant while the others aren't interested in living that way.

Parents sometimes become *baal teshuvas* when their children become observant, and this often leads to greater family bonding. Tragedies and crises, especially the loss of a parent, often motivate adults to become observant as they discover how Torah perspectives make sense of life and give a framework for coping and living.

THREE

Successful Change

Some *baal teshuvas* become observant almost overnight, while others do it over 10 or 20 years. Becoming highly observant within weeks or months is rarely ideal, because it takes far more than technical performance of rituals to become observant. It takes a long time to integrate the drastic changes one undergoes when becoming religious into a person's attitudes, personality, work life, social environment, and family.

Most people try to live in a way that they can be happy or comfortable rather than living by a commitment to truth. If they try to change their lives drastically and abruptly, their changes are likely to be short-lived. If religiously motivated changes prove to be uncomfortable for some time, people may regain their emotional equilibrium by dropping the rituals and beliefs that make them overly uncomfortable. While a small number of people can become stable, emotionally healthy *baal teshuvas* in just a few months or less, most *baal teshuvas* need to move slowly, consider each step along the way and the impact that it will have on their lives, and work through their feelings before moving to the next step.

Body without a Soul   For example, Nina was a young artist who attended a baal teshuva seminary. A few weeks later, she was advised to give up her art career, which involved painting nudes, and she did. She was told to give up her non-Jewish boyfriend and not date for a while, which she did. She learned how to observe Shabbos and kashrut (eating only foods that are kosher), to dress modestly, to pray every day, and to study Jewish texts and ideas intensively. Within a few months, she looked, walked, and talked like an observant Jewess. There was just one problem—she had made mostly behavioral changes without really understanding or internalizing what it meant to have a relationship with God and be governed by a Torah mindset. She had Judaism with a body but without a soul. Once she went back to the "real" world, mitzvah observance became difficult. She dropped her religious practices little by little because she had never learned how mitzvahs (plural of mitzvah) and Torah were to be integrated in her daily life outside of the seminary. When it made her miserable instead of happy to be observant, she stopped talking to teachers from her seminary and distanced herself from religious people who didn't approve of her backsliding.

It was a mistake for her advisors to have condemned her former way of life and encouraged her to change so abruptly. Tethering her down so quickly to behaviors that lacked spiritual or emotional richness was more than she could bear.

A *baal teshuva*'s changes affect every aspect of his or her life—worldview, one's integration into the secular world, work, relationship to family, life goals, and daily behavior. At the same time, their spouse, parents, siblings, children, friends, relatives, and co-workers react to each change. What an upheaval that can cause! When *baal teshuvas* are married or have families who are not on the same page with them, it is especially important that they give those close to them time and support to adjust at their own paces. Becoming *baal teshuva* is not an all-or-none phenomenon. Thinking through the impact that each change will make in different areas of life can help *baal teshuvas* to prepare themselves and those around them to adapt.

Slowly but Surely   Muriel and Alex intuitively understood this. They lived in a suburb of a large American city with their four-year-old son and six-year-old daughter. Muriel began studying Judaism with a teacher from an outreach organization and decided that she wanted to become more traditional. Before deciding to make the house kosher, she discussed her feelings with Alex. He was not ready to give up all non-kosher food and didn't want to resent being more observant, so they reached a compromise—they would make their home kosher, but he would eat whatever he wanted outside the house.

A few months later, they had to decide where to send their children to school. She wanted to send them to a Jewish school. He felt that it would be hard for the children to be around observant children and learn about rituals that Jews should observe while living in a family that didn't observe them. Muriel decided to defer to Alex.

By the end of the school year, Muriel wanted to begin observing some Shabbos rituals at home and to send the children to a Jewish camp. The couple decided to send the children to a camp that had both observant and not-observant children, where the counselors taught basic rituals and Jewish songs, and where the children were infused with good feelings about being Jewish. By the end of the summer, the couple felt that their children were ready for private teachers a few hours a week who would make learning about Judaism enjoyable.

That winter, Alex began making *kiddush* (sanctifying the Shabbos over a cup of wine or grape juice) and saying *hamotzi* (blessing over bread) Friday nights, and the family had a traditional Shabbos dinner together. Yet, Alex wasn't ready to give up playing tennis on Saturday mornings in order to go to synagogue. He didn't understand Hebrew, he couldn't relate to most of the prayers, and Saturdays were the one time that he had a chance to unwind. The couple decided that Muriel would drive the children to a synagogue that had beginner services for adults and fun groups for children while Alex played tennis.

Before Passover, Muriel asked Alex if he would mind joining a religious family in their home to see how a proper *seder* (Passover ritual dinner) was conducted, and he was fine with that. Their family had a wonderful time. By then, Alex no longer felt right eating *chametz* (leavened foods that may not be eaten on Passover) outside the house during Passover and was ready to eat only kosher food throughout the year. Soon afterward, the family decided to stop driving to synagogue and they rented a Shabbos apartment near it. Now that Muriel was no longer a beginner, she could follow the Hebrew services there.

Over a process of six years, Muriel and Alex's family became fully observant. They sold their home and moved within walking distance of the synagogue the same year that they enrolled their children in the synagogue's day school. By moving gradually and thoughtfully, the parents got used to each small change before making additional ones, and their children were slowly and comfortably integrated into a religious community.

Change: A Process with Many Choices

When a Jew decides to observe the Torah, where should he or she begin? Should a man buy and wear *tzitzit* (a 4-cornered garment with ritual fringes worn by Jewish males), or place a *mezuzah* (a biblically required piece of parchment with the *Shema* [fundamental Jewish prayer stating God's unity] written on it) on his door? Should a person start by keeping kosher? Should someone begin by saying a few prayers every day? By lighting Shabbos candles or staying home Friday night? By making time to study Torah every week or learn Talmud every day? When someone begins studying Judaism, what should they study?

How much should someone change at once? When is it time to make drastic changes, such as leaving a job that requires working on Shabbos or Jewish holidays? How long should it take for someone to become fully observant? How does a person prepare for the challenges to be faced as he or she changes?

Learning for Starters   There is no one right answer for these questions. It might be realistic for one person to start learning about Judaism for just one hour every week while it might be best for someone else to study full time. Generally, making a commitment to study Judaism on a regular basis and sticking with it are what's most important. We can't practice what we don't know, and it is easier to take on precepts that we understand. While having a study partner or taking classes is better than studying by oneself, some people don't have that option. Some people can only learn by listening to recorded Torah lectures, by reading Jewish books, or by accessing Internet sites. Some busy mothers only have time to listen to Torah tapes as they are making meals or nursing a baby. Some ill or handicapped people, as well as people who work in remote locations, such as park rangers or people in the armed forces, may not have access to in-person Torah teachers or classes. There are so many different kinds of Jews today, with such varied life situations, that the ideal way for one person to learn may be different from another. Regardless of how someone learns, it is important to have a religious mentor to whom one can address questions and get personalized answers.

Torah Mindset   Making behavioral changes and doing Jewish rituals can be the easiest part of becoming a baal teshuva. Developing a Torah mindset in all aspects of life and changing our character traits in line with that is the hard part. That is why some outreach professionals think that the process of fully becoming baal teshuva can require up to 10 years. The author thinks that it typically takes at least a few years, with the actual number varying according to the person.

Once we learn what Judaism requires us to do in our daily lives, we have to apply Jewish philosophy and ethics to everyday events. How are we supposed to relate to God; treat our families, other Jews, gentiles; and behave in the workplace? Relationships are very complicated! We need to develop faith and trust in the Almighty and to develop attitudes of appreciation, humility, kindness, and the ability to see good in others. We need to train ourselves to see Divine Providence in our lives and to come to terms emotionally and spiritually with challenges, crises, and suffering. We need to learn how to relate to the secular world and how to transform, transcend, or block out the negative influences that bombard us.

Personality Defects   We also need to refine our personality defects, such as tendencies toward anger, jealousy, impatience, judgmentalism, and hedonism. We are supposed to develop altruism and a God-centered view of life. We may have emotional problems that interfere with our religious commitments, relationships, and connection to the Almighty, and confusion about how to create holiness wherever we are. These issues should be worked out.

Community & Dating   Baal teshuvas are advised to find a religious community that is appropriate for them. If they are single, they will want to learn how religious people prepare for marriage, understand how to date in a religious framework, find out how to meet potential mates, and develop the knowledge and skills to stay married to a suitable spouse. Most will want to develop the emotional and spiritual wherewithal to raise religiously and emotionally well-adjusted children.

Old Friends & New   As we change religiously, we typically try to readjust our relationships with our relatives and former friends, while making new friends, finding religious mentors, and developing support systems.

No wonder the process of becoming observant can take 10 years!

How Much Should I Change?

Religious change should be a slow and steady process with emotional, behavioral, attitudinal, and practical adjustments. It is advisable to start a religious journey by making easy changes first and then making more difficult ones as one becomes ready. For example, praying every day is easier than giving up a non-Jewish partner, and eating Friday night dinner at home is much easier than fully observing an entire Shabbos. Each aspect of Judaism can be approached in quantitative and qualitative stages. Someone new to Judaism may be willing to devote 10 minutes a day to Torah study yet not be ready to take on new rituals. Years later, they might have daily study sessions and keep all of the *mitzvahs*, but their arena of growth is trying to pray and say blessings with concentration. We continually find many areas in which we can deepen our knowledge and practices as we become more and more observant.

At first, *baal teshuvas* should expect to be challenged often to change their ideas and ways of living. Some may need to give up their careers, to leave a secular community, to give up their desire to have their parents approve of what they're doing, to leave a non-Jewish partner who has no sincere interest in becoming an observant Jew. Whatever the challenges, people need to be practically and emotionally prepared when they make drastic changes in their lives or they may face negative repercussions later. It is usually best to first find substitutes for what one is giving up and sincerely believe that what one is gaining is worth much more than what one is sacrificing.

Working Things Out Fay was never encouraged to go through this process. She became a baal teshuva in college when she was very much in love with her non-Jewish boyfriend Keith. As she became increasingly observant, and he became increasingly bewildered, they decided to stop seeing each other. Fay then went to a women's seminary to learn about Judaism. A month later, she was set up on shidduch (arranged) dates that were unfailingly disappointing. One day her advisor asked her, "What were you feeling when you when out last night?"

Fay replied, "Nothing. No matter whom I go out with, I always compare him to Keith. I really loved him. I don't think that we ever fully discussed my interest in Judaism and what that meant to him. In retrospect, I think that breaking up the way that we did was a mistake. I keep wondering if I had given him time to adjust if he might have converted. Apart from our religious differences, which I never gave him time to work out, he was an extraordinary guy."

Until Fay works out her unresolved feelings about Keith, she won't be emotionally available to any other man, and dating will be an exercise in futility.

Baal teshuvas should expect to feel some tension about making changes. They don't have to feel 100% resolved before every change they make and many steps may stay a bit uncomfortable for a long time. On the other hand, changes should feel more comfortable with time. If someone feels overwhelmed or very anxious thinking about where their next change will lead, they probably need to talk it over with a spiritual mentor first and not change so much at once. An objective advisor can guide them as to whether they are ready to tackle the next hurdle or if they need to consolidate and strengthen themselves before moving forward.

How To Begin

In general, it is healthy to change one's life in small, but consistent, ways. As each new brick of the foundation settles in, the person will feel that they are on solid ground before going to the next step.

Learning Baal teshuvas should start learning what interests them most. Some suggestions are the Five Books of Moses, Talmud, prayer, Jewish meditation, or practical laws. Long ago, the basics of Judaism were learned in a structured order: Boys started learning the Five Books of Moses at age six, and then they studied the rest of Jewish Scriptures. Some years later, boys studied Mishnah. They began learning Talmud by age 15. Girls would learn practical Jewish laws and how to develop deep faith and good character traits, how to pray, and so on. Today, the topics and structure vary from school to school, and from person to person.

Besides studying what someone loves, newcomers to Judaism need to learn the Jewish laws that pertain to daily life, such as praying, keeping kosher, being careful not to speak badly about others, honoring parents, giving charity, and observing Shabbos and holidays. Getting a basic knowledge of Hebrew and Jewish prayers will facilitate newcomers' integration into a religious community and help them feel at home in the synagogue.

Kosher People who want to keep kosher might first stop eating pork and shellfish. Next, they might forego eating dairy and meat at the same meal. Later, they might buy kosher meat and poultry. Eventually, they will no longer eat in non-kosher restaurants. By that time, they will check food labels and make sure that products have proper rabbinical supervision, and they will buy only kosher food. Finally, they will be ready to ask a rabbi to help them make their house kosher. This entire process may span a year or more for many people but may take others considerably less time.

Hard for One, Easy for Another   Some commandments that are easy for many people are hard for others. Some men find it easy to put on tefillin (Biblically required special boxes containing Biblical verses that are tied to a man's head and wrapped around his arm during morning prayers) every day but don't want to study Judaism more than one hour a week. Others find it easier to study Torah every day and find it difficult to lay tefillin. When men put on their hand tefillin they say, "I will betroth You to me forever, and I will betroth You to me with righteousness, justice, kindness, and mercy. I will betroth You to me with fidelity and will know God." Putting on tefillin symbolizes marrying God, and men don't take marriage lightly. Some men don't want to put on tefillin even once before they are sure that they will continue doing it for the rest of their lives.

While every commandment that we do brings our soul closer to its Creator, *baal teshuvas* must be careful not to take on too much too soon.

Easing In   Pamela figured this out on her own. She was unemployed for nearly a year and was almost out of money when she got a job in another city. She was thrilled to have a source of income doing work that she enjoyed and which she found fulfilling.

As she settled into her new surroundings, a co-worker invited her to a class in Judaism, and Pamela went. It was so fascinating that she continued attending classes several evenings a week. She soon learned that she shouldn't work after sundown on Fridays or on Jewish holidays.

She realized that she could leave at the end of the work day on Fridays during the summer because the sun set late enough for her to get home in plenty of time to get ready for Shabbos. During July and August, she ate Shabbos meals with observant families in her neighborhood and learned from them what observing Shabbos entailed.

By the time Labor Day came, she had already worked for six months and was well liked at her job. A few weeks before the High Holidays, she asked to take off on the Jewish New Year (*Rosh Hashana*) and the Day of Atonement (*Yom Kippur*). Her boss agreed because she was such a valued employee.

As she broke the fast with friends after Yom Kippur, she found out about the holiday of Tabernacles (*Succot*). She had just learned about Rosh Hashana and Yom Kippur, and now there was another holiday?! She would have to take off four more days on short notice? What would happen to the important business presentations that she had to make? She decided to work on those days, but ate dinner those nights with some observant families.

By the time early Shabbos began in November, she had a good track record at work. When she asked her boss to leave at 2:30 pm on Fridays and make up the time during the week, he was amenable to her plan. Several months later, she was more observant and asked to take off for the first and last two days of Passover. This, too, was not a problem.

By making changes gradually, she was able to learn about Judaism and integrate into a religious community. This made her path to observance relatively uneventful. Had she decided to observe all of the holidays before she was ready, she may have lost her job and resented Judaism for "messing up" her life.

Having a religious mentor can be invaluable when these issues arise. *Baal teshuvas*-in-process can feel pressured to conform, either to gain approval of secular people who are important to them or to be similar to the observant people they want to be like. A mentor can help *baal teshuvas* make changes in a healthy way as they go through complex behavioral, emotional, social, and religious changes that lead to spiritual growth.

Keeping Things Positive

When a *baal teshuva* has a spouse and/or children, he or she must be aware that each of them has a different emotional makeup. Forcing religion on others is never good, nor is encouraging everyone to be religiously observant in the same way at the same pace. People are most eager to become observant when it is a positive experience for them and when there are substitutes for enjoyable activities that become proscribed.

For example, most American children and adults regularly watch television and movies. If someone wants his family to observe Shabbos and abruptly takes away their pleasures, the family may resent Judaism. So the *baal teshuva* will need to find enjoyable substitutes. Try replacing television time with enjoyable family dinners, fun or interesting board games, singing, or interesting discussions. Some families will prefer the change of scene if they substitute activities that are enjoyable to everyone.

The purpose of Judaism is to have a relationship with God and to live meaningfully, and the ideal is to do it in ways that are joyful and pleasant. Creating balance and normalcy are important keys to successful change.

Summary

To become an observant Jew, one must make behavioral, emotional, attitudinal, familial, social, and sometimes geographical, educational, and work changes! These are best done with the guidance of a sensitive and knowledgeable rabbi and/or spiritual mentor. Drastic changes usually don't last and usually impact adversely on oneself, one's family, and one's friends.

It is often best to change gradually, stretching oneself to do some uncomfortable behaviors that are not overwhelming. Try changing first in those areas that are least disruptive to your life.

When changes involve a loss of enjoyable activities, it is helpful to replace them with other enjoyable pursuits that are religiously acceptable. For example, it is important to have a support system of observant friends to replace those that one loses when changing communities or when one adopts a religious outlook on life.

As *baal teshuvas* change, they must also be mindful that what makes Judaism enjoyable or meaningful for others is not necessarily what makes it seem right for them. *Baal teshuvas* who want to encourage others to become more observant must do so with sensitivity to others' personalities, feelings, interests, and lifestyle. While Judaism is meant to help every Jew develop his or her spirituality, each of us must find the right path, at our own pace, to help us get there.

Part Two:
Becoming A Baal Teshuva

Finding the Right Approach to Judaism

When God created the Jewish people, we were 12 tribes from four different mothers. Had the Almighty wanted us all to be monolithic, our people wouldn't have started this way. Each tribe is supposed to have a slightly different path and every Jew has a different role to play in bringing spiritual perfection to the world.

Because we are all different, we each need to find our unique path within Judaism. We need a path to observance that fulfills us intellectually, emotionally, spiritually, and physically. The ways that we do Jewish rituals, pray, study Torah, raise a Jewish family, participate in a Jewish community, and generally live our lives should be emotionally and religiously fulfilling.

Newcomers to observance may not know that there are many different approaches to Judaism (sometimes called *Yiddishkeit*), all of which can be authentic. There is more than one "right" way to be and think like an observant Jew. There is an expression, "The Torah has 70 facets." The only way that a *baal teshuva* can discover the path that suits him or her best is to learn about, and experience, various approaches to Torah Judaism, aided by a religious advisor to guide him or her. This may include taking classes given by a variety of teachers in various venues. Such opportunities exist at retreats, conferences, community talks, local religious schools, seminaries or yeshivas, and synagogues. Thanks to technology, there are currently more than 15,000 taped Torah lectures on every topic imaginable that can be downloaded from the Internet, purchased or borrowed from Torah-tape lending libraries. This kind of exposure allows *baal teshuvas* to discover with which teachers and approaches to Judaism they resonate most.

Personalities   People don't become observant in a vacuum. We bring our personalities with us. Some people are more outer-directed while others are inner-directed. Some approach God, themselves, and others with an attitude of love and giving, while others are more tuned into the Almighty's awesomeness and power. They value the importance of submitting to His laws and justice. Thus, an emotional person is likely to gravitate to classes and to a flavor of Judaism that emphasize connection with God and people, love, and kindness. An intellectual is likely to thrive in classes that are intellectually challenging and that require studying and analyzing texts. A "free spirit" may gravitate to Jewish mystical ideas and meditation, while someone who appreciates order will study and practice Jewish ritual and self-discipline. If we can identify what predominates in our personality, we can more easily figure out which kinds of classes will speak to us and help us grow.

Teaching Approaches   With time, (potential) baal teshuvas learn that different teachers have very different styles. Each approach has merit for some students but may not speak to others. One teacher will focus on the Torah's psychological insights; another will teach how to work on character defects. Yet a third will describe how to draw spirituality into our daily lives. Some teachers teach how to live Judaism in the most careful way possible, hoping that students may do much of what they learn. Other teachers will try to present lenient approaches, expecting that people who hear reasonable ideas that are not too different from what they already know or practice are likely to wholeheartedly adopt these changes. Some classes emphasize the joy and emotional fulfillment that comes with having an intense connection to our Heavenly Parent. Some focus on textual learning, others on integrating spirituality into daily life. When baal teshuvas can identify a few local teachers whom they especially like, these people may be able to guide them in finding an approach to Judaism that will suit them the best.

Topics   People should start learning by studying a topic that interests them, then read books and take other classes that round out their knowledge of how to actualize themselves as Jews. Some baal teshuvas will really enjoy listening to Jewish history, while others will gravitate to explanations of the weekly Torah portion. Still others will find that Jewish philosophy is their cup of tea. Those with legalistic or analytic minds may love studying Talmud. There is not one "right" topic to study.

Perspectives   Since people are so different, potential baal teshuvas need to find a school, classes, and a community whose teachers, role models, and neighbors help them take away much that is positive and not be turned off by approaches that don't fit them.

A (potential) *baal teshuva* may come to a class or school and find it disappointing for any number of reasons. The person would be wise not to give up and think that those subjects, or those teachers' approaches, represent the only authentic forms of learning and practicing Judaism. An advisor, teacher, or *baal teshuva* friends can help the person find classes or a school that does speak to him or her. If that isn't possible, one can seek advice from a *baal teshuva* Internet site. Potential *baal teshuvas* should never be made to feel that there is something wrong with them if they can't easily find an approach to Torah learning that suits them.

In time, *baal teshuvas* hopefully balance their preferred approach with classes and teachers from other perspectives as well. One of the many beauties of Judaism is that it is "big" enough for every Jew to find his or her place in it.

Judaism Is Living, Not Only Learning

There can be a vast difference between admiring and loving someone's ideas and living the way that person does. If *baal teshuvas* love what they learn in their classes, some will also want to live as their teachers do. This can be a mistake for the *baal teshuva* if a teacher's ideas are wonderful in theory, but the teacher's lifestyle doesn't suit the *baal teshuva's* personality.

Living Like the Goldbergs   For example, Rabbi Goldberg was a popular Chassidic rabbi at a women's seminary. He was intense, handsome, funny, and very insightful. Women from all kinds of backgrounds enjoyed his classes. Some even dreamed of marrying a man like him. Yet, they knew very little about his real life and only extrapolated from knowing him as a teacher and counselor to what they imagined he was like as a husband. Marrying someone like him was advisable for those extraordinary students who were prepared to be the kind of wife that his wife was. Most of his students, though, would not want to make the necessary sacrifices nor work as intensely as he had on his spiritual self-development.

The reality of Rabbi Goldberg's (and his family's) life was that he got up at five o'clock every morning. He prayed at an early minyan, taught a Talmud class in his synagogue for an hour, came home, helped get his children off to school, grabbed a cup of coffee, and traveled to his first teaching job of the day. He taught at a boys' school all morning and ate lunch there. In the afternoon, he went to a seminary where he taught another class, followed by several hours of counseling students. He spent the next two hours preparing his classes for the next day. After driving home, he spent half an hour interacting with his children while his wife graded papers and prepared lesson plans for her classes. He ate a rushed dinner with his older children while his wife bathed the little ones and put them to bed. He then went out to evening services (*maariv*), returned home exhausted, and made necessary phone calls. He and his wife rarely ate meals or spent much time together except on Shabbos and Jewish holidays. His wife raised their large family while working as a teacher to augment his income.

This way of life was very fulfilling for the Goldbergs. They wanted to use every minute of life to spiritually perfect themselves and the world and to serve their Creator. They were beautiful models of how Jews can live fully, but the specifics of how they served God would not suit everyone.

Less-Intense Lifestyle Brett became a baal teshuva thanks to a rabbi on his college campus. The rabbi was very warm, attentive, interesting, and spiritually attuned. Brett had spent Shabbos at the rabbi's house many times and enjoyed the wholesomeness of the rabbi's family life. Brett decided that he wanted to be more observant, but he couldn't see himself living as the rabbi did. It was far too intense for him. While Brett wanted to emulate the rabbi's character traits and commitment to Judaism, the details of how the rabbi lived were not for Brett.

After Brett graduated from college, he moved to a community that had a modern Orthodox synagogue. He loved the way the rabbi integrated his knowledge of the secular world with Judaism. The rabbi had a warm personality, and his classes were a nice combination of intellectual ideas mixed with emotional impact. Brett's classmates invited him to spend Shabbos and Jewish holidays with them, and he enjoyed seeing how different Jews had a variety of approaches to observant Judaism. By year's end, Brett had settled into this community and had adopted a modern Orthodox lifestyle himself.

More Inspiring Lifestyle Gitty felt a great sense of urgency to make the most of her life. She lived in a modern Orthodox community and took weekly classes in the local synagogue. She walked away from each class knowing more Torah ideas, but she did not feel inspired, motivated to become a better person, or emotionally moved. Shabbos felt hollow, with conversations at the table often revolving around politics, money, shopping, dating, and other mundane topics. She never felt sanctity or close to God in that environment.

She started spending Shabbos in a *chareidi* ("ultra-Orthodox") neighborhood where the day of rest had a totally different character. The women had large families and often cooked for the less fortunate. They invited people to their homes who would otherwise be alone on Shabbos and Jewish holidays. Most of the conversations at the meal centered around Torah, self-improvement, or how to help others. There were women's classes on Shabbos afternoons that included saying Psalms to aid the recovery of sick people. The classes themselves were inspiring, always ending with practical ideas about how to become better people.

The more Gitty spent time in a chareidi environment, the more she was attracted to their way of life. The modern Orthodox world seemed too complacent and compromised for her. It was not long before she moved to a chareidi community and married a business-man who studied Jewish texts at least two hours every day. His rabbi became her rabbi, and he helped them grow religiously as individuals and as a couple.

As *baal teshuvas* visit religious Jews on Shabbos, holidays, or at other times, they should consider whether those Jews have the kind of religious life that the *baal teshuva* would like to live. When *baal teshuvas* listen to teachers or to taped lectures, they should think about whether the speaker's *hashkafa* (religious outlook) feels right to them. When they meet other *baal teshuvas*, or are hosted in different homes for Shabbos, they should discuss different approaches to observant Judaism and how each *baal teshuva's* religious advisor may or may not be suitable for themselves.

Even though there are general guidelines about how to live a "religious way of life," there is no one way to do this, nor is there only one "religious community." There is a wide spectrum of religious communities, a range of how rabbis *poskin* (determine how Jewish law should be practiced in specific situations), and a variety of Torah viewpoints on any number of topics. Becoming a healthy *baal teshuva* involves finding a rabbi, a *hashkafa* (a general religious outlook), and a community that best suits your personality and the way that you want to live for the next few years. As you grow and change, you may change your hashkafa and, with it, your community and rabbi.

Religious Pressures To Conform

Resisting Disapproval Baal teshuvas sometimes need to go against social pressures to conform and adopt a religious approach that is best for them. Since some people will always disapprove of others, most baal teshuvas will need to deal with others' disapproval of their choices.

What are some of these social pressures? In most religious communities, it is expected that singles of marriageable age should date in order to get married. Single *baal teshuvas* who are not ready to date shouldn't do so just because everyone around them is dating.

There are pressures in some schools or communities on *baal teshuvas* to adopt religious stringencies that aren't appropriate for everyone. In some places, there is pressure to give up parts of one's identity and personal preferences in order to fit in. Sometimes, observant people may be uncomfortable with the *baal teshuva's* style of dressing, acting or thinking even when there is nothing actually wrong with it. They may insist that a *baal teshuva's* ideas or behaviors aren't "kosher" because they make the first person uncomfortable. Yet, the Torah may not object to these diverging ideas or conduct. Some *baal teshuvas* need to find a different rabbi, advisor, community, or school for guidance when this happens.

Andy had an unfortunate experience with a narrow-minded religious advisor. He had just finished tenth grade at a public high school. He had studied Judaism on his own for three years, and was completely observant, yet lacked formal Jewish learning. He very much wanted to study intensively in a yeshiva high school. When he met with their *mashgiach ruchani* (religious supervisor), he told the rabbi that he wanted to study Torah, but he also needed to learn secular subjects and get a high school degree. The mashgiach wanted Andy to enroll full-time in the yeshiva and stop learning secular topics, but he didn't tell Andy that the school couldn't accommodate his request and leave it at that. Instead, he told Andy that anything other than learning Torah full-time would be a serious mistake that he should not consider. The mashgiach's refusal to legitimize Andy's path meant two things: a) Andy never found out about other programs in his city where he could have done what he wanted, and b) the rabbi's discomfort with secular education meant that Andy stayed in public school and got no formal Jewish education until after he graduated.

People shouldn't lose their individuality and uniqueness in order to become observant. A wise rabbi or advisor who is experienced working with *baal teshuvas* can be invaluable in helping newcomers navigate this challenging area.

Religious Leniencies Becoming observant involves molding one's personality, ideas, attitudes, values, and habits to fit into a new view of the world. In their zeal to become religious as quickly as possible, some baal teshuvas don't anticipate that they still need time to make a transition from their former way of life to their new way of life. Some do not appreciate the importance of making changes gradually and with less strictness at the beginning to help people stay their course. To this end, it is important to value the flexibility in halacha (Jewish law) and not think that stricter and restrictive are always better.

It is important to know that when a rabbi prescribes a leniency, one should use it—especially when domestic harmony is at stake. Leniencies are an integral part of Jewish law and of finding each person's rightful place in Judaism.

Do I Have To Give Up Me To Become Religious?

Frum is a Yiddish word that means "an observant Jew." A Chassidic scientist once told the author, "Every Jew needs a *'frumometer'* to tell you how religious you are compared to other Jews. You set the *frumometer* at relative zero, which shows how many mitzvahs you are doing at the time. Of course, whatever you do is normal. Any Jew who keeps at least one mitzvah more than you is *meshuggah frum* (crazy religious), and anyone who keeps at least one less is an *apikoros* (apostate)!"

Many a truth is said in jest. *Baal teshuvas* may need a lot of self-confidence to adopt a flavor of Torah Judaism that is different from that of their friends, from that advocated by their school, or from the one that predominates in their community.

When an author writes a book, she must decide whom she wants to address and whom she doesn't mind alienating. *Baal teshuvas* go through a similar process. They need to ask themselves, "With which approach to religious Judaism can I best live? Am I comfortable with other people who have those religious perspectives and practices? Will the version of observant Judaism that I adopt allow me to express myself most fully and joyously and feel close to God?" They can find answers to these questions in concert with a religious advisor.

Appreciating Baal Teshuvas   Most baal teshuvas want to be accepted by other religious people and fit into a religious community. Yet some lose something unique and precious about themselves in the process. Baal teshuvas need to recognize that they have made the religious Jewish world a far richer place by bringing with them their knowledge of the secular world and their unique experiences with it. Their backgrounds make Judaism more interesting, relevant, and vibrant. Their knowledge and talents in music, the arts, drama, technology, science, languages, writing, psychology, and education have opened doors for thousands of non-observant Jews to come to Torah observance and have made the world a better place. They have breathed life into educational methods and ways of transmitting Torah with their cutting-edge ideas. They have shown how God can be found in the furthest recesses of the universe by using scientific knowledge to understand Torah and by using knowledge of Torah to inform science. They have sanctified God's Name in public by being outstanding professionals and experts in a variety of fields where their expertise and caring has changed people's lives for the better.

Classy & Kosher   On a more mundane level, baal teshuvas have also made living Jewishly easier and more pleasant. Fifty years ago, there were three kinds of kosher wine—sweet, terribly sweet, and unbearably sweet. Then, it was unthinkable that kosher wines would some day win international awards and be served at formal dinners for US Congressmen and Nobel Prize winners. While Judaism frowns on hedonism, there is a place for quality kosher food, outstanding wine, and gourmet kosher restaurants. Every potential evil has an equal and opposite power for good. By bringing their interest in tasty, quality food and wine to the religious Jewish world, baal teshuvas have torn down many barriers to non-observant Jews' becoming religious and to traditional Jews' being derelict in keeping kosher. It is so easy to find delicious kosher food in so many parts of the world that the once-prevalent idea that kosher food means poor quality is no longer the case. In many cities, observant business people can take out clients to strictly kosher, classy restaurants without having to compromise their kosher or business standards. Non-observant people can now keep kosher without having to give up much gastronomic pleasure. Many relatives of baal teshuvas who are otherwise not observant have been willing to make their homes kosher for this reason.

World-Traveller & Kosher   Today, observant Jews can travel virtually everywhere in the world without compromising their observance. There are kosher tours everywhere, from Alaska to Antarctica, the Far East, and Africa. Observant Jews can find God in nature everywhere in the world, from the air and underwater, from tropical rainforests to ice-fields to deserts.

McKinley Marvel   A baal teshuva couple went on a trip to Alaska where they marveled at God's awesomeness and power. They saw an abundance of amazing wildlife and stunning natural beauty. As they were in the middle of nowhere, feeling awe of God as they admired the highest mountain in North America, they were shocked to see an entire busload of observant Jews filing past them. The people turned out to be from all over North America, on a tour organized by the Orthodox Union!

Healthy & Kosher   Unfortunately, the traditional diets eaten by Jews from Eastern European backgrounds are often correlated with major health problems. Challah and daily bread made from bleached flour; rich desserts laden with sugar and margarine; massive amounts of unhealthy candy given as rewards, at Shabbos parties, and for portions that Jews send to one another for the holiday of Purim; chemicalized foods and dairy substitutes; sweetened and colored sodas and drinks; and red, fatty meats have contributed to the epidemic of obesity, diabetes, heart disease, and cancer among religious Jews. Two decades ago, a study done at Maimonides Hospital in Brooklyn showed that observant Jews had the highest incidence of these health problems of any group of their patients. Baal teshuvas have brought awareness of these dietary issues to "always religious" (always know as frum from birth, or FFB) Jewish communities in cities like Brooklyn and Jerusalem.

Baal teshuvas also introduced dietary changes, including removal of chemicals and sugar from children's diets, and supplementation with fish oils and other nutrients. Hopefully, the knowledge that many *baal teshuvas* have of the relationship between diet and health will continue to impact observant communities to good effect.

Media & Mental Health   The explosion of Torah that is now on the Internet and CDs is partly thanks to baal teshuva computer and graphic experts. Baal teshuvas' influence has also resulted in the creation of performing and visual arts schools, as well as mental health training institutes, that conform to Torah (see Work and Money section). Baal teshuva filmmakers have even brought Jewish ideas and pro-religious and pro-Israel publicity to the world. By using mass media, they have dispelled many stereotypes about observant Jews and Torah Judaism and revolutionized the accessibility of Torah to all Jews.

Unique Gifts   I am from a family in which each child is very different from the next, and we have led unconventional lives. It once bothered me that I couldn't fit into any religious community. My sister, who believes in turning one's individuality into strengths that enrich the community, created a holistic, Torah-teaching farm to benefit religious Jews. Raising her children on this farm, she taught me she sometimes needed to "teach my children how not to fit in."

What wonderful words! How many *baal teshuvas* try so hard to fit into a religious community, only to be told directly or indirectly that they will always be different, or that they have to give up their individuality in order to be accepted? *Vive la difference!*

Sometimes, *baal teshuvas* need to take their holy sparks and channel them in unconventional ways so that they can make their spiritual contributions to the world. For example, I became one of the few observant, American-born, female clinical psychologists in the 1970s, despite criticism and disdain by some "always observant" Jews for choosing this career. Thirty years later, there are many religious Jewish women psychologists, and they are respected professionals. I was also among the first few observant women speakers who did international outreach and who wrote English Judaica books. This was despite not being taken seriously by many "always religious" Jews, who often disapproved of my ideas. A decade later, some of my ideas that they criticized most harshly proved to be both prescient and important enough for the "always observant" world to implement. Proper guidance can help *baal teshuvas* to make the world a better place by using their gifts instead of burying them.

Summary

God gave the Jewish people a Torah and system of living that is "big" enough to encompass every Jew. Since no two of us have the same spiritual task to accomplish, we were each given unique personalities, minds, interests, strengths, weaknesses, life circumstances, and challenges. We were meant to apply Torah to the lives that we have in slightly different ways in order to uniquely fulfill our purposes here.

There are many facets to authentic Judaism, and each of us needs to find the one that matches our soul and allows us to maximize our service to God. The nuances of our chosen path will govern our religious outlook, how we view the secular world and secular knowledge, how we observe Jewish law, what kind of Jewish community we live in, and where we send our children to school.

It is important for every *baal teshuva* to have models of the kind of Jew they aspire to be. A knowledgeable and sensitive spiritual mentor and/or rabbi can help guide us to be observant in a way that both respects our individuality and allows us to live a fulfilling Jewish life.

FIVE

Emotional Aspects of Becoming Observant

At some point, becoming observant means developing a healthy relationship with God. However, people who had bad relationships with one or both parents will often have a problematic relationship with their Heavenly Parent—the Ultimate Authority Figure—as well. Part of becoming observant involves working out these issues along the way. Otherwise, one's emotional blocks may limit one's religious growth, especially when challenges or crises occur.

Many observant people perform Jewish rituals without feeling connected to a God who loves us more than we can imagine. Many people mistakenly think of Judaism as a lifelong contest in which God keeps a heavenly scorecard and we try to accumulate enough spiritual "points" to win a place in the next world. In this view, life is about doing more good than bad acts in order to get a nice reward in the afterlife. People who live this way either don't know, or don't relate to, the idea that Judaism is about having an ongoing relationship with the Almighty.

Sadly, many Jews live only a "mechanistic" Judaism because they don't believe or feel that God loves them. In fact, a survey published in *Time Magazine*[1] revealed that 42% of American Jews believe in a distant God who does not interact with the world, who only set the laws of nature in motion. Some observant Jews never fully embrace the Jewish idea of God as a Being Who is All-Good, Who created the world and people only because He wanted to give of His goodness to us.

It is easy for people who go through painful experiences to lose faith if they don't feel close to a Heavenly Parent, or if they feel that God doesn't care about them. Part of being Jewish requires doing spiritual or emotional work to remove blocks that otherwise mar our close relationships with people and with our Creator.

People who can't trust people often feel that they can't trust God, although some of these people feel that they can *only* rely on Him. If people feel angry or hurt by their Creator every time they undergo painful circumstances, they will not use the difficulties that He sends their way to draw closer to Him.

We can only pray meaningfully if we can relate to a Being who loves and interacts with us. When prayer lacks a sense of relationship, it becomes either a rote exercise or a way that people try to manipulate the One Above to give us what we want. Its real purpose to intensify our relationship and bring us closer to our Creator is missed.

Gradual Changes

Healthy religious changes may need to be worked through emotionally before they are slowly integrated into one's life.

Some *baal teshuvas* gradually become observant by taking on one new "major" mitzvah and some "easier" ones, every year. Others do a bit of this and a bit of that, adding to their knowledge and repertoire of mitzvahs as time goes on.

Supportive Space   Manny understood very well that becoming observant would require a different path for himself than for his wife. He and his wife had been raised as religious Jews, but they left observance behind when they went to college. One day, Manny heard a charismatic rabbi speak about what being Jewish is all about. Afterward, Manny decided to return to observant Judaism, but his wife did not want to become observant when Manny did. Instead of pressuring her to observe what he did, Manny walked to the synagogue on Shabbos and holidays while she drove in their car. He kept her company while she ate in non-kosher restaurants but didn't eat with her. Each gave the other the space and support to embrace Judaism at his and her own pace. Their differences didn't threaten each other or their marriage. Change didn't mean, "I'm rejecting you," or "Your way of life is no good." Each was willing to accept the other without insisting that their partner change.

In time, he became a cantor, and she became modern Orthodox. Had he pressured her to change before she was ready, it is doubtful that she would have embraced observance again.

Internalizing Change   Obviously, people can vary greatly in how quickly they become observant and how fully they integrate Torah into their lives. Baal teshuvas should never be treated as one-size-fits-all and be told to become fully observant as soon as possible. Baal teshuvas need time to address the psychological and practical adjustments to life along the way. Some teachers place too much emphasis on baal teshuvas-in-process' looking like religious Jews and observing mitzvahs as quickly as possible, while neglecting to help them integrate changes into their lives and psyches. It is easy, yet potentially damaging, to focus only on the externals rather than being concerned with the whole person's adjustment to a new way of life. People who teach about Judaism or who do Jewish outreach should know this. Baal teshuvas should be aware that some teachers or well-meaning friends can push them along too fast and can focus on changes that don't result in well-rounded human beings.

Giving Up What One Values   When people give up something that is meaningful or important to them, they need something with which to replace it. For example, if spending the Jewish holidays with one's family of origin is important, baal teshuvas should strive to find a way that this can happen. A family that gives up driving to the beach on Saturdays should plan an alternative fun afternoon for themselves and their children so that they don't resent the sacrifice.

In one community, baal teshuvas made up for the loss of eating out in non-kosher restaurants by having their Shabbos lunches in a different family's home each week. Each host made a different kind of ethnic gourmet food—such as Mexican, Chinese, Indian, and Italian.

Sometimes, *baal teshuvas* can't find ready substitutes for what they are giving up, and they may need to work through their feelings about that. For example, if a Jew has a good emotional relationship with a non-Jewish partner or spouse, it is not always wise to give it up only because halacha says that it is wrong. The Jew must first work through his or her feelings about leaving their loved one or have reasons besides religion to end the relationship. If they leave the partner without doing this, they may become depressed and/or feel angry with God or Judaism for the sad repercussions. They may decide—if they are lonely and single a few years later—that observant Judaism wasn't worth the sacrifice. They may then walk away from it.

Ideally, those contemplating major religious changes should have a spiritual mentor who understands them and with whom they discuss their religious, practical, and emotional issues. It says in the Ethics of the Fathers, "Make yourself a rabbi/teacher and acquire a friend for yourself." It is important to have both as we become observant. A wise rabbi or friend can sometimes predict challenges that will occur down the line and help the *baal teshuva* preempt or prepare for them.

Realistic Expectations

Baal teshuvas have a variety of expectations about what will happen to them once they become observant, and these may or may not occur. Many feel more fulfilled, have a clearer sense of direction, set meaningful life goals, and find greater purpose in their everyday lives. They live with a structure and set of values that are conducive to emotional normalcy, balance, inner peace, and integrity. Many will create wonderful marriages and families and be part of supportive communities. Those who are single will have wholesome ways of dating, live in communities where they can socialize with other singles, and be close to observant Jewish families.

On the other hand, some *baal teshuvas* expect that once they become observant, they won't have to make any more hard decisions and that their lives will be easier. They are shocked to discover that Judaism only solves their existential problems! They not only have all the other challenges that they had before becoming religious, they also have additional ones that come with being religious! They may have difficulty finding a job in their field that does not require violating Shabbos or Jewish holidays. They may have additional conflicts with family. They may have to reexamine who they are, what their goals are, and how they can achieve them. There may even be times when observing Jewish law makes them unhappy instead of leaving them feeling fulfilled. Someone who is not emotionally prepared for this may walk away from Judaism or live in a state of great emotional turmoil.

Back to the "Real World"   Arlene was someone who had unrealistic expectations about what her life would be like when she became observant in her early 30s. She became a *baal teshuva* when she attended a seminary in Israel. Life there was intellectually stimulating, and she was surrounded by understanding and warm friends and teachers. She was invited to a nice family every Shabbos, she was largely supported financially by the seminary, and she was 6,000 miles away from a family that neither understood nor supported her decision to become religious.

After leaving seminary and a year of intense religious life in Jerusalem, she returned to the US where she couldn't find a job. To make matters worse, she couldn't find suitable religious men who were interested in marrying her. The single men whom she met were mostly interested in dating women in their 20s, or were men her age who had lots of emotional issues. She had a very bad relationship with her family, who thought that she was crazy for becoming observant. In short, she was ill-prepared to leave the seemingly idyllic religious world of Jerusalem and go back to a world that was neither supportive nor understanding of her new way of life.

Arlene felt overwhelmed by the triple challenges of unemployment, poverty, and being single. The religious women who invited her for Shabbos and holiday meals were all married with children. She had little in common with them and vice versa. Some of the religious people she met believed that all she needed to do was to get married and then all of her problems would be solved. Some assumed that she was still single because there was something wrong with her and they told her that she was too picky. She became very bitter and her commitment to observance waned.

As long as Arlene believed that had she not become religious, she would not have had these difficulties, being observant made her miserable. She needed to make an attitudinal shift in order to feel better about the fact that her life was so different from what she wanted. No one can say what Arlene's challenges would have been had she not become observant, but God always sends us challenges. These are custom-made to help us grow. Had she felt deeply connected to God, that might have been a gratifying relationship for her. Instead, she carried her bitterness and disappointment with her Creator into her relationships with people, making her unpleasant to be with. She was so negative that no potential spouse would want to spend time with her, thereby keeping her in a downward spiral. Working through some of her feelings with a spiritual advisor and/or a religious therapist could have helped her a great deal.

Proceeding with Caution

While Torah Judaism is real and lasting, the way some people approach it may not be. Judaism does not give a quick fix, a guaranteed high, easy answers to all of life's questions, or solutions to all of life's problems.

Emotional Deprivation　Some people are unhappy with their lives and hope that Judaism will magically change their circumstances. Some hope to replace an inner emptiness with a wholesome family life, structured time, and meaningful rituals. They enjoy the atmosphere at Shabbos tables, the closeness at holiday meals, and the intensity of the High Holidays. They find the delicious food at family meals, the singing, and Torah study very nurturing.

Yet, becoming an observant Jew doesn't overcome a lifetime of emotional deprivation or clinical depression. Most unhappy people still need to do a lot of emotional work once they become religious. These emotional issues are sometimes intensified by the interpersonal, life goal, and work problems that occur when one becomes observant.

Perfectionists, Dreamers Baal teshuvas who were idealistic or perfectionistic before becoming observant may be zealous about doing rituals "perfectly" and seem quite extreme in the Jewish ideas that they express. Just as they adopted a "black and white" approach with their prior pursuits, they are likely to do the same with Judaism. It may be hard for them to see the shades of gray that are part and parcel of authentic religious life.

Another form of extremism sometimes occurs with people who are "dreamers" or who get passionate about causes. They may have patterns of becoming infatuated with new pursuits and then quickly get bored with them.

An advisor or religious therapist may help people who tend toward extremism for any of these reasons to stay on an even keel when becoming religious. The goal is to be an observant Jew who is balanced, neither being overly perfectionistic and fanatic, nor becoming so intensely passionate that the fire soon dies out and with it, one's commitment to observance.

The long-term fulfillment and joy that come with observance are outgrowths of a long process of emotional and spiritual work. The goals of such work include achieving closeness with God and others, feeling good about observing commandments and exercising self-discipline, getting pleasure from studying Judaism, and appreciating what one has.

Empty Restlessness Some people who seek religion to unrealistically fill an emotional void may find that their religious commitments don't last. For instance, George was fascinated by New

Age for six months. Then he studied Buddhism, living in India and moving to an ashram in Vermont for a year. He next went to college, then dropped out in his sophomore year and went on a road trip for six months. In his travels, he spent a weekend at a religious retreat where he experienced his first Shabbos and heard many lectures about Torah Judaism. He then became infatuated with observant Judaism, just as he had done with the Far Eastern religions that he had explored.

George may float in and out of Judaism the same way that he was in and out of so many other pursuits if he is looking to fill an emotional void. As soon as the novelty of each religion wears out, George may feel restless and unfulfilled. He will only be able to "stick" with Jewish observance if he resolves the emotional problems that cause him to feel restless with routine and the mundane and finds realistic ways to feel satisfied with his daily life.

Depressed Vicky came from a very dysfunctional, wealthy family. Her mother was constantly worried about something and her father was distant, stoic, and harsh. Vicky was often depressed and lonely and desperately wanted to find meaning in her life. She had a wonderful Jewish boyfriend whose family was everything hers was not. His family was warm, accepting, uncritical, and loving, and her boyfriend was everything that she could ever have wanted. Yet, she just couldn't be happy. At one point, she thought that she would solve her problems by moving to Israel and living on a kibbutz. Her therapist recognized that Vicky couldn't fill the void in her life so simplistically. There was no reason to believe that she would magically become a different person by moving 7,000 miles away. If she didn't change the ways that she viewed herself and her life, she would only take her depression and dissatisfaction with her.

Vicky sought help from an observant therapist who explored with her what she thought would happen if she went to a kibbutz. Vicky hoped that a warm family would "adopt" her and give her the nurturing that was so lacking in her own family. She also expected the kibbutz to be a type of paradise, devoid of problems. The reality, of course, is that she might meet some wonderful families, but that they would have little time to spend with her except at Shabbos and holiday meals. Unless she spent the rest of her life living on a kibbutz taking care of animals or harvesting fruits, she would still have to deal with issues of how she would find meaning in life. She would still have to decide how she wanted to earn a living and what kind of career she wanted. Plus, she would need to change her attitude so that she wouldn't become disappointed with everyone she met. How would she find meaning in day-to-day life and not be bored with everything she did? How would she overcome her difficulties sustaining a close relationship with a man and eventually get married?

It soon became apparent to Vicky that she was not likely to escape all of her problems on a kibbutz. She would just transfer them to a new environment. It took months of therapy before she realized that she would have to change her ways of thinking and learn how to make herself happy instead of depending on others, or on Judaism, to magically make her feel good.

While religiosity isn't an antidote to loneliness or depression, that doesn't mean that lonely or depressed people shouldn't become observant. Becoming observant always has positive spiritual effects. In addition, much research has shown that the support systems in a religious community, the structure of religious rituals, finding meaning in life, and belief in God all have very positive effects on one's emotional and physical health. However, many people still need to do emotional work along with their religious journey for a religious way of life to be emotionally satisfying. Judaism gives us tools to live a happy, productive, fulfilled life, but if our emotional limitations prevent us from using those tools, we won't feel fulfilled.

The Mid-Life Crisis

Financial & Family Disappointments Another issue that some baal teshuvas face is the mid-life crisis. When many secular Jews become observant, they believe that their lives will become better, easier, and more fulfilling, yet that is not always how it feels. It is wrong for anyone to teach non-observant Jews that observing

Torah Judaism will result in their becoming wealthier, automatically having stable and happy families, and feeling satisfied with their lives. Observing Torah typically results in giving away more money to charity and paying more for children's Jewish education. It sometimes requires giving up lucrative careers that conflict with observance, and it occasionally causes observant Jews to lose profits that less scrupulous people would keep.

Becoming observant is also no guarantee that people will have good marriages or well-adjusted families. Using Torah guidelines can help people to become good marriage partners and parents, but we have to continually apply these ideas to marriage and child rearing. Even after doing so for many years, living by Torah guidelines can't ensure that one will have healthy, well-adjusted offspring.

Fifteen or 20 years after some people become *baal teshuvas*, they may not have attained the financial status they had expected. They attribute this to diminished savings due to their children's tuition bills for religious education. Their marriages seem humdrum: not the sparkling, vibrant, romantic relationships that they believed keeping the laws of family holiness would ensure. Others don't have the harmonious relationships with their children that they thought would come with observance. They and their children argue about many things, including about Judaism. Some children even decide that they don't want to stay observant. Now in their late 40s or 50s, the parents realize that they are in dead-end jobs and they feel that they will never achieve what they had once hoped they would in their careers or at work.

Blaming Judaism   Some will complain to their rabbi or to a therapist, as Berel did:

"If I hadn't become observant, my life would have been so much better! The rabbis who taught me about observant Judaism years ago led me to believe that Judaism would make my life better. It didn't. I would have had a better life if I'd stayed secular. I would have had a lot more savings. I could have advanced in my career without being restricted to jobs that allowed me to take off early on Fridays and on the Jewish holidays. My kids and I wouldn't be fighting about issues like dressing modestly, playing ball on Shabbos, and hanging out with teenagers of the opposite sex. Even keeping the laws of family holiness didn't give me a fantastic marriage. My wife isn't as attractive, or as interesting, as the secular women in my office are. When my wife and I are together, she mostly complains about problems—our teenage kids, problems with the house or car, the latest episode with her elderly and sick mother—you get the picture. I have enough problems at work. I don't want to hear about more problems when I am home."

Some men like Berel attribute a variety of disappointments to their becoming observant. While it is true that Berel might have earned more money and had more job opportunities had he not become religious, there are several flaws in his beliefs:

1. Wishful Thinking

First, Berel lives in a world of wishful thinking. No one knows what his life would have looked like if he had stayed secular. God might have chosen to send him different challenges than the ones that he had. For example, had he invested the money that he used to pay for his children's tuition in the stock market, who knows that he wouldn't have lost much of it?

2. Tendency toward Dissatisfaction

Second, Berel attributes all of his unhappiness to his becoming religious. Yet who is to say that if he were secular, he wouldn't also have been unhappy, for either the same or different reasons? He might have had his mid-life crisis despite having a lot more money, a nicer house, and living in a fancier neighborhood. This is because his emotional dissatisfaction had to do with his sense of self, his expectations, and how he saw himself as a passive victim of circumstances.

Some people live in a fantasy world rather than doing the hard emotional and practical work that is necessary to have more fulfilling lives. Rather than develop healthy attitudes and fulfilling endeavors that keep life interesting, and successfully adapting to changes around us, some people attribute their unhappiness to their spouse, their kids, and/or to becoming religious.

If people want to stay physically healthy, they may need to forego eating the unhealthy foods that their emotions or body crave and they may need to exercise regularly to stay in shape. Staying emotionally healthy and happy also requires work. The older we get, the harder we sometimes need to work to keep ourselves in good emotional and physical shape. Unfortunately, the older we become, the more we may expect to relax, have an easy life, and be able to enjoy ourselves. God often has a different agenda for us.

3. Lack of Effort in Marriage

Third, fulfillment in marriage often has a great deal to do with both partners' contributions. People like Berel often contribute to their lack of a fulfilling marriage, yet see their partner as the source of the problem. We want our spouse to look great, be interesting, and admire us, yet we may not want to discipline ourselves to exercise and restrict our eating, dress attractively, talk about topics that interest our spouse, and make our spouse feel admired, desired, and appreciated. We want marriages that don't have problems, but how many people are willing to develop the tools necessary to make our marriages as exciting after 20 years as they were when we first got married?

Good marriages don't happen simply because someone observes the laws of family holiness. These laws give couples an opportunity to spiritually enrich their marriage and to connect physical intimacy with a great love for one another and for their Creator. Whether or not they have an emotionally fulfilling marriage, though, depends upon many other choices that a couple makes. Do they set aside time to work on their marriage every day? Do they make time to enjoy each other and create ongoing intimacy and love? Do they exercise the self-control necessary to stay attractive, not gain weight, and dress nicely when their spouse is around? Do they continually give their spouse the affection and respect that is a foundation of marriage? Do they learn the skills to resolve conflicts, use them when necessary, and make sure to say nice things to their spouse every day?

As one divorced man rued, "If I'd only put as much effort into making my marriage work as I did dating women who seemed to be better than my ex-wife, I would have had the marriage that I always wanted."

The only way that Berel would have had a happy marriage, regardless of whether he was religious or secular, is if he and his wife worked hard to make that happen. If he had stayed secular, he might even have gotten divorced (as do at least half of American couples), because he and his wife would have had so little binding them together.

4. Wanting Payoff Now

Fourth, Berel has lost sight of the fact that Judaism sees this world as a place of struggle, challenge, and hard work—the payoff for which occurs primarily in a spiritual afterlife. Why doesn't he feel that the spiritual work that he has done these many years is real and worthwhile? Why does he blame everything that he is lacking on Judaism?

Anything that we invest in spirituality is never lost, yet spirituality gained had lost its meaning for Berel. Berel didn't feel a sense of accomplishment in meriting to give his children a Jewish education, from which they and their offspring would benefit. The many years that he had observed Jewish rituals did not seem to have a tangible payoff. The sacrifices he had made to observe the laws of family holiness were not emotionally rewarding to him. His entire focus was on how little he had, not on what he had accomplished.

There are often trade-offs between what feels good to the body and what is best for the soul. That which is real and lasting often requires our making short-term sacrifices. For example, do most people feel better after fasting for 25 hours on the Day of Atonement? Hopefully the person feels spiritually revived and cleansed at the end of the day, and while one may not feel physically better, it is an elixir for the soul.

If we continually forego the emotional pleasures that are spiritually unhealthy, we need to find some way of feeling good about the
sacrifices we make. That often means working hard in other ways so
that our sacrifices will feel worthwhile.

Judaism can only tell people how to behave; it can't make us feel
the happiness and fulfillment that we should feel as a result. We
have to have the proper attitudes in order to reap those emotional
benefits of our sacrifices and hard work.

Too Much, Too Fast

Judaism encourages us to have a joyful relationship with God, yet
some *baal teshuvas* give up so much that they don't feel happy after
they become observant. Instead, they feel restricted and deprived
and grieve for lost opportunities. They also miss the closeness they
once had with non-observant or non-Jewish friends and with family
members from whom they are now estranged. If *baal teshuvas* speak
to wise counselors who help them anticipate practical and emotional
challenges they will face, they might pace their changes differently,
and develop coping skills and attitudes that will help them during
their often-difficult journeys.

When *baal teshuvas* gradually become observant over a period of
years, rather than over a few months, they have time to readjust their
relationships and develop these coping skills and changed attitudes.
They can also integrate changes in lifestyle, goals, and attitudes into
their personality and being. When they change too quickly, they
often have second thoughts or regrets about who they've become and
what they have missed.

Making Up for Lost Time   Ethan became attracted to observant Judaism during his senior year in high school. The following
summer, he went on a Birthright trip. Instead of going back to
America when the trip was over, he stayed in Israel and enrolled in
a yeshiva.

He was so excited about making up for lost time that he observed
everything that he knew with zeal and joy. He awoke at 6:30 every
morning, practically jumped out of bed, and was one of the first

students at the 7:00 am minyan. He was also one of the last to finish praying. He spent more than an hour reading every word in the prayer services plus some translations. He prayed with concentration and devotion.

Except for socializing and eating meals, Ethan basically learned Torah or prayed from 6:30 am until 10 pm five days a week, and spent the better part of Fridays and Shabbos doing more of the same. Ethan loved living this way.

In the midst of his second year in yeshiva, Ethan's excitement with Judaism started to cool. His high school friends were having fun in college. He wanted more fun in his life. His friends were all dating. He hadn't spoken to young women for months. His former buddies went out to movies, sports events, parties, and rock concerts. He went from his dorm to the yeshiva and back again. His former friends were getting exposed to worldly ideas and he was getting exposed to inner worldly and metaphysical ideas. He started feeling confined and frustrated.

As Ethan thought about leaving yeshiva to catch up with his friends, his wise spiritual advisor told him to take as much time as he needed to "chill out" in healthy ways. The advisor guided Ethan in how to do this. They chatted every week about how Ethan was feeling, and Ethan's advisor soon recommended that he attend a less intense yeshiva part-time and study for a career as well. With his advisor's help, Ethan left that yeshiva and not Judaism. He realized in retrospect that he had become too frum too fast, and he appreciated his advisor's wisdom in helping him get back to where he needed to be.

Depression

Pre-Teshuva Depression   Depression is fairly common among Americans, so it is not surprising that many baal teshuvas are also depressed. Many people expect that becoming religious will treat their emotional states, as if faith in God is a panacea for all emotional and medical problems. That is a mistake.

Some seminary and yeshiva students are depressed before they become observant, but they temporarily feel better when they are excited with Judaism and with their new way of life. They meet new people, hear new ideas, are welcomed into families, and are made to feel special by rabbis and teachers. But, the novelty of this often wears off. Unless a depressed person fundamentally changes the ways of thinking and acting that result in depression, the depression is likely to recur.

Teshuva-Based Issues   A person who believes that keeping Torah is the right thing to do may give up familiar sources of happiness and pleasure without having replacements. Some simultaneously get lots of criticism and harshness from their families and former friends. They may have fights with their parents and siblings about their not attending family functions. They no longer party with their friends as they once did, and shopping or going to sports events with friends on Saturdays is out of the question. Some stop watching television and going to movies, no longer listen to music that they formerly loved, and read little other than Jewish material. They stop going to discos, parties, to the beach, and hanging out with the opposite sex. They stop wearing sexy clothes, going to the health club (not that there is anything wrong with exercising, they just tend not to make time for it), jogging, and lounging around the swimming pool. Women who now dress modestly tend to stop getting the kinds of compliments about their looks that they once received. Some gain at least 10 or 15 pounds when they attend seminary if they eat lots of unhealthy food and don't exercise. Their clothes no longer fit and they may lack the money to buy attractive new ones. No wonder they are depressed!

Remedies   Depressed people can usually benefit from cognitive-behavioral therapy. They can develop internal coping skills, eat healthy food, and/or take nutritional or biochemical agents to change their brain chemistries. They can monitor their emotional states and "treat" their low moods before they develop into full-blown depression. Walking briskly for half an hour a day is as beneficial for many people as is taking an antidepressant. Keeping away from processed and junk foods and eating a healthy diet help stabilize and nourish the brain. Learning how to deal with parental conflicts, adapting to the pressures of religious dating, resolving financial worries, and maintaining some formerly enjoyable activities within a Torah lifestyle can often make the difference between a baal teshuva's feeling fulfilled instead of miserable.

A seminary principal told a depressed student who formerly enjoyed movies and novels that she *must* watch some movies and read some novels (of course, using discretion about the content). She also encouraged seminary girls to participate in exercise and dance classes led by instructors on the school premises. Many young women's depression can be ameliorated by following this good advice. Exercising in a natural setting, getting fresh air, and spending time away from the confines of buildings does wonders for many people. Cognitive-behavioral psychotherapy and exercise have helped countless people overcome depression and deal with their problems without needing antidepressant medication.

Coming to Terms with One's Past Some baal teshuvas become depressed when they get the sense that their former lives were worthless and that activities or goals that once gave them meaning or pleasure are pointless or bad. How do you fix your life when nothing about you—nothing that you have done, or enjoyed, for the past 20 or 30 years—is "good"? While Judaism doesn't say that everything about a person's past life is worthless, some baal teshuvas are either told this or decide this on their own.

Secular Pursuits Someone who has been observant for years may think that every baal teshuva is much better off now than when life was filled with "nonsense." Yet, those secular pursuits aren't nonsense to the person struggling to become more observant.

No one should be told—directly or indirectly—that everything that used to feel good, or that he or she thought was positive about himself or herself, was bad or only an illusion. Nor should *baal teshuvas* who still yearn for past involvements in secular pursuits be belittled or insulted by those who insist that there is nothing about their past lives that they should want.

If someone still yearns for what he or she once had or was, there must be something positive about those experiences, even if the form that it took was not ideal. The *baal teshuva* needs to identify what about those experiences is meaningful to him or her, work through their feelings, and try to recapture in spiritually healthy ways what those inappropriate pursuits gave him or her.

Some former pleasures may be irreplaceable when one adopts an observant way of life. In this case, the *baal teshuva* may need to mourn for those lost feelings and involvements that they are giving up.

At the same time, *baal teshuvas* need to see their prior lives as stepping-stones to their present lives and they need to hold onto parts that are valuable and important. Maintaining strengths and positive aspects of one's former life will allow for healthy growth. Hopefully, the *baal teshuva* will find other pleasures and fulfillments to replace those they've lost, but that process may take a long time.

We should never throw out the baby with the bath water. We had our good qualities when we weren't observant, and we have them after we become observant. In time, we may even make some of our most unique and important contributions to the world because of who we were in the past.

Spiritual Greatness   A trap that some baal teshuvas fall into is to believe that their entire identity or former life was worthless because only learning Torah and keeping mitzvahs are worthwhile. A person must sometimes hit rock bottom and be steeped in less-than-desirable activities to search for greater meaning in life. Once someone turns to a life of Torah, it doesn't negate the value of activities that moved him or her to where he or she needed to be. In fact, the Talmud teaches that in a place where a baal teshuva stands, even a person who was perfectly righteous—who never yearned to do the inappropriate things that some secular Jews do—cannot stand. An "off-track" past can be a necessary impetus to walking toward the Divine Presence. When one's sins lead to love of God and regret over one's shortcomings, they are especially precious to the Almighty. Such Jews need to appreciate their spiritual greatness and the Divine image inside that makes them like priceless gems.

Itzik, a man in his early 30s, lamented, "God made me pure, and I destroyed myself. I have gotten so used to using women as objects, I can't ever get back my naivete. How can I even pray? I totally corrupted the beautiful soul that the Almighty gave me."

The Kotzker Rebbe once said, "There is no one as whole as he who has a broken heart." A sinner who regrets his wrongdoing is so precious to God. The book of Joshua tells a story of a harlot (some say that she was an innkeeper) in Jericho named Rachav who practiced her profession for 40 years. When she knew that the Israelites were about to conquer Jericho, she abandoned her immoral ways and became a righteous convert. None other than the prophet Joshua, Moses' successor, married her.

Acher The Talmud recounts a story about a brilliant Jewish sage, Elisha ben Abuya. When he became an apostate, he was nicknamed "Acher," meaning "other" or "outsider." When former student Rabbi Meir asked him why he didn't repent, Acher replied, "I heard a Divine voice call out, 'Everyone may repent, except Acher.'" Elisha ben Abuya didn't feel there was any hope of his redeeming the Divine image in himself. He died an apostate.

The sad part of the story is that there was no such Divine message. Acher misinterpreted what he heard. The Heavenly voice said, "All can repent except for someone who sees himself as 'Acher,'" i.e., who views himself as outside the fold. God's loving embrace is always extended to each and every Jew when we want to be close to Him. In fact, if we regret our past misdeeds and that regret intensifies our love for the One Above, our misdeeds are even considered as mitzvahs—Godly acts.[2]

We must strike a balance between not feeling arrogant, yet not feeling so inadequate that we can't see ourselves as beloved of God. No one can build self-esteem believing that his or her entire life was a mistake and that it's too late to make up for lost time. Whatever we did that brought us to presently yearn for a deep and fulfilling relationship with our Creator cannot be worthless. It's never too late to take our qualities, talents, desires, and drives that we used in the wrong places and use them constructively.

Voice of Experience   Margie became observant when she was 14. When she went to college, she sat next to a very cute young man, Nigel, in her English literature course. Nigel was very funny and charming and he asked Margie out. Margie asked him if he was Jewish, and he said that his father was Jewish but that his mother was not, and that he didn't consider himself "anything." Margie hesitated, so Nigel suggested that they just have a cup of coffee together in the student lounge. After all, what harm could that do? Margie agreed.

After seeing each other twice a week in class and eating lunch together in the lounge a few times, Nigel invited Margie to a concert. One thing led to another, and they were soon dating each other exclusively. It was so easy to talk to one another and to be together; they were deeply in love by the end of the summer. They continued to date for the next two years. Margie exposed Nigel to her religious way of life, but he found it too confining. Little by little, some of her religious commitments dissolved until she admitted to herself that she was compromising her life as an observant Jew. Every day, Margie would resolve to break up with Nigel, and every week she continued to see him.

After much heartache and soul-searching, Margie flew to Europe for the summer in order to put distance between them. She sent Nigel a letter telling him that she couldn't see him any more. She spent the rest of the summer coming to terms with her decision.

After Margie finished college, she began working for a college outreach organization. Many of the Jews that she met on campus were either dating non-Jews or saw no reason not to date non-Jews. She could speak from the voice of experience with an authenticity that others lacked when she told how difficult it was to break up with a gentile partner, and why it was so important not to start. Her support and genuineness helped other Jews to break up with non-Jewish partners and helped others not date them in the first place.

Summary

A man who felt like he lived from one disaster to another once asked his rabbi if he thought that the man would have better luck with his finances and social life if he moved to another city. The rabbi indicated that it was possible. On the other hand, the rabbi advised, "You'll take yourself with you."

Becoming observant helps put some existential issues to rest, but it is common for one's emotional problems to remain.

To the extent that becoming a *baal teshuva* involves many changes in attitudes, expectations, and behaviors, slowly and gradually evolving can give people time to readjust their equilibrium. Having a relationship with our Creator and with other Jews also taps into many of the relationship issues that people carry with them from childhood. When these interfere with a *baal teshuva's* growth, it can be wise to work them out with a competent, religiously sensitive therapist.

Whether or not a *baal teshuva* brings emotional baggage with him or her, getting guidance from a wise advisor can often smooth the bumps that may otherwise make the *baal teshuva's* journey much more difficult.

SIX

Advisors

*B*aal *teshuvas* can have many needs. Some are financial, such as finding a benefactor or securing a scholarship to seminary or yeshiva so that the person can learn how to be a knowledgeable Jew. *Baal teshuvas* may have emotional needs, such as needing support when they are rejected or hurt by their family and/or when they need help making new friends. They may need someone to guide them through the process of religious dating and marriage. *Baal teshuvas* with children need to learn which religious schools and summer camps are suitable for their kids. They may need information about how to integrate into a religious community and what different religious communities and synagogues are like. They need names of contact people and hosts for Shabbos and holidays from whom to learn and with whom they can build a social network.

It is a rare rabbi who has time to be a *baal teshuva's posek* (decisor of how to apply Jewish law in specific instances), spiritual guide, support system, and counselor. Nevertheless, *baal teshuvas* need to find people who can advise them about many types of practical matters, such as how to deal with parents, how to tell a spouse that they want to start keeping kosher, or where to find modest and stylish clothes. *Baal teshuvas* may need a listening ear and suggestions from someone who has been around the block a few times who is not their rabbi. This is why most *baal teshuvas* will need at least one advisor in addition to a rabbi. This person may be a teacher or another *baal teshuva* who has been religious for many years, who is wise and supportive.

The advisor may be someone who can discuss with them the pros and cons of various seminaries and yeshivas. For some women, it might be a rebbetzin, someone who hosts the *baal teshuva* for Shabbos and holiday meals, someone who helps *baal teshuvas* to plan their weddings, or someone who takes *baal teshuvas* to the *mikvah* (ritual bath) before they get married. Whoever the person is, he or she should have the knowledge, sensitivity, and time to be the *baal teshuva*'s sounding board, advocate, friend, and religious advisor.

How does a *baal teshuva* find such a person? Often, they ask their teachers or other *baal teshuvas* to recommend someone. Some people connect well with their Shabbos hosts and ask if they will play this role. Some hosts even help *baal teshuvas* "try out" their community, and may even be able to provide names of real estate agents to help them locate a home to rent or buy in the area.

Having more than one advisor can ease the transition to observance. Advisors may have different strengths or knowledge, and the *baal teshuva* can pose their many questions to several people so that no one person feels overwhelmed.

Rarely, *baal teshuvas* may also need legal help when observance causes them to be discriminated against at work or when they must take university exams scheduled for Shabbos or Jewish holidays. An advisor may know just the organization or attorney to help with these matters.

Someone Who Can Be There for You

Not everyone with good intentions has the wherewithal to advise *baal teshuvas*, though. Some don't understand *baal teshuvas* so well, and some have an inappropriate agenda that they foist upon *baal teshuvas*. Advisors may want *baal teshuvas* to adopt the advisor's "brand" of Judaism, his way of thinking and living, instead of ones that might be more suited to the *baal teshuva*'s personality and spiritual needs. There are many beautiful ways to observe Torah and serve God, and an advisor should help the *baal teshuva* to find the path that suits him or her best.

Following One's Inclination   Jean was raised in a family without much structure and she yearned for the intensity of a religious way of life. A few years after becoming modern Orthodox, she attended a chareidi seminary for baal teshuvas in Jerusalem. She studied there for two years. She loved the learning and the families that she met in the community, yet she felt that something was missing. She spoke to her advisor about this several times, but her advisor kept telling her that she had unrealistic expectations.

Finally, Jean heard about a Chassidic seminary where the girls studied meditation and Chassidic texts and lived a Chassidic way of life. At the same time, a matchmaker recommended that she go out with a Chassidic young man. Jean went out with him and found that they got along very well with each other. Against her advisor's recommendations, Jean enrolled in the Chassidic seminary and was very happy with her choice. She began consulting with her to-be-fiance's rabbi and moved to his Chassidic community. It was a great choice for her, and she and her husband thrived there.

Too Extreme   Charlotte had different spiritual needs than Jean did. Charlotte knew from the time that she was a young girl that she wanted to be a doctor when she grew up. She become observant in high school, and decided to study in seminary in Israel for a year before she started university. The chareidi seminary that she chose espoused many ideas that she found close-minded, unscientific, and extreme. When Charlotte discussed with a teacher her objections to what was being taught, the teacher insisted that Charlotte had been indoctrinated by an anti-religious world-view and assured her that the seminary was teaching truth. Charlotte spoke to another teacher about her discomfort with the seminary's perspectives, and the second teacher backed the views of the first teacher. Charlotte could not accept these ideas and changed to a different seminary that was more open-minded and which focused on textual learning. The teachers there validated Charlotte's perspectives, and they introduced Charlotte to an advisor who was herself an observant physician who had integrated Judaism with the secular world.

Mediator's Role   Sometimes, mediators try to help ease the tensions between baal teshuva children and their parents. Although not everyone who teaches baal teshuvas has the psychological awareness or the sensitivity to be effective in this role, there are—thankfully—many effective teachers and spiritual advisors connected to outreach programs, seminaries, and yeshivas. Such mediators should be skilled in working with the parents of baal teshuvas and appreciate and empathize with the parents' concerns. Even where the mediator disagrees with the parents' beliefs or lifestyles, he or she should be able to empathize with the parents' feelings and treat them respectfully.

A mentor needs to see both sides of the story—that of the parent and that of the child—even while believing that living by Torah is ideal. The advisor should value, whenever possible, maintaining or improving the relationship between a child and his parents. That is not always possible, but the mediator should do his or her best to try when it is.

Anticipating Problems

Advisors and religious hosts often invite newcomers to observant Judaism to their homes for meals. This helps *baal teshuvas* feel that they are part of a religious community and belong to a religious family. Yet, simply doing this is usually not enough to help potential *baal teshuvas* make a smooth transition to the world of observance. *Baal teshuvas* typically need guidance in many areas along the way. Advisors need to listen to the newcomers' hopes and expectations, help them to formulate realistic religious goals, and put together a plan to achieve them. Advisors need to have the experience and wisdom to anticipate where certain challenges are likely to occur and to help *baal teshuvas* anticipate and prepare for them before problems arise.

Roller-Coaster Relationships   Sam was a wonderful teacher of potential baal teshuvas, but he was not a very good advisor. One night, Sam met Mark at a Jewish concert. Mark was an attractive, charismatic, ambitious businessman who was still single in his 30s. When Sam invited Mark to his house for a Shabbos meal, Mark was both touched and flattered and accepted the invitation.

Mark and the singles at the table that night spent the better part of the meal flirting with each other, and Mark asked the women for their phone numbers before the evening ended. Sam told them about the synagogue's beginner service, which Mark decided to attend the next day—partly to learn more about the prayers, partly to meet some single women and to be invited to more warm homes, the likes of which he had never known growing up.

Mark became progressively more observant over the course of the year, until he was observing Shabbos and holidays. However, he had a lot of unresolved emotional issues that ultimately undid his religious fervor. He was a lonely man who had mostly superficial relationships with others. He very much wanted others to accept him, but as soon as others got to know him well enough to see his flaws, he bolted. His "relationships" with women were brief emotional roller coasters. As soon as he got a woman interested in him and he no longer had to "chase" her, he got bored and tried to find someone new and exciting.

After going to a number of religious Jewish singles' functions, Mark burned out. Although Sam saw Mark at his synagogue every few weeks, Sam thought that it would be intrusive to ask Mark about how his dating was going. Had Sam asked, Mark would have told him that he had a pattern of getting infatuated with women, dating each one a few times, losing his excitement with her, and searching for the next woman. Sam would have realized that Mark wasn't ready for the kind of goal-oriented, serious religious dating that observant Jews did. Mark would have told Sam that so much meaningful conversation that centered on goals and revealing oneself was too intense for Mark, and he hated feeling that *baal teshuvas* were sizing him up and might quickly reject him! They expected him to know what his religious goals were. They asked him where he wanted to be Jewishly in five years, what kind of a family he wanted to have, and what kind of religious community he wanted to live in.

He had no idea! He felt overwhelmed having to define his life goals with so little experience and knowledge about what each choice implied. The more he dated, and the more women didn't want to go out with him more than once or twice, the more inadequate he felt. He realized that as much as he wanted to get married, he didn't have a clue about how to make a marriage work. It was only a matter of time until he went back to the singles' bars and party scenes on Friday nights, resumed eating non-kosher food, and was soon living exactly as he had before he became observant.

Mark needed an advisor who could point out that his tendency to get excited about new things and people would soon result in his feeling bored or dissatisfied, and he would likely grow disenchanted with observant Judaism and with observant women. He needed someone to suggest that he refrain from religious dating until he worked out these issues and had figured out his life goals. If Sam wasn't able to do this, he should have suggested that Mark find an advisor or therapist who could help him.

One prominent outreach rabbi estimated that about half of recently observant Jewish singles give up observance if they don't get married within a few years. Singles often lack the support systems and emotional resources that married *baal teshuvas* have, so it is especially important for outreach teachers to help newly observant Jews find social networks, synagogues where they will feel welcome, religious families who will host them for Shabbos and holidays, and people who can set them up when they are ready for religious dating. It is important that Jews not only become ritually committed, but also fit in emotionally and socially with their new way of life.

An experienced advisor can help prepare *baal teshuvas* for the challenges that they are likely to encounter. When necessary, he or she can usually recommend a religiously sensitive therapist with whom the *baal teshuva* can work out emotional issues that are barriers to becoming an integrated observant Jew.

Support Groups

It takes a very strong person to deal with the many challenges that *baal teshuvas* typically confront. Many *baal teshuvas* can benefit from help with the kinds of friction they face as they make a series of changes in their lives. One *baal teshuva* advised that there should be a *Baal Teshuvas* Anonymous support group in his city. I advised him to start one!

How wonderful it would be if *baal teshuvas* would establish support groups in their synagogues or homes! Thankfully, there are now websites for *baal teshuvas* (see the Appendix) that provide forums for discussing their problems, answering their questions, and helping them find support. Keeping in touch with Judaica teachers or friends who have become observant can also be important components of the support system that most *baal teshuvas* need.

Summary

Ideally, every Jew should have a spiritual advisor. However, not everyone who thinks that he or she is a good counselor, advisor, or mediator, is. It is important to find advisors who are experienced and sensitive when talking to parents of *baal teshuvas* and who can appreciate the psychological and practical issues involved. In cases of conflict between parent and child, a mediator must recognize the validity of the parents' feelings and concerns and respect them. That doesn't mean that the *baal teshuva* should stop learning about Judaism or stop observing Torah just because others are opposed to it. It does mean that how they do both should be with the support and guidance of those who can help them become well-rounded, emotionally healthy people.

SEVEN

Choosing a Rabbi

In addition to teachers and a spiritual advisor, every Jew needs a rabbi whom they trust and who relates well to them. In some ways, finding the right rabbi is like searching for a soul doctor. We not only want a rav who knows Jewish law well, we want him to understand where we are coming from when we ask questions. It is ideal when a rav knows when a question is the tip of the iceberg for a larger issue and responds accordingly.

Choosing a Rabbi   One of a baal teshuva's most important decisions is choosing a rabbi. The rabbi will not only influence the details of how a baal teshuva observes Jewish rituals, but the rabbi's responses will affect all aspects of the baal teshuva's life. Some Jews will consult their rabbi about day-to-day questions as well as about all of the major decisions in their lives. These issues may include who to marry (if they are single), how to raise their children, where to send their children to school, where they should live, what career to choose, which house to buy, and so on. Rabbis can wield tremendous power and baal teshuvas should trust only those who have proven themselves to be worthy of such a role.

Baal teshuvas can find out who might be a good rabbi or advisor for them by asking others what their experiences have been. Some *baal teshuvas* rave about the sensitivity and knowledge of the same advisors and rabbis. Such people may be good choices of advisors and rabbis for newcomers to observance if such people have time for them. A new *baal teshuva* should ask if those advisors and rabbis have qualities relevant to their particular circumstances. For example, does the rabbi have experience dealing with issues involving Jews who have a non-Jewish father, who want to go to college, who have conflicts about the role of women in Orthodoxy, who need help dealing with a non-observant spouse and children, and so on? The answers to such questions will help the *baal teshuva* decide if such a person is suited to advise them in their individual circumstances.

We should look for a rabbi who acts like a *mensch* (a decent person), is knowledgeable about Torah, and can sensitively inform us about how God wants us to live. Great rabbis are concerned about the person asking the question, not only about the questions that are asked. They will try to hear what the *baal teshuva* is not saying as well as the actual question being asked.

The Passover Milk   The Brisker Rav once asked his wife for some money for charity shortly before Passover. His wife asked him why he needed money just then, since they had already disbursed all of the community funds buying food for indigent Jews for the holiday. The Rav responded,

"A man just came to me asking if he could use milk to fulfill the commandment to drink four cups of wine at the seder. I told him that one must use wine. However, I understood from his question that he would only ask about using milk if he didn't have enough money to buy wine. If he is so poor that he can't afford wine for the seder, he certainly doesn't have money to buy chicken and *matzot* for the holiday meal. I want to give him enough money so that he can buy the food that he needs to properly enjoy Passover."

A rabbi who advises *baal teshuvas* needs to be very sensitive to human relationships. This is because he will be a model from whom the *baal teshuva* will learn how to relate to others. The *baal teshuva* will also need a lot of guidance about how to deal with many people in his or her life.

The kabbalists would choose a rav who not only was an expert in Jewish law but who had an exemplary relationship with his wife. Such a man would model how being a righteous Jew is not only about what one knows, but is also about living the fundamental rule, "You should love your fellow Jew as you love yourself." This begins at home, especially with one's wife.

Jewish learning involves more than discovering what one may or may not do in a given situation. It is about becoming a decent human being who tries to be moral and holy in all of his or her involvements. A learned rabbi who has an exemplary marriage shows that he takes this seriously and does whatever is required to mold his character and behave in a Godly way.

Few *baal teshuvas* today have any idea what kind of marriages their teachers or rabbis have. Not knowing that, they should seek teachers and rabbis who act in a *menschlich* way—who are shining examples of decency. There is a Jewish saying, "Decency preceded the Torah (*derech eretz kadma l'Torah*)." Since much of Judaism involves how we relate to others, a rabbi should model how to be a Godly person around others.

The Scholarship Shoshana was a baal teshuva who sought a roommate. A few months after Malkie moved into Shoshana's apartment, Malkie acted very disrespectfully toward Shoshana and violated the rules that they had formulated before Malkie moved in. Malkie used Shoshana's phone without permission, invited friends to stay in Shoshana's room without Shoshana's permission when Shoshana was away, and repeatedly left Shoshana's dishes dirty and the kitchen a mess.

One Friday, Shoshana planned to go away for the weekend but suddenly fell ill. She decided to go home instead of to her planned destination. She arrived home an hour before Shabbos, only to find that Malkie had invited her two brothers to spend Shabbos in her apartment, and they had already moved into Shoshana's room! They were lounging on her bed, listening to her CDs, and were reading some private letters from Shoshana's desk drawer.

Shoshana was livid. She ordered Malkie to move out within the week, which Malkie did when Shoshana was at work one day. When Shoshana returned home, she looked forward to having peace for the first time in months. Instead, the apartment looked as if a hurricane had struck. Shoshana sighed as she started cleaning up and then gasped when she realized that Malkie had stolen Shoshana's new, expensive linens that she had bought to replace the ones that Malkie had ruined! Shoshana was ready to explode.

Just then, the phone rang. It didn't surprise Shoshana that it was for Malkie. Malkie had given everyone Shoshana's phone number as Malkie's own because Malkie couldn't afford a phone.

The voice on the other end of the line told Shoshana, "I am from the Financial Aid department at Hunter College. Malkie has been awarded a full scholarship to attend graduate school here. If she doesn't accept the scholarship by five o'clock this afternoon, we will have to give it to another applicant. Do you know where we can reach Malkie?"

Shoshana knew exactly where to reach Malkie, but she certainly didn't want to. Shoshana took down the Financial Aid officer's number and hung up the phone.

It was four o'clock. She called her rav, told him her predicament, and asked what Jewish law required her to do.

The rabbi replied, "According to Jewish law, you don't have to call her. But, the Temple was destroyed because of causeless hatred between Jews, and we are still in exile because of it. If you can overcome your anger about all of the terrible things that Malkie did to you, imagine what an incredible effect your causeless love will have on the world. We all know how much we need spiritual goodness these days."

After Shoshana hung up the phone, she called Malkie and told her the incredible news. Malkie got her scholarship. Shoshana never did get back her linens. Nevertheless, Shoshana got something worth far more. She had the good feeling of having done a spiritually heroic deed and had an opportunity to appreciate what an amazing rabbi she had.

What Rabbis Are and Aren't

All people who call themselves "Rabbi" do not have identical knowledge or expertise in dealing with different aspects of Jewish law, ethics, and familial relationships. Many non-observant people call themselves "rabbi" despite the fact that they are not knowledgeable about the Five Books of Moses, the Oral Law (explications of the Written Torah that were given by God to Moses for oral transmission to the Jews; they were written down in the sixth century as the Talmud), nor about how Jewish law is supposed to be practiced. Many can't even read or understand Hebrew. This is very confusing to Jews who are not observant. They tend to think that everyone with the title rabbi knows the same information and gives equally valid advice about how to live as Jews.

History The process by which the rabbinate began dates back to the time of Moses. Rabbis were all knowledgeable and observant Jews who were originally ordained by Moses or by one of his ordained disciples. Although the transmission of Torah remained intact over time, this chain of actual ordination or semicha going back to Moses broke down due to the persecutions of the Jews in the fourth century. Since that time, observant rabbis have been ordained by observant Torah scholars once the students have shown that they have mastered the requisite knowledge.

The use of the term "rabbi" by non-observant Jews began in the 19th century with the creation of Reform Judaism. Subsequently, other sects such as Conservative and Reconstructionist developed, and began using the term "rabbi" as well. Today, almost no one with the title "rabbi" who affiliates with these groups is fully observant. A Torah-observant Jew does not pose their religious questions to non-Orthodox rabbis because such rabbis reject traditional Jewish beliefs and do not have the requisite knowledge of Jewish law and practice.

For example, a survey commissioned in 1972 by the Central Conference of American [Reform] Rabbis reported that "Only one in ten [Reform] rabbis states that he believes in God 'in the more or less traditional Jewish sense.'" The 90 percent who did not believe in a traditional Jewish God said that they were "agnostic," "atheist," "Baha'i in spirit, Judaic in practice," "polydoxist," "religious existentialist," and "theological humanist."[1]

Types of Rabbinic Ordination   There are currently two types of rabbinic ordination in the Torah-observant world. The first level is called "*yoreh yoreh*"—literally, "Can he teach? He can teach." Such a rabbi minimally knows what foods are and are not kosher. He typically knows the practical laws of Judaism as well.

The second level of rabbinic ordination is "*yadin yadin*"—literally, "Can he judge? He can judge." Such a rabbi knows Jewish law thoroughly and can be a judge in a Jewish court of law known as a *bet din*.

There was once a third, and highest, level of rabbinic ordination that required detailed knowledge of sacrifices in the Jewish temple. This was called "*yatir bechorot yatir*"—literally, "Can he release a firstborn due to a blemish? He can release it." While many Jews today study the ritual laws of Temple sacrifices, no one has the highest level of ordination today. Practically speaking, some observant men who hold the title "rabbi" only know the laws of kashrut and basic Judaism. Others have studied intensively for years and have encyclopedic knowledge of Jewish law. Some rabbis have extensive experience in practical rabbinics. Others have studied a lot but have little experience applying it to a *baal teshuva*'s circumstances.

Which Rabbi To Ask   There are many practical situations where a "run of the mill" Orthodox rabbi can easily answer questions about Jewish law. For example, a woman may want to know the basic laws of modesty, or whether her food is kosher after someone stirred hot chicken soup with a dairy spoon. On the other hand, if a man with a questionable genealogy wants to know whether to consider himself a cohen (a man of Jewish priestly lineage) and take upon himself the privileges and restrictions of Jewish priesthood, or whether Jewish law recommends that someone undergo a risky medical procedure, he should ask a rabbi with expertise in these areas.

Some *baal teshuvas* live in a place where the local observant rabbi(s) may be fine for deciding most religious questions but lacks the knowledge or sensitivity to give Jewish legal opinions appropriate for the *baal teshuva*'s circumstances. Rabbis with lots of experience dealing with *baal teshuvas* understand that a seemingly simple question may have great ramifications for the person's domestic harmony or for their future Jewish observance. A question about kashrut may imply a need to discuss what a *baal teshuva* should do to keep peace in a parent's house or how the answer will impact his wife and children. In this case, the *baal teshuva* should call a posek elsewhere who has that expertise.

In today's global village, dilemmas about how to find a posek can be easily remedied by speaking with observant people who have a posek, consulting Internet *baal teshuva* or Judaica sites, getting a referral from the local rav, or reading certain Jewish books. *Baal teshuvas* can consult rabbis whom they don't personally know by telephone, e-mail, or via Internet sites.

If people are fortunate enough to attend a *baal teshuva* seminary or yeshiva, they will find most of their rabbis and teachers happy for alumni to stay in touch with them. Before leaving the school, *baal teshuvas* should get contact numbers of rabbis and advisors in the community in which they will be living, whom they can consult when necessary.

Leniencies

Baal teshuvas sometimes think there is something wrong with following a lenient religious ruling, and that a lenient opinion is less valid than a strict one. However, it is fine to rely on a rabbi's leniencies as long as one abides by his stringencies as well.

Four Types   There are four circumstances that require giving a lenient ruling: When peace is at stake, when a significant financial loss can be avoided, when the strength of Torah observance may be affected, and when someone's health or life is at stake. A rav's greatness is not measured by his ability to give the most stringent rulings possible. Rather, a true Torah scholar sometimes advocates following leniencies that other rabbis might not dare advise. The Torah's ways are meant to be as pleasant, not as restrictive as possible.

Same Question, Different Answer   Baal teshuvas are sometimes surprised to hear that Jews with the same questions may get different answers, sometimes from the same rav! This is because rabbis have different approaches and because a prescription that is right for one person may not be right for someone else. One individual's circumstances or details might warrant being lenient while someone with a similar situation may have circumstances that warrant a stricter answer.

All such cases must be decided by a rabbi who is an expert in Jewish law, and people should not decide for themselves that another person's circumstances apply to them. It is always a good idea to discuss religious issues with such a rabbi when one is not certain of what Jewish law requires or when domestic harmony is at stake, rather than deciding such questions for oneself. Just as the doctor who treats himself has a fool for a patient, so is the person who acts as his or her own rabbi. Rather than being too strict or too lenient on ourselves, we can learn much Torah by going to an expert in Jewish law—often in ways that we would not otherwise learn it.

Personal Factors

Rabbis have different levels of sensitivity to baal teshuvas, and their personalities and Jewish views may affect the way each responds to Jewish legal questions. Some rabbis are especially sensitive to women. Some are especially knowledgeable about the secular backgrounds from which baal teshuvas come when they ask their questions. Some rabbis believe that Jews should be insulated from the secular world while others are more open to the secular world. It is important to choose a rav whose flavor of Judaism and way of relating to baal teshuvas match the person asking the question. Rabbis' different religious perspectives sometimes affect their Jewish legal rulings (piskei halacha), also known as how they poskin shailas. For example, a Chassidic rabbi and a modern Orthodox rabbi may give diametrically different Jewish legal rulings when asked the same question.

The Double Oven This disparity in religious perspectives was unknown to Betty when she became observant in college. She learned Jewish law from a Chassidic rebbetzin. When the rabbi kashered her home, he told her that she needed separate ovens for milk and meat. Years later, she discovered that non-Chassidim use the same oven for dairy and meat, provided that it is clean and that certain other qualifications are observed.

Lakewood vs YU Yirmi and Avital discovered how different rabbis could be when they were engaged to be married. He took premarital classes with a rabbi who learned in Lakewood yeshiva, while she took classes in the laws of family holiness from a rebbetzin whose husband learned in Yeshiva University. After the couple got married, they were shocked to discover that they learned different things about how to properly observe the laws of family holiness! After speaking to their rabbi, they discovered that this is not uncommon, and he advised them how to reconcile their differences.

Finding the Right Rabbi

Finding a rav is not easy for some *baal teshuvas*. They may not know the differences between one rabbi and the next and what those differences imply. It can also take time for *baal teshuvas* to find a rabbi to whom they can relate. That is why it makes sense for *baal teshuvas* to initially ask their questions of their teachers or to the rabbi in their community. As they learn and observe more, they may feel that their local rav does not have the knowledge or sophistication necessary to answer some of their questions. (In other cases, they may discover how much their rav does know, and how fortunate they are to have such a person to consult.) If a local rabbi isn't suitable for them, they may then find a different rav, at least for questions that their local rabbi can't handle.

Some rabbis are so popular and busy that they aren't available for answering general questions or for giving ongoing advice and guidance, but they can be consulted when an expert opinion is necessary. In some communities, the local rabbi handles most questions during the year. When people have questions about whether certain food products are kosher, or whether certain products are kosher for Passover, they should call national kashrut hotlines or rabbis who specialize in such food supervision (see Appendix).

Teachers or spiritual mentors can often help *baal teshuvas* to find an appropriate rav. If a *baal teshuva* doesn't feel comfortable with the person who is recommended to them, he or she can discuss this with the person who made the recommendation. The teacher might then recommend someone else. As a *baal teshuva* becomes more knowledgeable and more connected to other *baal teshuvas*, those friends may also recommend rabbis with whom they have had positive experiences.

Baal teshuvas who don't yet have a rav may initially ask different questions to a variety of rabbis. This will give them an idea of how different rabbis approach various issues. Although it is tempting, *baal teshuvas* should not "shop around" by asking different rabbis the same question until they get the answer that they like. Also, the fact that a rav is stringent with himself or with his family is no indication that he will be more stringent than Jewish law requires with *baal teshuvas*. A good rav will give answers that suit each person and that person's circumstances.

Checking Out a Rabbi It can be helpful for baal teshuvas to have an advisor "check out" a rabbi they are considering consulting if he is not widely known in the Torah world. Was the rabbi ordained in a recognized Torah institution or by a Torah scholar? Does he have broad and deep knowledge of Jewish law? Are his approaches and understanding of how to poskin generally accepted? Does he understand and respond sensitively to baal teshuvas? Does he have integrity in his personal behavior? Most rabbis will need to have studied a minimum of four years in a yeshiva in order to have enough knowledge to address the complex issues that baal teshuvas might encounter. Rabbis should continue their learning after getting rabbinical ordination in order to maintain and expand their knowledge.

Hashkafa When baal teshuvas identify the hashkafa with which they are most comfortable, they can ask friends or teachers to recommend a rav whose approach is similar. Ideally, there should be a match between a community rabbi's general hashkafa and that of the baal teshuva. Unless someone is a Torah giant, he may not have the sensitivity and knowledge to address questions coming from someone from a totally different world than he lives in. To find out if a local rabbi would be suitable for a particular individual, it can be helpful to find out in which yeshiva he studied—for example, in Yeshiva University, Lakewood, Brisk, Telz, Mir, Aish HaTorah or Chabad, to name a few. What kinds of people ask him shailas (questions of Jewish law)? Does he teach any classes and, if so, in what subjects? Is he affiliated with a particular synagogue, school, Jewish institution, or community kollel? [A kollel is a yeshiva where (usually married) men study Talmud full time. In a community kollel, the men also teach members of the community.] Does he study Torah every day? What does he study? Even if the baal teshuva doesn't know what this information means, his or her spiritual advisor might use it to help determine if this rabbi will be a good match for the baal teshuva.

Circumstances There are times when a baal teshuva has questions that require a rav's knowing their circumstances and other times when that is not necessary. For the former type of question, it is best to contact your own rav; if that's not possible, explain your circumstances to an alternate. For the latter type of question, it is fine to get answers from other qualified rabbis when one's primary rav is not available. One can call a community rabbi or experts in Jewish law who make themselves accessible by phone at specific times every week. There are also halacha hotlines for questions such as kashrut, lashon hara (harmful gossip), and issues relating to Shabbos, including whether an eruv is up in an area, using cosmetics on Shabbos, and having blood tests for infertility treatments on Shabbos. (Contact information for the first two is listed in the Appendix. The third can be accessed by searching the web for the words "Hilchos Shabbos hotline.")

Trust

Besides being a fount of Torah wisdom, a true Torah scholar has impeccable integrity. Unfortunately, there are also some unethical charismatic Jews who market themselves as kabbalists, miracle men, rabbis, and the like. Their main objectives are to get honor, self-gratification, and/or money from unknowledgeable or desperate people. All Jews should avoid these characters. Jews should do background checks before they run to see rabbis who come to town offering blessings (usually expecting donations), *kabbala* (Jewish mysticism) for the masses, and spiritual quick fixes. Some are truly holy men, yet others have left behind a trail of disappointed (and poorer) people.

Scam Artist   Noah was an attractive, articulate rabbi who got semicha (rabbinical ordination) from a well-known yeshiva in Jerusalem. He applied to be an assistant rabbi at a synagogue that did Jewish outreach. After being interviewed by the synagogue's rabbi, Noah got a year-long contract to start a beginner's service, run outreach Shabbatons, teach beginner's classes, and do spiritual counseling.

Noah was very successful on all counts. He was a great "people person." Within six months, at least 50 new people were regularly attending services and classes. He was soon telling newcomers about the importance of Jewish outreach and soliciting donations to expand his programs. By the end of the year, Noah had solicited thousands of dollars from unsuspecting Jews to support his expensive apartment, buy himself custom-made suits, eat out in costly restaurants, and make deposits into his personal bank account.

The rabbi who hired him heard of his shenanigans when several Jews from whom Noah solicited funds asked the rabbi whether they should give Noah donations. The rabbi checked out Noah's background and discovered that Noah had conned many "donors" in Jerusalem before he had fled to America, where his reputation wasn't known.

Unfortunately, when Noah quietly packed his bags and slipped off to another city, he plied his wares to others for a long time before his reputation caught up with him.

The moral of this story is never to give money to anyone unless you can check and make sure that the receiver is who he purports to be, is reliable and honest, and that your money will go for intended purposes.

Personal Decisions

Baal teshuvas need a rabbi to answer their questions and guide them toward spiritual growth. Yet, as Dennis discovered, there are some decisions that only the *baal teshuva* can make.

Dilemma Dennis and Alexa had been married for more than 20 years. While those years hadn't always been happy ones, they had weathered the bad times and were still in love with each other. He had a small, successful business, they lived in a beautiful neighborhood, and both of their sons were doing well in good colleges. One day, Dennis went on a business trip and sat for five hours on a plane next to an Orthodox Jew. One thing led to another, and Dennis was soon taking Judaism classes. Slowly but surely, he became increasingly observant.

This created problems because Alexa wasn't Jewish. Dennis was born Jewish but never had any Jewish education. He had never minded the fact that his wife was from a Methodist family because she wasn't much of a churchgoer. They had raised their boys as secular. The boys had attended a private Protestant high school and had non-Jewish friends. Every winter, they had a Christmas tree, but it was more of a social convention than a religious object.

Alexa was taken aback by Dennis' religious transformation and was completely uninterested in Judaism. The spiritual gulf that began to separate them became wider and wider. Still, when Dennis wanted to keep kosher at home, Alexa was willing to conform to the restrictions as long as she could eat anything she wanted outside the house. He wanted to observe Shabbos, but this put a crimp in their social life and made her very unhappy. They stopped going out on Friday nights and spending Saturday mornings playing golf. He no longer went to Saturday matinees of opera or concerts, and he gave up eating out. Dennis felt lonely staying at home on Shabbos or being a guest in others' homes while Alexa went out with friends on Saturdays.

He got to a point where he couldn't move forward with his Judaism as long as he lived with a non-Jewish wife, yet he also didn't want to lose her. He asked his rabbi,

"Do you think that I should divorce my wife?"

The rabbi wisely replied, "No rabbi can tell you to do that. That's a decision that only you can make."

When *baal teshuvas* want a rabbi to make their tough decisions for them, the rabbi's refusal to do so may be one of the best reasons to trust him!

Advice

Sometimes a rabbi or spiritual mentor will give what seems to the *baal teshuva* to be bad advice. If that happens, it can be useful to discuss the matter with a Torah teacher or objective advisor.

Baal teshuvas may not know when they are getting good advice or Torah wisdom and when they are hearing misguided opinions. Not hearing what you want to hear does not mean that someone isn't giving you appropriate information.

In addition, *baal teshuvas* may get "bad advice" about what to do if they give a rav only partial or misleading information, if they ask a question inappropriately, or if the rav lacks sufficient factual information about the matter to give an informed response. There are also times when a rabbi does not have the background to answer questions posed to him, yet he oversteps his bounds and answers anyway. Rabbis who aren't objective may sometimes interject their personal opinions into the advice that they dispense, and those opinions may not be in the person's best interest. And, of course, there are times when people assume that if the rabbi's answers aren't what they want to hear; the rabbi must be wrong.

Misinterpretation Baal teshuvas must be careful not to confuse what everyone else seems to be doing with Jewish law. For example, there are many synagogues where congregants sit down when Kaddish is recited and people are supposed to stand up, and they stand up when it is fine to sit down. Even worse, there are synagogues where people talk throughout the prayers and during the Torah reading even though that violates Jewish law. Much of what we learn as Jews is by imitation. We need to ask if what others do is based in Jewish law, and if so, are we supposed to conduct ourselves that way?

For example, Toby came to a *baal teshuva* seminary in New York one winter and became observant during the next few months. In July, there was a sweltering heat wave, and temperatures soared to a hundred degrees during the day. The humidity locked in the heat. There was no respite from this sauna even at night, when temperatures remained in the mid-80s.

The seminary girls, like many poor souls in New York, had no air conditioners. Yet, Toby wore a heavy bathrobe over her nightgown. As she perspired profusely, another young woman asked her why she was dressed that way.

Toby replied, "I thought that was the way women are required to dress at night." It never occurred to her that when she had arrived in the seminary in February, it was cold in the dormitories. Naturally, the other women were dressed in heavy bathrobes so that they could keep warm. Their behavior had nothing to do with modesty. Tobi never realized that until someone confronted her about her behavior during a sweltering summer.

It is sometimes difficult for *baal teshuvas* to ascertain what is right for them without consulting their rabbi or advisor. Just because a teacher or role model lives by a certain standard, that isn't necessarily the ideal for which they should strive.

We should all strive for greater spiritual connection with the Almighty. As individuals, though, we have unique paths that differ from person to person. We need to rely on the good advice of someone who is knowledgeable and objective to help us find our way.

Ignoring Advice Samantha was a young woman with unique abilities who was quite unconventional. As she became observant, she asked a rav if it was okay to socialize with non-religious men. The rav explained why that wasn't a good idea. She decided that the rav gave her bad advice because what he said wasn't what she wanted to hear.

She was lonely and hadn't dated in awhile, so she went to a secular Jewish event hoping to meet someone nice to date. She did, and he asked her out. It soon became apparent that he wasn't Jewish, but she figured, "What's the harm in one date?" She accepted his invitation.

By the end of their six-hour date, they had "fallen" for each other. When he asked her out again, she didn't want to say 'no', and she accepted again. They continued to see each other a few more times and each date was better than the one before.

When he went away to college, he ended their relationship. Both of them went through a lot of needless emotional pain having to break off a relationship that never should have happened. Samantha realized too late that her rabbi understood far more than she did about life.

Know A Rabbi's Limits Being a rav and being a counselor/therapist often overlap. Since Judaism has a perspective about every aspect of life, people ask rabbis' advice about almost anything and everything. People ask rabbis to advise them about legal matters, problems with their children, spouses, neighbors, careers, and even business decisions. Sometimes people ask rabbis' advice about matters that are beyond the rabbis' expertise, especially when it comes to some relationship and emotional issues. Most rabbis aren't equipped to help someone choose a marriage partner, resolve marital discord, help children with learning problems, and resolve emotional conflicts. While a rabbi can give spiritual approaches to these matters, professional therapists and specialists are usually the best address for help with such matters, even if one has to pay for such help. Otherwise, people might get what they pay for.

Some people who need professional advice go to rabbis instead of therapists because that allows them to deny that they have a "real" problem. The rabbi's advice is also free! Unfortunately, a rabbi who does therapy without proper training can do people a real disservice.

Simplistic Advice   Dean, a 30-year-old bachelor, asked a rabbi whether or not he should marry Aliza after dating her 10 times. She was pretty, had good character traits, was religious, and had life goals that were compatible with Dean's. Yet, he wasn't excited about marrying her.

"Is there was anything wrong with her?" his rabbi asked
"No," Dean said.
"Have you ever dated a woman whom you wanted to marry?"
"No."
"Then you should marry Aliza," concluded the rabbi. "The feelings will come once you're married."

Needless to say, the feelings didn't come after marriage. Dean spent the first few years of their marriage confused, agitated, and aloof from his wife. He deprived both of them of the pleasures that they could have shared had he worked out his issues with a competent therapist instead of taking simplistic advice from a rabbi.

Simplistic ways of responding to emotional issues may prevent the *baal teshuva* from dealing with what really needs to be addressed— possible problems with intimacy, fears of making commitments and decisions, not feeling chemistry with a woman, depression, and so on. A rabbi who has trained as a professional counselor or therapist would be an excellent choice to give people with real emotional problems the psychological help that they need.

Wait a Year Elaine and Simon got married in college and became baal teshuvas in law school. After they finished their training, Elaine wanted to have children, but Simon was working terribly long hours and did not want any more responsibilities. He had no place in his life or his heart for children.

Elaine felt her biological clock pounding. When she was 32 years old, she went to her rav for advice about how to deal with her husband. She didn't know that the rabbi had such a happy marriage and loved his children so much that he could not understand how others did not feel the same way. He advised Elaine to give Simon another year. By then, the rabbi was sure that Simon would come around. Elaine followed the rabbi's advice.

When Elaine was 33 years old, Simon was in exactly the same emotional place as before. It was only when she sought professional help that she realized the extent to which she and Simon had serious marital problems and different goals. Listening to the rabbi's advice had only made Elaine lose another year of precious time. The couple got divorced. Years later, Simon still had no interest in having children.

Raising Children Sandy and Jacob had three children. The youngest, Meir, was floundering in the intellectually-demanding day school that he attended. Sandy took Meir to an educational consultant for an evaluation and he was found to have some severe learning disabilities and an attention-deficit disorder. The consultant recommended that Meir be removed from Hebrew classes because he couldn't handle learning a second language and was overwhelmed by the additional pressures that the Hebrew studies placed on him.

Sandy and Jacob consulted their rabbi, who pooh-poohed the idea that Meir had such difficulties. He insisted that Meir would outgrow his learning problems, and that removing him from Judaica studies was a terrible idea. The parents followed their rabbi's advice instead of having Meir learn secular subjects in school with remedial help and learn about Judaism from a private tutor. Instead of Meir being a well-adjusted child who learned in school for half a day and was tutored about Judaism at his own pace, he was crushed by his constant failures in school. The rabbi's disastrous advice ruined Meir's self-esteem, his ability to value being Jewish, and interfered with Meir's ability to use the potentials that he did have.

Some rare rabbis without formal counseling training give good advice based on their intuition and experience. Yet, most rabbis should refer *baal teshuvas* with emotional or complicated family problems to a competent therapist or other experts and not try to be all things to all people.

Rabbis Who Are Professional Counselors

Fortunately, many rabbis today have MA or PhD degrees in counseling and are professionally trained to help with grief or family problems. It can be useful to determine this before one assumes that a rabbi will be equipped to help with certain issues. When a rabbi is well trained in the proper techniques, he can be a tremendous help in dealing with family problems that *baal teshuvas* encounter.

Four-Way Meeting Harlen and Audrey started becoming more observant before their first baby was born. Audrey's mother, Carol, came to town to help Audrey but insisted that the "antiquated rules" that her daughter was observing were ridiculous and certainly not necessary in an era when we have refrigerators and good hygiene. She brought non-kosher food into their home and made it clear that she thought that having her grandson ritually circumcised (bris milah) was barbaric.

Carol and Audrey were in a tug-of-war over who would control the baby. When Harlen told their rabbi (who often used his master's degree in counseling) what was going on, the rabbi suggested having a family meeting.

"Carol, you must have been very surprised to see how much Audrey has changed in the last year," the rabbi began.

Carol: *You bet. I was so happy when she got married. I thought that she and Harlen would have a won-*

derful family together. Now that they've become so fanatic, I don't know what's happened to them.

Rabbi: *What did you hope their family life would look like, and how is it different from that?*

Carol: *Well, I hoped that they'd be modern, successful people who loved each other and who had good, happy, successful children.*

Rabbi: *I guess that your idea of normal meant eating the way most Americans do and living without Jewish rituals.*

Carol: *That's right. Don't get me wrong, Rabbi, I don't mind going to Rosh Hashana services or to a Passover seder as long as the religious stuff isn't overdone. But I want my grandson to be raised as a normal child. Audrey's gone overboard with these rituals. These rituals were fine when Jews didn't know about hygiene, but we don't need them any more. They only draw a wedge between us and other people and make us stand out in bad ways.*

Rabbi: *I could see how some people think that the Jewish laws were made up for hygienic purposes. Can we come back to that later?*

Carol: *Sure.*

Rabbi: *First, I want to agree with you that Jewish laws can certainly set people apart from one another. Are you concerned that Audrey's keeping Jewish traditions will make it hard for you to be close to her, or to have a loving relationship with your grandchildren?*

Carol: *Of course. If I don't keep kosher, my grandchildren are going to think that I'm not Jewish and they won't be able to eat in my house or go to restaurants with me. Half the fun of being a grandmother is feeding them and taking them out to eat.*

Rabbi: *I certainly agree with you there. If you knew that Audrey and Harlen would raise their children to respect and love you, would it bother you so much that they kept kosher?*

Carol: *It would still bother me, but not as much. I don't want my grandchildren to lose out on wonderful experiences because their parents want them to be religious.*

Rabbi: *We all want the best for our children and grandchildren, but we can't guarantee that they'll have everything we want for them. Do you think that most children are well adjusted and happy today? If you saw that your grandchildren could have wonderful lives, even if not exactly the way you had envisioned, would that upset you?*

Carol: *I could deal with that.*

Rabbi: *You know, Carol, we all have to let go of our children, and let them make their own choices. We also have to change and compromise. If I were in your shoes, and were as caring a mother as you are, I would also be concerned about my daughter's becoming more observant. On the other hand, she's an adult now, and she's entitled to make her own choices. Don't you agree?*

Carol: *Within reason.*

Rabbi: *Well, from what I know of Audrey, she seems to be a very reasonable person, and I think that she'll be a great mother. Have you been curious as to why someone like her would choose to take on religious observances like keeping kosher and having a ritual circumcision for her baby?*

Carol: *Well, now that you mention it....Audrey, why in the world did you want to change your life so much*

*and do these things? They're so archaic, they're so re-
strictive...*

This rabbi has masterfully given Carol a chance to talk about her
feelings, and he empathized with her deepest concerns. Once Carol's defenses are down, he can raise questions in her mind as to why
Audrey has chosen the path she has. He has set the stage for the
mother and daughter to engage in a productive dialogue, mediated
by him.

The Art of Asking Questions

While some factual questions such as "How do I get to the train
station?" are straightforward, seemingly simple questions about Jewish law can be more involved. There is an art to asking shailas, and
the rabbi sometimes needs to hear many details that the *baal teshuva*
would not even think to include.

Imagine a patient asking a doctor if penicillin is good for bacte-
rial infections. The doctor might say "yes." Were the doctor to know
that the patient is allergic to penicillin, or that the patient actually
has a viral infection, the doctor would answer the question very differently.

Until a person knows how to ask halachic questions, or has a rav
who knows him or her well, it can be helpful to request that an advisor ask the questions, preferably with the *baal teshuva* present. Shailas
requiring straightforward, factual answers can be asked of a halachic
expert by telephoning a rabbi whom the *baal teshuva* doesn't even
know. For example, if someone wants to know if a kashrut symbol
on a food is reliable, he can phone a rabbinic expert on kashrut and
ask the question.

The real question, though, might be, "My parents have gone all-
out to make me kosher food when I stay with them for the first time
since I became observant. My mother bought food supervised by
this rabbi. Should I eat the food?" If the rabbinic expert on kashrut
says that the products can't be eaten, he will need to tell the *baal
teshuva* how to diplomatically handle the host of relationship issues
that will follow.

Once someone asks a shaila, he or she is supposed to abide by the answer. *Baal teshuvas* sometimes avoid asking a shaila because they believe that they won't get an answer they can live with. At other times, they don't ask a rabbi important questions because they are embarrassed asking something so personal. It is sometimes easier to discuss these situations with an advisor, who can then ask the shaila on the *baal teshuva's* behalf. If that's not possible, the *baal teshuva* can ask a rabbi on an Internet site or anonymously on a telephone without the posek's knowing who they are.

E-mail Advisor Alan didn't feel comfortable asking his Torah teachers his questions, so he went on an Internet site geared to baal teshuvas. He wrote about his concerns and asked some detailed questions. Although he didn't always get the answers that he hoped to hear, his e-mails set up a dialogue with a wonderful rabbi with whom he continues to correspond when he has questions about Judaism. That rabbi has become his religious advisor.

Summary

Choosing the "right" rabbi can be one of the most important decisions that a *baal teshuva* makes. In some ways, it is like finding a marriage partner. *Baal teshuvas* can find a rabbi by asking their teachers or friends whom they recommend. It is important that a *baal teshuva* feel comfortable talking to the rabbi he or she chooses and feel that he understands him or her. A rabbi can guide people in so many areas of life, including how to grow religiously, how to build a Jewish home and educate one's children, what Jewish outlook to adopt, and how to relate to others. A *baal teshuva's* rabbi should be knowledgeable in Jewish law, be experienced fostering good relationships between people, and have personal integrity.

Due to the limited time that many rabbis have, it is often wise to have a spiritual advisor who can guide *baal teshuvas* in concert with one's rabbi. The right advisor can teach the *baal teshuva* how to ask religious questions, what religious questions should be asked, and who to ask questions of when one's rabbi is not available. As in a good marriage, a good fit between a *baal teshuva* and his or her rabbi can go far in helping *baal teshuvas* enjoy and feel fulfilled by a Torah lifestyle, have good relationships with their family and other Jews, and provide healthy ways to continually grow.

EIGHT

A Jewish Community

Observant Jews need to be part of a Jewish community and find a synagogue within walking distance of their homes where they are comfortable praying. *Baal teshuvas* want supportive friends who can understand and relate to them and who share their values, interests, and concerns. They enjoy having friends with whom they can celebrate Shabbos and religious holidays, baby namings, circumcisions, bar and bat mitzvahs, and weddings, and who will comfort them if they lose a loved one or suffer a tragedy. Singles will seek a community where there are other religious, potential marriage partners and where families will host them for Shabbos and holiday meals.

Comforting Loss Judi and Jack were fortunate to have found a religious community that was perfect for them. They became baal teshuvas and joined a religious community just before their baby was born. Tragically, the infant died, and the community rallied around the stunned parents. The rebbetzin organized people to bring chairs and food to the house for the week of shiva. The rabbi brought a Torah scroll to read at services in their house that week. A third person organized men to come for a daily minyan. In addition, many people from their new community came over to comfort them for their loss.

Judi and Jack felt so supported that they recalled their community's kindness every year at their child's yahrzeit (anniversary of death).

Baal teshuvas may feel comfortable in one community for many years, or they may outgrow it as Emily did as their religious and personal needs change.

Matchmakers, Dates   Emily became a baal teshuva in a religious community with many families. The people were warm and inviting and a family always hosted her for Shabbos and holiday meals. The rabbi was wonderful, too. Yet, after being observant for a few years, she knew every single religious man within a few hundred miles of her city, and none was a potential mate for her. The rabbi advised her to move to a city with many religious singles.

She followed his advice and moved to New York. She missed the warmth of her home community and felt lost in the sea of singles. She moved to a cozier community in New Jersey that was within commuting distance of New York City. There, she lived close to host families, yet she had easy access to matchmakers and potential dates.

Baal teshuvas need to find a religious community with affordable housing within commuting distance of work or the place they study. Ideally, it should also offer a high-quality spiritual, if not material, life. *Baal teshuvas* need to find out if the religious values and lifestyle of the people in a community will match their own. Are there good religious schools for their children and Jewish classes for themselves? If single, will they be able to meet other religious singles, attend singles' events, and find matchmakers who will introduce them to potential marriage partners? Will parents and children find peers their ages who have compatible religious approaches and interests?

Moving Up   Ruth and Jeff were Reform Jews who began attending a nearby synagogue with a wonderful observant rabbi. Although the synagogue was Orthodox, there were only a handful of observant people in the entire town. Ruth and Jeff became observant over the next two years, along with their three school-age children. The rabbi insisted that they move to a larger Jewish community with a religious school where the children and parents could have a more fulfilling Jewish life. A year later, Jeff found a job in Boston and moved his family to Brookline. He sent his children to the wonderful day school there and found a place among the many observant professional families in the area.

How Do Communities Differ?

There is not one "right" community for everyone, and each has many options to consider.

Approaches to Judaism   Communities may be on a spectrum of religious observance, ranging from modern Orthodox to yeshivish, chareidi, and Chassidic, including a variety of groups in-between. There are cultural and lifestyle differences between communities in California, the mid-West, the South, New England, Canada, New York, Baltimore, and Jerusalem, to name a few.

Origins   Some communities are largely composed of one group of Jews. For example, there are communities of émigré Ashkenazic Israelis, Iranian, Iraqi, and Syrian Jews. Some communities are largely composed of third- or fourth-generation Americans with many baal teshuvas among them, while others are mostly FFBs (Frum From Birth Jews: born into observant families).

Ages   Communities vary in the ages of people who live there. They range from senior citizens, to young couples, to families with young children, or even singles. Some are largely homogeneous, while other communities are more mixed.

Professions   People sometimes seek neighbors who work in similar professions. Communities near universities often have many academics. Some communities have many Yuppies (young, upper class, professional), business people, or high-tech and computer people; others are poor, still others are middle class. Some communities have people who work in a variety of jobs, from blue collar, to teaching, to professional. Some have primarily men who study Torah full time and whose wives work to support the family.

Learning Opportunities   Some towns or cities have lots of Jewish learning opportunities, including a variety of classes, guest lectures, community kollels, yeshivas, and/or seminaries. Other places have daily services and only one or two Jewish classes given by the local rabbi. Some places have many Jews with yeshiva backgrounds, while others have members with strong secular education. Some communities have people with both.

Settings   Religious communities are in urban, suburban, and rural settings. Some communities are even near beaches [such as Onset (Cape Cod), Fire Island (NY), Deal (NJ), Nice (France), and Kiryat Sanz (Israel)] or in the mountains (such as the Catskills, Tannersville, and the summer Chassidic community in Burlington, VT).

Amenities   Most families with young children seek a community with an eruv, a series of wires and other devices that enclose the Jews in one area and permit carrying outside one's home on Shabbos. An eruv permits people to carry outside the home and use strollers on Shabbos.

Some communities have at least one mikvah, which is very convenient for married women who need to use it on Shabbos or Jewish holidays. If a community lacks a mikvah, women will have to drive to another town or wait an extra day or two to immerse if their immersion night falls during a multiple-day Jewish holiday or on Friday night.

Some communities have a variety of shuls (synagogues) and schools to choose from while others may have only one synagogue, with children commuting to school in another town. In some places, children move out of town to attend high school because there are no local Jewish schools beyond eighth grade.

Neighborhoods populated by many observant Jews tend to offer conveniences such as kosher stores, kosher restaurants, Jewish bookstores, Torah audio-lending libraries, Judaism classes, and beginner's services.

Some communities have Jewish schools for learning disabled or deaf children. Jerusalem and New York City have institutes with many resources for Jews who are blind. A few synagogues have interpreters who sign the rabbi's sermon, announcements, and Megillah reading for hearing-impaired and deaf people. Some synagogues, Jewish community centers and mikvahs are handicapped accessible.

Some baal teshuvas will want to know if a community has a good quality of life apart from its religious aspects. For example, are there parks, libraries, community centers, secular classes, and activities such as sports leagues, and tennis courts nearby?

Costs Housing, tuition for Jewish education, and living costs vary greatly from one community to another. Homes that are outside a community's eruv may cost considerably less than homes that are inside, but will usually entail a longer walk to the synagogue on Shabbos.

Safety is of utmost concern to some families, who seek a community in a low-crime neighborhood. Unfortunately, the cost of housing in many cities rises with the safety of the surroundings.

Getting Information

Baal teshuvas can begin their search for a community by asking a teacher or advisor to suggest appropriate options and to describe their pros and cons. They can get basic information about many synagogues and their communities by visiting the websites of the Orthodox Union, Young Israel, Agudas Israel, and Chabad. Each lists affiliated synagogues with their location, contact information, and name of the rabbi. Googling specific Orthodox synagogues in an area can yield additional leads. Once you have contact information, call or e-mail the local yeshiva or synagogue to find out about other synagogues or Jewish resources nearby.

A community kollel can be a main source of classes and support for *baal teshuvas*. The rabbis' wives in a community kollel often teach women's classes, and the kollel typically has evening learning sessions for men and some classes for women. Kollel couples usually invite Jews from their community to their homes for meals on Shabbos and Jewish holidays. Information about a variety of community kollels is available by googling the city desired with the words "community kollel." Some of these can be found by contacting www. torahmitzion.org.

Some religious communities have their own community directory. If you can get a copy, it can be a treasure trove of practical information!

Experience the Community

Once you have narrowed down the information you have accumulated, visit the communities that interest you most. Try to spend a Shabbos plus a weekday there. You might get a taste of how warm the people are, how alive and vibrant the classes and children's programs are, and what the people there are like. Are the people well learned in Torah? Do the adults and children have nice character traits? Do they seem to have a good balance between materialism/ spirituality and religious/secular involvements? Do the people live Judaism in a way that suits you? Do you feel that you could fit in? Does the neighborhood have schools that would be suitable for your children? Are the people there happy with their community and their way of life?

Wonderful Fit   Annette and Brian became observant in a mid-Western city that limited their possibilities for spiritual growth. After getting advice about other communities that might be more suitable, they decided to spend a weekend visiting a place that reportedly had a vibrant religious community, good religious education for children and adults, and a good quality of life.

Their experience surpassed their wildest expectations. There were many other *baal teshuvas* there. There were two synagogues with several minyans where they felt comfortable. The community had an eruv, which made it easy to take their two young children to shul on Shabbos, and there were children's groups during Saturday prayer services. The parents they met spoke well of the local religious school. Brian was especially impressed by the large number of people who attended the early minyan on Saturday morning, then stayed for a Torah class afterward, and came back to the shul *motzei Shabbos* (Saturday night) to learn together with their children.

It is worthwhile asking religious Jews in a community what they think are the pros and cons of their neighborhood. After speaking to several people, you might get a picture of whether this community might be appropriate for you.

Persistence Pays Bonnie and Ron were modern Orthodox baal teshuvas who were expecting their first child. They wanted to buy a house in a suburb that had many observant Jews. They got names of three couples who lived in a recommended community. These families offered to host them for Shabbos meals. This allowed Bonnie and Ron to spend each of the three meals with a different family. They stayed with a fourth family, and went to three different synagogues during their whirlwind tour. They liked the Torah ideas that the rabbi spoke about in the synagogue that they attended Friday night, but the service was staid and they were disturbed by the incessant talking. They liked the vibrant Saturday morning services at a different shul that they attended. The people there were friendly, down-to-earth, and had nice manners, but the rabbi's sermon wasn't very meaty. The third "synagogue" was a minyan in someone's home. Ron liked it, but Bonnie wasn't happy that the women had to sit in the family's kitchen.

The hosts had mostly positive comments about the Jewish school. One synagogue also offered a few beginner classes for men and women.

The main downside to the community was that people were so busy during the week that it only felt like a community on Shabbos and Jewish holidays. Most of the women had jobs and there were few stay-at-home mothers like Bonnie planned to be. She believed that she would feel lonely there. She needed a core of women whom she could befriend and spend time with during the week while her children were small.

Bonnie was advised to check out a community where the Jews were more religious and knowledgeable than Ron and Bonnie were, and where many women were full-time mothers. They found the religious standards there to be intimidating. So, they continued asking questions about other options, now realizing what was critical to them in a community and what wasn't.

It took about a year, but they finally found a community with a spectrum of modern Orthodox Jews that was a good choice for them. Ron ended up going to the religious Zionist community kollel minyan, and Bonnie ended up feeling at home in the modern Orthodox shul. They found a young rabbi from the kollel who suited them both, and his wife and Bonnie became good friends.

Questions To Ask

Baal teshuva women often have some concerns about a community that are different from those of men, and they should discuss these with their religious mentor or advisor. For example, in which religious communities do *baal teshuvas* who are similar to themselves feel happiest, feel most fulfilled, and feel they have meaningful lives? Does the *baal teshuva* think that she will fit in there? Are women there generally respected? Do the husbands and wives have the kinds of relationships that the *baal teshuva* would like to have with her spouse? Do the women get support raising their families or are they overwhelmed? Would the *baal teshuva* feel fulfilled by the kind of life that most women there have? If a woman is single, how are singles integrated into, and treated by, various communities? If the *baal teshuva* has, or hopes to have, a university education and a career, how is that viewed?

Does the *baal teshuva* want to live in a community where men and women are largely segregated from one another or where there is more mixing? Which community is most conducive to the *baal teshuva's* feeling able to express her creativity and individuality and experiencing the kind of religious intensity that she hopes to have?

Feeling Understood

One of the nice things about being part of the right community is that *baal teshuvas* can relax and feel understood. No one wants to feel that he or she will never fit in, never be understood, always have to explain himself or herself, and always be regarded as somehow inferior or an outsider. As one *baal teshuva* put it, "Perhaps part of the lyrics from the TV show 'Cheers' said it best:

'Making your way in the world today ...Takes everything you've got... Sometimes you want to go where everybody knows your name ... And they're always glad you came ...'"

Scuba Lesson Marlene was a baal teshuva who was exploring different religious communities to see where she could fit in. She ate dinner one Friday night with a host family who were European FFBs. The couple was kind and very hospitable, but Marlene had little in common with them. The mother was a full-time wife and mother who had little secular education. The hosts had spent their lives among Chassidim, and their closest friends were European. Marlene felt like the man on the moon when the conversation went like this:

Hostess:	*Where did you get such a nice tan in the middle of December?*
Marlene:	*I just came back from a scuba diving trip in Bonaire.*
Hostess:	*What is Bonaire, and what is scuba diving?*
Marlene:	*[excitedly] Bonaire is a small Caribbean island, about a two-hour flight south of Miami. Scuba diving is going underwater with a tank of air on your back, swimming with a glass mask on, and seeing all of the beautiful coral, sea animals, and fish that our Creator put in the undersea world."*
Hostess:	*[slightly horrified that anyone would swim with the likes of the gefilte fish that she had just served] And you like this?*

That, and many experiences like it, convinced Marlene that she would have to move to a community where people were very observant but also had university degrees and broad life experience. Not long afterward, she spent a Shabbos at the home of a *baal teshuva* marine biologist who scuba dived. When Marlene was able to discuss many beautiful Torah ideas in the context of her travel and life experiences, she appreciated finding people who could relate to God's wonders as she did. Theirs was a community where she could fit in.

Compartmentalization

We live in a very complex world and it is not always possible, or even desirable, to seek one friend, synagogue, or community that meets all of one's needs. Some *baal teshuvas* have fulfilling lives by satisfying different needs in different places.

Supplementing Marcia is a mother and housewife in a chareidi community where her children go to school. She is not happy with their secular education so she and her children join home-schooling mothers and their children two afternoons a week to supplement her children's secular studies. She further supplements their secular studies at home using Internet resources and CDs from enrichment programs.

There are many pluses to her community. Her neighbors are warm, and her children have good friends down the street with whom they play on Shabbos and during the summer. Marcia and her husband also have good friends there, mostly other *baal teshuvas*. Marcia attends a Torah class on Saturday afternoons, which she enjoys immensely. She listens to Torah lectures on CDs while driving or cooking.

On the other hand, she doesn't like Shabbos prayer services at her neighborhood's synagogue. So, her husband goes to a "no-frills" 7 am minyan on Saturday mornings. He then comes home to take care of the young children while the older ones go to shul with their friends. Marcia goes to a 9 am service in an adjacent neighborhood. They have a women's section that is esthetically pleasing, the women can see and hear what is going on in the rest of the sanctuary, she likes the melodies that they sing, and the congregants don't talk, allowing her to concentrate on her prayers.

During the week, Marcia takes a ceramics class. She also drives to a Jewish community center in a nearby town where she takes women's exercise classes three times a week. Combining life in a strong religious community with some secular involvements has been a good mix for her.

Unconventional Lifestyle   Oren became a baal teshuva in high school. He always had a variety of interests in and out of school and was a non-conformist. He got a bachelor's degree in political science and a master's degree in ecology. Before he started working, he traveled around the world for a year. He eventually settled down and married a baal teshuva who shared his love of adventure and nature. In his thirties, he realized that most people had conventional lives and were not comfortable with his unconventional lifestyle. He and his wife ended up moving to a community in Los Angeles that had a diversity of observant Jews and where they didn't feel pressured to be like everyone else.

Oren joined a modern Orthodox synagogue that had many professionals. He attended lectures at different synagogues that addressed a plethora of topics from ecology to medical ethics to politics. He and his wife mostly hosted Shabbos guests who were not-yet-religious Jews or who were *baal teshuvas.*

Baal teshuvas may find that they have a variety of friends for different occasions. They study Torah and share Jewish ideas with some and travel or go on vacation with others. They may socialize with parents whose children are in their children's school but have other friends who share special interests with them.

Baal teshuvas may need to compartmentalize themselves such that they don't share religious ideas and concerns with certain secular people and don't share their enthusiasm for some secular interests with religious people. Otherwise, they may find that when they wistfully say, "Gee, I really miss those McDonald's cheeseburgers" or "I still listen to rock music," their religious Shabbos hosts will look askance at them. Those same listeners may not want to hear *baal teshuvas* discussing what is great about the secular world or other cultures. Such ideas are best left to discussions with like-minded friends and family.

Deflated   Aaron loved to hike, ski, and go whitewater rafting with friends. They all went on a camping retreat in the mountains twice each year where they spent Shabbos in tents or cabins, put up an eruv, and spent time feeling God's greatness and power in nature. There, outdoors, they were able to appreciate the amazing care with which the Almighty watches over so many creatures, great and small, and how much beauty He puts in the world for people to enjoy.

One Shabbos after returning from his nature retreat, Aaron gushed to his hosts about how he had spent the prior Shabbos. His excitement was met with blank stares. No one seemed to care. He felt like a deflated balloon and realized that it was pointless to share his feelings about nature with people who didn't appreciate it.

The Invisible Folk Dance   Sabrena and Paul became observant in a city where there were almost no observant Jews, where they had no rabbi, and where finding kosher food and a minyan on Shabbos were difficult. Yet, they took on mitzvah observance with joy. There was only one thing that they regretted about becoming observant. They were both avid folk dancers who for years had spent every Wednesday night folk dancing at a local university. They felt that it wasn't modest to be dancing and holding hands publicly, but they weren't ready to give up the folk dancing. So, he put on a Greek fisherman's cap, she wore a long skirt and wig, and they went folk dancing at a venue where no one would know that they were Orthodox Jews. There, they joyfully danced around the outside of the circle. This fueled them to get through the rest of the week and serve God with happiness. Many years later, Paul was able to find a job in a city with a large observant population and they moved their family there. By then, they no longer felt the need to go folk dancing, and they got their sense of joy in other ways.

Community Standards

Baal teshuvas sometimes need to know about a community's religious standards, politics, and idiosyncrasies before deciding to move there. This is especially true for families who are planning to move to Israel, where a religious community's behavior can be very different than what *baal teshuvas* are used to in America. Such communities may have far more stringent religious standards, different methods of teaching and disciplining students, a vastly different curriculum and school schedule, and a bureaucratic structure impervious to parental input.

Pizza Picketers   In an Israeli town with many observant American Jews, a group of Israeli-born observant Jews picketed a local religious girls' school largely serving the American Jews and harassed the students every day. The Israelis did this because they did not consider the school religious enough. The same men also harassed patrons and workers at a local kosher pizza shop because the owner allowed boys and girls to eat there at the same time.

One needs to be aware of such frictions before moving to—or deciding not to move to— these communities.

Schooling   Finding a religious school for American children in Israel is not simple. Some FFB communities do not welcome baal teshuvas, even if the baal teshuvas are exemplary, because those FFBs feel that baal teshuvas's children bring unwanted secular influences into their community. Some schools even tell baal teshuva parents not to apply.

Some religious schools in the United States and in Israel require parents to agree not to have a television in their homes. At least one community now requires that homes be computer-free as well, to avoid potentially bad influences from the Internet. In addition, some schools have people who report to the school if a parent is lax in their religious standards. Roberta and Mike were shocked when they experienced this.

Bounced for Bowling   Roberta and Mike were Reform Jews when they got married. Over the next five years, they became observant and moved to a wonderful, observant American community. The rabbi encouraged his shul members to move to Israel, and Roberta and Mike did. They found a community of people like themselves in Israel and quickly made friends there. Their friends recommended that they enroll their children in a reputedly excellent school, and the couple did. A few weeks later, Roberta got a call from the principal because someone had seen Roberta in a store with her hair uncovered, and this was not acceptable. She either had to cover her hair in accordance with Jewish law or take her children out of the school.

It was extremely difficult for her, yet she decided to make the sacrifice for the sake of her children's education. The next month, she got another call from the principal. Roberta's non-Jewish housekeeper had worn pants when picking up the children from school. This could not continue if the children were to stay in the school.

On another occasion, one of their daughter's friends had a birthday party at a bowling alley where adults also played pool. The principal found this unacceptable. He called in the parents and suspended the girl.

By then, Mike and Roberta realized that this school was not for them. They took their children out and enrolled them in a religious school that was much more liberal.

Shunned over Sports   Frank grew up in an easy-going, tolerant Jewish community where many people became baal teshuvas. There was an eruv in his community, and even the rabbis played baseball with the children of baal teshuva families on Shabbos. When Frank's family relocated to a more observant community, he never thought to ask how their standards would differ from what he was used to. He found out a few days after he took his son to the park on Saturday afternoon that playing any form of sports on Shabbos was not acceptable in his new religious community. Frank really wanted his family to fit in, so they gave up Shabbos baseball.

Soon, Frank's family adopted their community's religious stringencies and had integrated into the community. A few years later, the family excitedly moved to a community in Israel where some of their former neighbors lived. Much to his shock, Frank's son Yehuda came home crying one day. Yehuda's classmates had heard that Yehuda played baseball and soccer after school during the week and they ostracized him for it. The religious Israelis in his school considered playing sports at any time *treif* (spiritually inappropriate). At that point, Frank had to reconsider how his family could, or should, cope with their community's expectations.

Meals Issues   A family's religious standards may determine who will eat in their house and who will socialize with them. It is the policy of many religious schools that children can only bring to school foods that are certified to have stringent rabbinical supervision. Even if baal teshuvas do not personally hold by these standards of kashrut, it can simplify matters when they buy and cook foods that anyone who might eat at their home or who might socialize with their children would find acceptable.

The Birthday Party   Aviva was so excited about her upcoming birthday. She had just moved to a new community two months earlier and couldn't wait to celebrate with her new classmates. She and her mother planned a wonderful party with a clown and juggler, followed by games, then birthday cake and do-it-yourself ice cream sundaes. Aviva wrote invitations to about 20 girls in her class, delivered them, and waited with baited breath for everyone to RSVP. Much to her chagrin, only three girls called that night, and by the end of the week, only two more had accepted her invitation. Aviva was devastated.

When her mother called a teacher and asked if she knew why Aviva was so unpopular, the teacher confided, "I don't know if Aviva is or isn't liked, but I did hear some girls saying that they weren't sure if they could trust your kashrut. Some mothers were also concerned that the party activities might not be suitable. Rather than call and interrogate you, they decided that it would be best if their children didn't attend."

The mother phoned another mother to find out exactly what food and activities would be acceptable so that other children would come to her party. Aviva's mother then followed those instructions to the letter. Thanks to this bit of advance planning, Aviva had the birthday party that she wanted and which her classmates felt comfortable attending.

Community Politics

Two Shuls   There is a story about a man who got shipwrecked and swam to a deserted island where he lived undiscovered for many years. One day, a boat passed by, and a traveler came ashore. As the newcomer explored the island, he came across a weathered old man tending his garden. The traveler introduced himself.

"My name is Marvin Silverberg," the traveler announced as he shook the islander's hand.

"I'm Jewish, too," said the islander. "My name is Herman Gertner. Nice to meet you."

The two men then played Jewish geography and discussed how each happened to come to the island.

After serving Marv some fresh coconut milk, Herman said, "Come, let me show you around the island." Marv followed him, marveling at the lush plants, trees, lizards, and multi-colored birds. Finally, they came to a clearing where two buildings stood facing each other.

"What are these two buildings for?" Marv asked, bewildered.

Herman smiled as he replied, "This first building is my synagogue. This is where I pray every week."

Marv wondered, "And what is that building opposite it?"

Herman cast a nasty glance and pointed with contempt at the second building. "That," he sneered, "is the synagogue that I won't set foot in."

Unfortunately, many Jewish communities experience a variant of this story. Some groups get along with each other and others don't. Frequently, as soon as one synagogue gets established, some people think it's too religious, others think it's not religious enough, some want a different rabbi, and others want a different way of praying. In the blink of an eye, there is a breakaway minyan, sometimes in the same synagogue. Soon, there is a breakaway synagogue whose members feel that they have a better service, standard of Judaism, rabbi, and congregation than the original group has.

The Second Temple was destroyed due to causeless hatred between Jews and that has been the bane of our existence since. There can be many religious groups in a community and they can all get along if they respect one another. Every Jew should strive to develop his or her spiritual potential without judging other Jews negatively. We can practice Judaism differently than Jews whose standards vary from ours without looking down on them or causing bad feelings between one group of Jews and the next.

One small way of showing respect for other Jews is by having a community calendar where every Jewish group posts their major events—bar mitzvahs and weddings, synagogue dinners, charity auctions, carnivals, speakers, and so on. Each group can be careful not to schedule any event that would conflict with events that are already posted. Rather than being concerned with how religious or not religious people are, or with which brand of Judaism is best, there is at least outward respect between the various segments of a community. They can collaborate for the sake of the community instead of being divided by their differences.

Mikvah Money   A community of observant Jews once needed a mikvah but didn't have enough money to build one. The leaders of several groups of Jews in that community met and discussed how they could work together to raise funds to build a mikvah that suited everyone's needs. In the end, two of the groups couldn't agree and the community ended up not having a mikvah at all. Years later, those groups are still at odds with one another.

Eruv Plans   Another community had many young, observant couples and wanted to attract more Jews. A rabbi decided to build an eruv so that people could carry and take young children out of the house in strollers on Shabbos. A large group of anti-religious Jews opposed the plan. The building of the eruv was delayed for years because Jews acted as their own worst enemies.

Community Politics   Baal teshuvas need only ask what a community's politics are and they will probably hear more than they bargained for. Since such conversations can easily degenerate into forbidden gossip, one should ask for only concrete information, without mentioning any names. The information requested should be relevant to someone's specific concerns about whether or not to move into a community. Useful questions might be: What are the religious flavors of Jews in the community? Do people get along with one another? How do people in the community relate to Jews with my background and practices? Do groups collaborate? What religious direction are the school and community taking? Is the atmosphere in the community conducive to raising children who will practice "love your neighbor as yourself?" Do the adults practice this? What kinds of Jewish organizations are in the community? Do people in the community try to be honest and ethical in business? What kinds of children do the schools turn out? Which organizations do kind deeds and who in the community is involved?

Behind the Scenes

Many *baal teshuvas* become observant because they appreciate the good that Judaism has to offer. They experience how observant Jews make the world a better and more spiritual place. They see the extraordinary kindness and hospitality of religious Jews and how studying and living according to the Torah can make people into exemplary human beings. They are proud to be part of a people that contributes so much to the world.

Unfortunately, *baal teshuvas* eventually also see a darker reality. There is sometimes a vast gulf between how truly righteous people live and the way that outwardly observant Jews practice Judaism, and so there are some who look religious on the outside but don't act it. *Baal teshuvas* may read in the newspapers that a very "religious" rabbi, who has a long beard and *payos* (side curls) and who wears a long black coat, cheated taxpayers out of millions of dollars. They may read stories about drug abuse in the religious Jewish community. Or, they may hear about religious Israeli politicians or builders who engaged in unethical or illegal acts.

At first, *baal teshuvas* may rationalize these distressing reports by saying, "Oh, rabbis from that sect can be corrupt. Politicians in Israel aren't representative of the people I know. No religious people whom I know use drugs. I'm glad that I'm not part of those groups." Later, they may be shocked to hear that a rabbi or teacher in their community engaged in, or advised being involved with, immoral activities. Finally, they are defrauded or are cheated by someone "religious." Now they are outraged. How could a religious person be dishonest? Who wants to be part of a religion that doesn't make people better?

Corruption & Misdeeds   Doug and Tzippi were recent baal teshuvas who had to confront these questions. They had become observant due to their interactions with an outreach couple named Basya and Zelig. Basya and Zelig, as well as other couples in their neighborhood, hosted Doug and Tzippi for every Shabbos and Jewish holiday for nearly a year. One couple was nicer than the next. They were scrupulous in not speaking badly about others. They had loving, well-adjusted families. They applied Jewish ethics in their business transactions and were very caring to others.

Doug and Tzippi then moved to a chareidi community where Doug enrolled in a *yeshiva* and Tzippi took care of their new baby.

A few months later, Basya invited Doug and Tzippi to spend Shabbos with them. As they relaxed around the dinner table, Basya asked Doug and Tzippi how they liked their new community.

Doug replied, "I hate it. I can't wait to leave. When we moved there, we signed a lease on an apartment for a year. The observant Jewish landlord reneged on the contract a week before we were supposed to move in and rented it to someone else. We found a second place owned by a different religious Jewish landlord and moved in there. That place turned out to have major problems, including a leaky basement. When he refused to fix the problems, we wanted to move out, but he wouldn't give us back our security deposit. We took him to the local Jewish court (bet din), but he has those judges in his back pocket. We still haven't gotten our money back.

"The Jews in our neighborhood also disparage non-Jews. The non-Jews that I work with have always been very decent. When we do business deals together, they are always honest and live up to their word. They are nice to be around, they don't drink or use vulgar language, and they care about their families. Why do religious Jews speak so badly of non-Jews, especially when the religious Jews where we live are not so decent?

"We seriously thought about giving up Torah observance. After all, if this is the way Torah makes people behave, who needs it? The only reason that we didn't turn our backs on Judaism is because we know people like you, and we have experienced that religious Jews can be very good."

Doug caught his breath and calmed down for a minute, then asked, "How is it possible for religious Jews to be so corrupt?"

"It *is* shocking to learn that frum Jews can behave very badly," Basya replied. "I myself have a hard time with that. I try to view it in several ways. First, people who seem to be observant are not necessarily religious. A religious person wants to know what God wants of him or her, then tries to act that way all of the time, not only when it suits them. Unfortunately, some people pick and choose the laws they feel like observing and ignore what is inconvenient or difficult, especially the importance of treating well those who are different from us and of being scrupulously honest in business.

"Some Jews grew up in an observant family, and/or have a feeling that following the Torah is generally the right way to live. Yet, they may have learned corrupt values or lack the self-discipline to always do the right thing. Many observant Jews don't feel that they are constantly in a relationship with God. They keep kosher or observe Jewish holy days because it is second nature to them, just as many Americans eat turkey and watch football on Thanksgiving, or party on New Year's Eve. They are used to these rituals, but the rituals lack the religious significance that they were meant to have. Others observe some laws and not others because their logic or emotions tell them that it is not necessary to follow all of the rituals. They convince themselves that some behavioral observance is enough, but they haven't internalized the deeper ethics and attitudes of being a Jew.

"Of course, there are also times that we are just human, and we make mistakes. Our greed or other negative emotions sometimes get the better of us. If we don't regret the path that this puts us on, we then justify our misdeeds instead of admitting that we are doing the wrong things. If we do that long enough, our inappropriate behavior sometimes takes on a life of its own.

"If a Jew doesn't feel that life is about having an ongoing relationship with God, it is easy to stop behaving morally when doing so is inconvenient.

"Secondly, the Torah has to command Jews 'to love your neighbor as yourself' because it doesn't come naturally to us. We are likewise commanded in the Shema prayer to love God with all of our money because money is more real to many people than the Almighty is. The Talmud states that it is forbidden to leave money lying around where others might be tempted to steal it. One might say, 'But Jews aren't supposed to steal.' The Talmud replies, 'You're right, but we have to assume that most people will succumb to certain temptations given the right circumstances.'

"Just because someone is stringent about not eating foods that most observant Jews would eat, wears a black hat or *kapota* (silk caftan to honor Shabbos or holy days), wears a yarmulke, or covers her hair, it doesn't mean that the person fears God above all else. People's emotions get them to rationalize doing the wrong things. Some Jews dress the way they do or observe commandments as long as they feel comfortable, or they do what everyone else in their community does. They aren't necessarily committed to acting ethically because that is what God wants of them. Their religious practices are more social conventions than principled commitments.

"Never trust people just because they have the title rabbi or look religious. We should still take the same precautions with a seemingly observant Jew that we would take with anyone in business, financial, or personal matters. We ignore common sense at our peril."

Basya insisted that Torah was intended to make us good people. We shouldn't deride the Torah when people misuse or ignore it, then claim that they are acting as pious Jews. She encouraged Doug to see the good that being observant creates, while recognizing that among good people there will always be some bad apples.

Despoiling the Hosts   Menashe was a bad apple. He grew up in an observant home, but rebelled against his parents and against Judaism in his teens. He became a very successful con man, infiltrating one Jewish community after another. He would go to the local synagogue on Shabbos, meet people there who invited him for meals, and make them feel as if he and they were best friends by the time the meal was over.

By the time Menashe had parted from his hosts or from the other guests, he had assessed their vulnerabilities and had given them advice. Some time later, he offered them a helping hand, or brought his hosts an expensive thank-you gift. Soon, he was renting an apartment in their community, fell into arrears on the rent, and borrowed money from his new "friends." Sad to say, he never repaid it. He also found single women who were desperate to be loved. He dated them, and then convinced them to join him in investment opportunities. Little did they know that each "opportunity" was a scheme to garner him more money before he left town and moved to the next unsuspecting community. The religious communities' goodness and naivete allowed him to con people for decades. When he was last heard from, he had checked himself into a hospital (where he got three free days of room and board) for a non-existent intestinal problem. His roommate was an Orthodox Jewish man in his 70s. Menashe charmed the man during his stay. When Menashe was ready to leave the hospital, the man graciously gave him the keys to his apartment so that Menashe could stay there until he found his own place. When the man came home two days later, Menashe had cleaned out his place and the sobbing, frail man could only stare at his four bare walls.

By nature, people are self-centered and self-serving. We need to follow the Torah to become better human beings. Studying Torah doesn't automatically make people decent, compassionate, ethical human beings. During the Second Temple era (around 2,000 years ago), Jews studied, and were well versed in, the Torah. Yet, their causeless hatred led to the exile that we are still in. We have to internalize Torah's values and live by them. When we see that some "religious Jews" observe some laws of the Torah but do despicable things, imagine what they would be like if they didn't even abide by any of the Torah's limitations!

We shouldn't blame God or Judaism when people pervert the system for living that He advised us to adopt. We shouldn't stop doing what is right when we see that others don't take Judaism as seriously as we do. On the other hand, if we live in a community where the lack of proper values and behaviors impacts negatively on us or on our families, it is time to consider moving to a different neighborhood.

Summary

Every Jewish community has its strong and weak points. The trick for *baal teshuvas* is to find a place where they can benefit from the strengths and grow despite the weaknesses. When we choose where to live, we should always consider whether our neighbors will be good influences on us and our families.

It is useful to ask advisors or friends about what characterizes different communities and to get firsthand information by staying there for at least one Shabbos or Jewish holiday.

Some *baal teshuvas* will have some family members who go to different synagogues to suit their different needs. Some needs may be best met outside of the community. Having a variety of friends, hobbies, and classes that serve different purposes will help *baal teshuvas* to feel more at home.

NINE

Synagogues

There are many flavors of observant Judaism but even more varieties of synagogues. This is partly because the Jewish nation began as 12 tribes, each of which had a slightly different version of praying. These ancient paths, called nusachot (nusach, sing.), are the roots of modern variations in prayer services and in prayer texts.

Nusachot Different communities of Jews embrace different nusachot. Sephardic Jews (from Mediterranean countries) and many Chassidim pray using the Sephardic nusach. Ashkenazic Jews (from Western Europe) pray using the Ashkenazic nusach. Lubavitch Jews pray using nusach Ha'Ari. Within each general version of prayer are slight differences, depending upon the specific community that is praying. Thus, for example, Syrian, Moroccan, and Spanish Jews all pray using the Sephardic nusach, but there are slight differences in some of their prayers. These variations are mostly noticeable in the extra prayers that are said on Jewish holidays.

The same is true for German and Lithuanian Jews. They pray using the Ashkenazic nusach but each recites some holiday prayers that the others don't say and there are slight variations in their daily prayers. Thus, Ashkenazic Jews who attend Ashkenazic Shabbos services of Jews from another country are likely to be able to follow the services without much difficulty. On the other hand, if they attend a Sephardic synagogue for Shabbos services, they may find the services difficult to follow, and vice versa.

Where's Lecha Dodi? Liz was a baal teshuva who was familiar with the Ashkenazic prayers and melodies from her synagogue. She once spent Shabbos in a Sephardic neighborhood and attended their services Friday night. Much to her dismay, she was completely lost. Her custom was to say Kabbalat Shabbat that consisted of six Psalms, followed by Lecha Dodi. Their custom was to preface those prayers by first chanting the Song of Songs. By the time Liz had figured out what was going on, the service was nearly over!

Baal teshuvas should try to pray in a synagogue whose nusach is appropriate for them. If someone's family is Ashkenazic, they should follow the Ashkenazic nusach. If their parents were Sephardic or Chassidic, they should follow the Sephardic nusach. If someone (or someone's ancestors) are Lubavitch, they should pray nusach Ari. Once Jews regularly pray with a Sephardic nusach, they are not supposed to change it to Ashkenazic. Ideally, Jews of Iraqi heritage should pray using their nusach, Jews of Polish extraction should pray using their nusach, and so on. In reality, though, if an Ashkenazi becomes Chassidic, he or she may switch to nusach Sephard or Ari, and many *baal teshuvas* follow the nusach of the people who teach them about Judaism.

We are supposed to pray using the same nusach that our fathers did. Yet, if *baal teshuvas* all did that, some wouldn't say any Jewish prayers at all because their fathers hardly ever set foot in a synagogue!

Dad's Custom Reuven, a baal teshuva, called a rabbi to find out whether he should put on tefillin during Chol Hamoed, the intermediate days of the Jewish festivals. Most Jews do not lay tefillin on these days, yet some do. The rabbi, not knowing who the caller was, told Reuven to follow his father's custom.

"Fine," responded Reuven. "My father never put on tefillin in his entire life, so he certainly never wore them on *Chol Hamoed*. I'll do the same!"

Synagogue Layout   The structure of Ashkenazic and Sephardic synagogues differ slightly, with Ashkenazim leading their prayers from the front of the synagogue and Sephardim from the middle.

Chanting & Scrolls   The two groups also vary in their synagogue rituals. For example, Sephardic prayer leaders chant every word and use Sephardic pronunciation. Ashkenazic prayer leaders read only parts of the service aloud, and typically use an Ashkenazic pronunciation. The exact dialect will differ according to whether their ancestors came from Lithuania, certain parts of Russia, Germany, and so on. The melodies that are sung also vary from one service to another.

Sephardim read the Torah and *haftarah* (selections of Prophetic writings) from scrolls that stand in upright cases. Ashkenazim remove the cloth mantle that covers their Torah scroll before placing the scroll on a table and reading from it there. They read the haftarah from a book.

Choosing a Synagogue

Getting There   The most important initial consideration in choosing a synagogue is that one can get to the synagogue and pray there in accordance with Jewish law. Many not-yet-observant Jews drive to a synagogue on Shabbos while they learn the basics of Judaism. As they become more observant, they may continue attending that synagogue, but no longer drive there. If the synagogue is too far from their home to walk, some might rent a place for Shabbos and Jewish holidays that is within walking distance, or buy a home near the shul. Other Jews stay with families who live near the synagogue on Jewish holy days. Some baal teshuvas find a different shul they can walk to on Shabbos or move to a different community.

Non-Orthodox Synagogues   There are sometimes only non-Orthodox synagogues in one's area. What does one do then?

Philosophical Issues   By definition, these other streams of Judaism either don't believe that God gave the Torah to the Jewish people, and/or they posit that its traditional system of interpretation needs to be modified. As mentioned before, some of their spiritual leaders don't even believe in God. Their "innovations" have destroyed traditional belief and practice and replaced them with substitutes that sometimes violate the very essence of the religion that they claim to protect.

Note: Reform houses of worship are called temples because Reform leaders didn't believe there will ever be a third Jewish Temple in Jerusalem. They wanted German Jews to believe that Berlin, not Jerusalem, was their real home, and they rejected prophetic predictions that Jews would some day return to Israel. (Boy, have they been proven wrong!) The Reformers adopted church customs, such as having an organ, a mixed choir, and mixed seating, as part of their "temple" rites to fit in with the way the Christians around them worshipped.

Inasmuch as a synagogue is supposed to be, first and foremost, a sanctified place where we worship God on His terms, it is problematic for a Jew to pray in a house of worship led by people who reject God's Torah and His Oral Law.

Unfortunately, most non-observant rabbis today are not guided by, nor are they well versed in, Jewish law. When they are asked to give Jewish legal opinions, such as whether or not it is permitted to drive on Shabbos, who one may marry, and how one converts to Judaism, their responses tend to be at odds with observant Judaism.

Mechitzah & More   Apart from being centers where Jewish leaders teach philosophies that contradict observant Judaism, non-observant synagogues are not built according to Jewish law. Synagogues are required to have a women's balcony or a mechitzah (a physical divider between men and women) that is at least 40 inches high. If the men and women aren't separated by a physical divider, it is problematic to pray there. Other problems with non-Orthodox synagogues are that the rabbi and prayer leaders use microphones and electronic systems whose use is forbidden on Shabbos, someone plays musical instruments during services (which the rabbis barred since the Second Temple was destroyed in 70 CE), congregants are given the honor of opening the ark using electric switches that violate Shabbos and non-kosher food is often served at their functions.

Minyan Men who pray in a non-Orthodox venue may only say public prayers such as Kaddish if there are at least ten men who are halachically Jewish present. The prayer leader must also be halachically (according to Jewish law) Jewish. If the only place where one can pray does not fulfill these requirements, he should consult a rabbi about what to do.

Daily & Shabbos Minyan

Men and women tend to have different considerations when choosing a synagogue. Men may have mostly pragmatic concerns, such as the schedules of the prayers, being able to pray at a pace that is comfortable for them, and knowing that there will always be 10 men present. Some men prefer to pray in a particular synagogue because they like the Torah or Talmud class that is taught before or after services.

During the 11 months that a mourner says Kaddish, a synagogue can be a place where a Jew finds a supportive group of fellow worshippers. He will want to pray in a place where he can say the prayers at his own pace and have listeners respond to his Kaddish. If a *baal teshuva* isn't yet fluent in praying, he will want to pray among people who are sensitive to his need to pray more slowly than others do. Not everyone is fortunate enough to find this. When one can't find an ideal situation, he should discuss with his rabbi what to do.

Women may be concerned about the social and esthetic aspects of a synagogue—whether they can see and hear the service, if they enjoy the way the prayer leader sings, whether it is quiet enough to concentrate, whether the women's section is esthetically pleasing, and if it is comfortable. They don't want to hear men talk about sports, politics, money, or the stock market instead of concentrating on the prayers. Women with children may want a synagogue that has babysitting, a playgroup, or a children's service on Saturday mornings and holidays. Nursing women will appreciate a synagogue where they can feed their baby comfortably and unobtrusively. They will also want to find a shul that has women with whom they will enjoy socializing—preferably not during the prayer services!

Mechitzah

Some observant Jews pray in places where men and women can't see each other at all. However, there is no requirement that women be blocked from seeing or hearing the services. Many synagogues have attractive ladies' sections with nice mechitzahs. Some have mechitzahs made of one-way glass: women can see through the glass into the men's side, but the men only see mirrors when they look toward the women's section.

Other Considerations

Shteiblach   While many baal teshuvas pray in a synagogue, many communities also have shteiblach. A shteibel (plural—shteiblach) is an apartment, basement, or part of someone's house that is used for public prayers. Shteiblach are often started out of convenience, such as when a man in that house can't walk to a synagogue. Some people prefer to pray in shteiblach because they have a different hashkafa from those who pray in the nearby shuls, while others prefer shteiblach because they like the intimacy of a small shul, the schedule suits them, or they don't want to pay shul membership fees.

Singing   Apart from differences in their structure or architecture, synagogues vary in other ways. Some are "no-frills," with prayer leaders saying out loud the minimum verses necessary while each congregant reads along silently. Others have a lot of singing, led by a cantor and choir, using traditional European or modern melodies. Some shuls have a prayer leader who sings in a way that encourages the congregation to join him.

Time Considerations Some synagogues are renowned for the rapidity with which they "get through" the services, while others—especially yeshiva or yeshivish minyans—take much longer. Some services start so early that they say the Amidah (main prayer) at sunrise. These are called hashkama (early rising), or netz (sunrise), minyans. Other minyans (typically Chassidic) start as late as 10 am. Some communities offer a beginner's or explanatory service in which a leader explains the main prayers and the participants recite or sing the prayers together in Hebrew and/or English.

Learning Some synagogue rabbis give a sermon or say a few words of Torah (dvar Torah) during Shabbos services. Many teach a Talmud class before or after weekday services. Some synagogues offer Judaism classes throughout the week as well.

Social Centers Some synagogues are primarily places to pray while others are social centers as well. Member families celebrate bar and bat mitzvahs there, socialize over kiddush after services on Saturday mornings, and have functions such as sisterhood lunches, annual dinners, charity affairs, and Shabbatons. Some also hold cultural, singles, and holiday events, as well as other community activities.

Paying Your Dues

Synagogues can only function if the people who pray there support them financially. Someone has to pay for the rabbi's and Torah reader's salaries (and cantor if there is one), mortgage and maintenance expenses, publications, mailings, and food. The cost of membership varies greatly from synagogue to synagogue. A student may pay only $50 to be a member of one synagogue, while members of a large synagogue may pay thousands of dollars per year, including annual contributions to a building and/or school fund. If people can't pay the full membership fee, many synagogues offer a sliding scale. If someone regularly attends a synagogue, they should pay what they can of the membership fee.

Hopping   Moira was an unmarried computer programmer who "hopped" from one synagogue to another. When she had religious questions, she asked them of the rabbi of the shul where she went most often.

From time to time, people with questions about their computers asked Moira if they could "pick her brain," and she often helped them to fix their computer problems. One man, though, became especially irksome as he kept trying to get free advice from her rather than pay for technical support.

"I didn't go to school and get years of experience to give advice for free," she finally told him with annoyance one day.

That Shabbos, someone made an appeal for people to contribute to her synagogue maintenance fund. The speaker emphasized that people go to school for years and expect to get paid for their knowledge and hard work, yet they expect rabbis and teachers to give of their knowledge of Judaism for free. It was only fair that people who used the synagogue, or who availed themselves of the rabbi's services and knowledge, support those people and their institution financially.

Moira got the hint. From then on, she paid membership dues to her shul.

Summary

The synagogue is often a focus of communal Jewish life. Besides praying, members attend Torah classes and celebrate holidays, Shabbos, life cycle, and community events there. A synagogue that suits the *baal teshuva's* needs is a combination of many factors: location, the rabbi, the types of classes and services offered, its flavor of observant Judaism, and feeling a commonality with the other members. *Baal teshuvas* sometimes try out more than one synagogue in their search for a place that they can feel at home. Finding the right synagogue is often the key to finding the right community as well.

TEN

Learning About and Living Torah Judaism

Judaism is not an academic subject that one can "master" by simply reading about it. Since Judaism teaches us how to live, it encompasses a breathtaking array of topics. The material world has the Divine Presence hiding within every facet of it, and we learn how to discover Him by learning Torah, which expresses the Divine Will for us. Yet, unlike topics such as history or geometry, knowing facts alone can't adequately prepare us to become well-informed Jews who have a relationship with our Creator. We must experience how others think, speak, and act Jewishly in a living laboratory. This is best done by spending time with religious families, especially on Shabbos and Jewish holidays.

We should ideally attend classes, listen to taped lectures, and/or read books from which we can enjoyably study Judaism. We need to also find a rabbi and spiritual advisors who can tell us how we, as individuals, should live it. We need to join a religious community where we can avail ourselves of, and support, institutions such as synagogues, schools, adult education classes, kosher markets and restaurants, Judaica stores, *mikvahs* (ritual baths), religious youth groups, *Bikur Cholim* (those who visit the sick), *gemachs* (organizations that provide free loans, clothing, wedding assistance, and more for the poor), and *chevra kadisha* (Jewish burial societies).

Types of Seminaries/Yeshivas   Baal teshuva seminaries for women and yeshivas for men offer part-time and full-time study programs for Jews. They typically offer financial assistance to needy students who want to formally learn about Judaism. Some yeshivas are set up to teach baal teshuvas, the main goal of others is to grant rabbinical degrees, still others are primarily places where men can engage in advanced Talmudic studies full time, sometimes for life. Most seminaries and yeshivas are in New York and Israel, although there are programs in many other cities as well. They offer a wide variety of classes, schedules, and perspectives.

Seminary/Yeshiva Life   In some ways, living and learning in a yeshiva or seminary is idyllic. The learning is stimulating and fulfilling. It is easy for most students to make new friends and develop relationships with wonderful advisors. The baal teshuva lives in a very supportive environment where their former existential and personal problems are either resolved or put on a back burner. They have few responsibilities and can fully devote themselves to studying.

Questions To Ask   Seminaries and yeshivas differ in their locations and size, as well as in their religious outlooks and emphases. Some of the better-known ones are listed in this book's Appendix. It is advisable to ask oneself the following questions, and formulate answers with one's religious advisor, when trying to choose an appropriate place of Torah study:

1.   Are there Judaism classes in my city that are suitable for my level and interests?

2.   What can I study that fits my schedule and interests?

3.   Do I want to study part-time or full time? If part-time, how many hours a day or a week?

4. Do I want the intensity and spirituality of studying in Israel? This requires, at a minimum, taking a break or leave of absence from work or school for several weeks to several years.

5. Can I afford to relocate or take a leave from my job or school? *Note: Studying in Israel has the potential challenges of needing to make cultural adaptations to a new country, adjusting to life in a dormitory or communal apartment, and living far away from home.*

6. Would I prefer a small school with a limited number of classes where I can get to know my fellow students and teachers in an intimate setting or a large school that has a greater variety of teachers, students, and subjects?

7. Do I want a school that offers a lot of individual attention, emotional support and nurturing, help finding a religious approach that is appropriate for me, and/or tutoring?

8. Which schools offer the level of teaching or learning that I am seeking—beginner, intermediate, or advanced?

9. Do I want a school that emphasizes textual learning, where I can develop the skills to understand Jewish texts on my own? If so, which schools will help me become self-sufficient in understanding Hebrew (the language of the Jewish Bible and the Jewish Oral Law known as the Mishnah) and/or Aramaic (the language of the Talmud)?

10. What religious approach suits me best? Do I want a school with a modern Orthodox, religious Zionist, chareidi, or a Chassidic orientation, or a place that exposes me to a variety of approaches?

11. Do I want coed classes or only same-sex classes? Most seminaries and yeshivas are for women only or men only. How-

ever, some Jewish learning institutes, universities, and synagogues offer coed classes.

12. What is the curriculum at different schools? Are there specific topics that I want to study? Which schools offer classes in those subjects or will find me a tutor with whom I can learn about these topics?

13. Would I prefer teachers who mostly lecture on topics that impart basic Jewish information, a chavrusa system where I will learn one-on-one with another student, or some independent study where I can also learn in classes or with a study partner?

14. How much do I want teachers to impart a specific religious orientation and outlook versus giving me information and letting me develop my own ideas about how to integrate it into my life?

15. Do I want teachers who will monitor my spiritual self-development and work with me to improve myself, or do I want a more hands-off approach?

16. Where can I find classes with students my age and of similar secular educational or vocational background?

If you are unfamiliar with the schools and classes that are available, ask your religious advisor about what he or she would recommend. If you have heard recommendations but don't know enough about what the various choices imply about the above issues, ask the school's principal or administrator to clarify them for you. It is important that there be a good match between what a school offers and what a student wants and needs to get from studying there.

Develop Connections and Support Systems

Besides studying texts and learning how to apply Judaism to their lives, it is advisable for *baal teshuvas* to build strong connections with a rabbi, teachers, religious families, and advisors. By talking to, and spending time with, these people, a *baal teshuva* can see how Judaism is lived. The personal connections create opportunities to ask knowledgeable Jews questions and learn how to integrate one's thinking and behavior into the religious world.

Fellow students from Judaism classes may become friends and important support systems for one another as *baal teshuvas* experience tension with their former friends and families. Many religious schools have alumni organizations that offer continuing education and support through publications, lectures, annual retreats, seminars, and/or reunions.

Summary

Judaism is a way of life, not an intellectual pursuit. We need to learn about Judaism in an environment in which we can assimilate information about how to live as Jews, as well as find models of how to live an observant Jewish life. Whenever possible, *baal teshuvas* are encouraged to learn in a seminary, yeshiva, or classes that offer the best curriculum and teachers for their needs. Schools tend to teach different subjects, vary in their emphases on studying texts and acquiring textual skills, and have different hashkafas. Some stress intellectual ideas and development, others have a more emotional focus, and some blend both. It is important to match the personality and interests of the *baal teshuva* with a school. A spiritual mentor can be invaluable in helping with this process.

Baal teshuvas who want help choosing a school can read the Appendix of this book for more information about many (but certainly not all) *baal teshuva* yeshivas and seminaries. By asking themselves and the school administrators the questions in this chapter, *baal teshuvas* are likely to find a match between their personalities and interests and what a school has to offer.

Part Three:
Parents and Siblings

ELEVEN

Guess Who's Not Coming to Dinner?

It is normal and healthy to change as we get older. Children continually do this as they mature and separate from their parents. Parents change as they go through life, especially when their children leave home. Yet, no matter who we are at different times in our lives, we want others to love and appreciate us. No one wants to feel that he or she is loved conditionally.

Yet, that is what happens to many *baal teshuvas* whose family and friends try to talk them out of their newly found religious ideas and lifestyle. Some people react to a *baal teshuva's* becoming religious as if he or she fell to Earth from the planet Mars. Others cannot understand how and why the person whom they used to know has become so unrecognizable. Some even sabotage the *baal teshuva's* efforts to grow so that they won't have to examine their own beliefs and seriously think about changing how they live. Some feel an inner guilt that the *baal teshuva* is living with an authentic Judaism that they discarded but which, in their heart of hearts, they believe they should be practicing. They then camouflage their inner turmoil by being angry with the *baal teshuva*.

To be honest, some mothers' worst nightmares about their *baal teshuva* children do materialize. Their child does not join them in some family celebrations. Some parents may not be able to use their favorite dishes, pots, and pans when cooking for their child. The *baal teshuva* won't eat her mother's cooking unless the mother makes or buys kosher food. The family can no longer eat together in their favorite restaurants. If the *baal teshuva* gets married and moves far away, the parents may not have a strong relationship with their children or grandchildren. Many children who went to temple with their parents on the Jewish High Holidays will never spend the holidays that way with their family again.

Like the Shtetl　One mother voiced her deepest fears when her baal teshuva daughter, who had observed Shabbos and kept kosher for years, stopped wearing immodest clothes.

The mother sighed, "I bet the next thing that you're going to do is to get married and wear a wig, like those women from the *shtetl*." The mother was right. The daughter did exactly that.

Parents' fears about their child becoming *baal teshuva* are very important. Even small changes in a family's relationships can be very traumatic and shouldn't be dismissed. It can go a long way for the child to acknowledge a parents' fears by saying things like, "This must be so hard for you. I can't imagine how I would feel if my child went off to college and came back so different than the way that he or she left."

Overnight Morph　Baal teshuvas may not realize that what they view as a gradual metamorphosis looks to others as if they have become foreigners almost overnight. Baal teshuvas eat foods like challah (those "ch" sounds are so annoying to secular ears), kosher wine, a Shabbos stew called cholent, and seudah shleesheet (the third Shabbos meal). They eschew delectable foods like crabs, oysters, shrimp, clams, lobster, pork, McDonald's, and Burger King. They don't do fun things any more like getting drunk or stoned, partying and getting inebriated on Friday nights, gossiping, dancing or swimming with the opposite sex, wearing revealing clothes, spending Saturdays at the mall, eating in non-kosher restaurants, eating at non-kosher family celebrations, or watching racy TV shows and movies.

Weird Concerns   Baal teshuvas pepper their speech with strange words like divrei Torah, treif, tznius (which requires covering the knee-us), kedushah, and davening. They live in the past, being concerned with the ideas of medieval rabbis named Rashi and Tosfot. They worry about when sunrise and sunset are. They are concerned with how many ounces of food or drink they consumed, and they wash their hands in strange ways numerous times every day. They wonder how invisible influences will affect their souls. What kind of bizarre Jews talk about religion and God?

Strange God-Talk   Many secular Jews think it is normal to discuss a deity only in college courses and that it is absurd to place a Supreme Being at the center of one's life. Some think that a Jew who takes religion seriously was brainwashed by a cult. They can't believe that a formerly normal friend or relative, who was once just like them, is now a "fanatic" who really believes in this weird stuff!

Ruining Dreams   Let's face it. A baal teshuva's changes can seem very strange, and they can cause lots of emotional upheaval. These changes are stressful to most families and can bring to the fore other emotional issues that have plagued a family's relationships for years. For example, a mother who has tied up many hopes in her children's vocational success will be absolutely devastated if her son, whom she hoped would be a doctor, now wants to cancel his acceptance to medical school and study in a yeshiva for the next few years. A mother who had hopes that her daughter would marry a professional or someone who is financially "successful" will feel anxious when her daughter goes to Israel and dates men without her input. A dependent mother who expected her only child to stay nearby forever is beside herself when her daughter moves to New York to attend Stern College and live with religious Jews. A father who rejected Judaism in college and hoped that his son would join his lucrative law practice is dismayed when his son decides instead to get a dual degree in rabbinics and counseling.

Baal teshuvas should expect their families initially to be upset when they become observant. Most of us would feel that way if our child totally changed his or her life in the space of six months to a year, moved to a religious community thousands of miles away, and announced that he or she was getting engaged to someone that we felt he or she barely knew.

Patience & Respect   Sometimes we need to see how our changes look to others, especially to our parents. We need to be patient with, and extraordinarily respectful of, our parents and to make halachically permitted compromises as our parents try to catch up with who we have become.

When Leib became observant, his rabbi advised him, "The more stringent you become observing Jewish law, the more stringent you must become honoring your parents."

Sage words indeed!

Summary

While becoming observant may seem a reasonable choice to a *baal teshuva*, it raises many emotional issues for their loved ones—especially their parents. The fact that parents are critical of a *baal teshuva's* changes doesn't automatically mean that the parents have no legitimate concerns, even if some negativity is unwarranted. For example, parents might think that a child is changing too fast and doesn't understand why he or she is doing what he or she is doing. They may feel that their child's behavior is extreme. They may be concerned that their child is following a cult-like leader. When parents feel this way, it may be helpful to have a three- or four-way meeting between the parent(s), the child, and the child's rabbi and/or spiritual advisor (see the dialogue above with Claire and Audrey).

It is important for *baal teshuvas* to appreciate how their religious changes look to others. They should not cause their parents undue hardship by imposing upon them unnecessary religious strictures or by overwhelming them with too much information. Guidance by a religious mentor or rabbi can be invaluable in helping *baal teshuvas* maintain the best relationship possible with their family as they go on their religious journey.

TWELVE

Family Challenges

One of the most daunting challenges that *baal teshuvas* have is explaining their new life to their parents or to other non-observant people. Some *baal teshuvas* do this by gushing about why the Torah is true, why Jews should keep mitzvahs, how exciting and wonderful everything Jewish is, etc. When they pause to catch their breath, they are surprised to see the listener standing in stunned silence instead of sharing their excitement.

Take a Deep Breath The pace and process of our broaching the topic of our religious change can affect how well others come to terms with our becoming baal teshuva. While this is difficult enough to gauge, a baal teshuva's real troubles may begin when they try to convince their family and friends back home to become observant. Instead of embarking on a knock-'em-dead-by-sharing-everything-I-know-about-Judaism-approach, baal teshuvas need to consider how their ideas sound to others. Bear in mind that discussing your religious transformation will not be as neutral a discussion as whether you prefer chocolate or strawberry milkshakes. Whatever you say might be used against you. It will be heard in the context of the listener's feelings about observant Judaism, how your observance will affect their life and their hopes for your life, and how open someone is to changing their ideas and lifestyle.

Bottom of Totem Pole   A secular Jewish organization surveyed a representative cross-section of American Jews in the late 20th century. The respondents were asked to rate the desirability of potential husbands for their daughters. A majority of the Jews polled preferred their daughter to marry a gentile rather than a religious Jewish professional. In fact, there was almost no group that fared worse in desirability for non-observant Jews than the religious Jewish husbands.

Extreme Interpretations   Many parents of *baal teshuvas* have negative interpretations of their child's changes. Something as moderate as keeping kosher can be interpreted as the adoption of primitive rituals.

In 1977, Woody Allen produced an award-winning movie called *Annie Hall*, in which he played a neurotic Jew and Diane Keaton played his WASPy girlfriend. In a famous scene, she invites him to eat Thanksgiving dinner with her parents. As they sit at the table, the gentile parents mentally transform him—a secular American who disdains Judaism—into an unlikeable, bearded, ultra-Orthodox rabbi. People with preconceived stereotypes about Orthodox Jews sometimes project similar pejorative views onto *baal teshuvas*. Some parents make their child's changes far more disturbing than they objectively are.

Slowly, with Humor   How baal teshuvas present their religious changes to their families can set the stage for how the families will relate to them. The more you gush about Torah and doing mitzvahs before others have come to terms with your changes, the stranger they may think you are. It is great that you are enthused about Torah, but others won't think so as long as they feel threatened by your changes or think you have been brainwashed by a cult.

Don't discuss Judaism with others unless those people have expressed interest in knowing more about it, or unless you have reason to believe that they might be receptive to it. It is not useful to tell parents everything about your new religious views and beliefs, what Jewish law has to say about how you will face every aspect of life, and your future plans. Try to gauge what they can hear and give them time to digest what you tell them. For example, consider initially only summarizing your religious changes to your parents. You can even do this with some humor. Being able to poke fun at oneself can go a long way toward easing the friction over how "abnormal" you may seem to have become. Acknowledge that you would also be taken aback if someone you loved went through such a metamorphosis, but reassure the person that you are still the person they know and love, and that you always want to have a good relationship.

How To Disclose that You Are Observant

Many *baal teshuvas* say too much to their family and friends about their new ideas, classes or behaviors, thereby intensifying the listener's fears and feelings of alienation from the *baal teshuva*. Say only what you need to, and focus on the listener's feelings when you respond to their questions. You may find it easiest to talk about your newfound observance with one person at a time. Some children find it easiest to do this first with the parent they get along with the best.

The Disclosure Baal teshuvas might preface a conversation with parents by first thinking about the education and values that the parents gave them to do what they feel is right, to find their own truth, to do something meaningful with their life, and/or to make themselves happy. The child can express gratitude for this base. They can add, "I've applied those ideas to studying Torah and I've started living by its ideas. For now, I'm finding it very gratifying."

Their Response Wait for a response. Don't detail what you feel, have learned, are doing, etc., until the person has had a chance to process what you've said. If they are feeling alarmed or angry, the best thing to do is listen, empathize, and perhaps reassure.

Some parents will be worried and say something to the effect of, "What in the world has happened to you?" or "You're not going to end up like your brother and not eat in my home, are you?" or "I hope that you're not serious!"

Your Response   If they react this way, you could say, "I know that this must seem like it's coming out of left field. Don't worry—I won't become a religious fanatic. We'll both need time to get used to my changes which must seem pretty weird right now. If we can keep our lines of communication open, there's no reason why my changes should interfere with us having a close relationship, even though it might take a bit of work on both our parts to adjust."

A similar response might be, "I'm sure that some of my changes might make you feel as if I've rejected your values. You must be worried that we won't be close any more. I want to reassure you that you gave me the strength to be who I am and that I will always value our closeness."

What Will Happen?   Your parents may ask you specific questions about what will happen or what you might do or not do next. For example, "Are you going to marry someone who will sit in a yeshiva and not work?" or "Are you still going to spend the holidays with us?" or "How long are you going to stay in that religious school before you come back to the real world?"

It is not usually productive at this time to give specific or detailed answers. The best answer might be, "I don't know all of the answers to the questions that you are asking. Right now I am going through some changes and I'll need some time to sort out exactly where they will take me."

How Different?   At this point, a parent's real questions may be, "How different are you going to become? Will this break up our family? Are you ever going to be part of the real world again? Are we going to have to support you financially for the rest of your life?"

You might generally respond to such concerns as follows: "I can see that you are very concerned about how well thought-out my changes might be, where they will take me, and how they will affect our family. Let's both give it some time before we decide exactly where I will end up. I am concerned about your concerns. Let's try to work them out together."

Why Do You…? If a parent asks why you plan to observe certain rituals, or will no longer do things that you once did: "You're asking some very good questions. Let me research the answers before I get back to you."

You should talk to an advisor or rabbi before giving detailed answers to others' questions. It is okay not to have all the answers, even though questioners may be quite demanding about wanting an answer on the spot.

Rhetorical Questions Some people make rhetorical or incredulous statements with a question mark at the end. Don't try to answer "questions" that express the intensity of someone's feelings about what you have said, or are doing, when they are really statements. Try first to respond to the person's feelings instead of answering their questions directly.

Scenario #1:

A mother may ask, "Does your becoming religious mean that you won't be spending Rosh Hashana with our family at our Temple and in my house any more?"

Son: *It sounds like you're concerned that my becoming observant means that we can't celebrate holidays together any more. Tell me about your concerns."*

Mother: *Well, I'd always like the family to spend New Year's together. If you won't go to my Temple, and you won't eat in my house, and you won't travel on the holidays, then you'll break up our family!"*

Son: *I can see that this is something that's really important to you, and spending time with the family is important to me, too. There should be ways that we can share the holidays, even if it's not the way that we used to."*

Scenario #2:

A father says to his son, "You know, Joey, I spent a lot of money so that you could get your MBA, and my friend Blaine and I are hoping that you will come and work for our business. You're not going to do something silly like becoming a rabbi, or dropping out of school and learning in a yeshiva, are you?"

Joey: *Right now, I'm keeping lots of options open, Dad. But since you raised the issue, how would you feel if I didn't go into your business?*

Dad: *[after a few moments of horrified silence] I would feel very bad. I hope that I didn't waste $100,000 on your education. I worked very hard to support you and make sure that you got a great education. I also worked my tail off to develop a business that you could take over some day and use to support your family. I can't even imagine you turning that down.*

Joey: *Well, Dad, thanks for letting me know how you feel about this. Your thoughts and feelings are important to me.*

In time, Joey may decide to let his father down, but at least he will have some idea of what that will mean to him.

Respecting Parents Since most baal teshuvas change over months or years, their parents (or other relatives and friends) will need lots of time—sometimes many years—to adjust. Many parents will eventually do that, and baal teshuvas owe it to them to be patient. While honoring and respecting one's parents can be hard when parents do not readily accept their child's observance, the reward for doing this mitzvah increases according to the effort we put into it.

Humor

Jay became a *baal teshuva* in college. For the next few years, he knew far more about what he was supposed to do or not do than he knew about the rationales behind many Jewish rituals. When he went overnight camping with his family, he slipped away from them for a few minutes and unwrapped a new mess kit so that he could prepare his dinner. He then trudged off, unnoticed, to the nearest pond because Jewish law requires that vessels used to prepare or serve food that were owned or produced by a non-Jew must be immersed in a natural body of water or ritual bath before a Jew can use them. (This immersion is not because the vessels are physically dirty or spiritually contaminated; the purpose is to spiritually elevate vessels which will be used for foods that Jews spiritually elevate.) Jay said the appropriate blessing, then dipped the metal utensils into the muddy water and muttered with irony to himself, "You see, I am doing this to make these dishes clean and pure."

Jay understood that what he was doing had spiritual value but that it would look ridiculous to most people, including his parents. They cared about hygiene and could not accept Jewish ideas of spiritual blockage (called *tumah* in Hebrew) and spiritual free-flow (*taharah*). He knew not to tell his parents what he was doing or they would think that he was a lunatic.

Having a sense of humor instead of only being overtly serious about religious changes can reassure some people that you are still "normal." Giving funny responses to rhetorical questions can help diffuse tension and show the questioner that you are still the person that you used to be.

Yid with a Lid   When Mordechai (formerly Murray) came back from a year in yeshiva, his father took one look at him and scornfully shook his head. The father ruefully asked his son, "Do you have to wear that awful thing on your head all of the time? It looks so conspicuous."

Mordechai chortled, "No, I don't have to wear it all the time." He smiled gently at his worried father and continued, "I do it because it reminds me that God is above me and that I shouldn't become too egotistical." After a few more moments of his father shifting uncomfortably, Mordechai added, "It also has a side benefit. It keeps the flies off my bald spot." With that, he gave his father a reassuring pat on the back.

Who's in Control?

When a child becomes observant, many parents feel that they've lost their ties to him or her. *Baal teshuvas* control how quickly they become observant while their parents watch, sometimes feeling terrified and helpless, from the sidelines. Parents often worry about where this process will stop. For some, it feels like watching their precious child in a car with no brakes careening at breakneck speed toward a busy intersection.

More Stringencies   Once some parents get used to the idea that their child has become a baal teshuva, the child may adopt even more stringencies or customs that seem bizarre to the parents. Will their child end up so far away geographically, emotionally, and spiritually that the parents and child will never live in the same universe again?

Fiddler Wedding   It was hard, but Genine finally accepted that her daughter Rose had become Orthodox. Rose did things on Shabbos and Jewish holidays that her mother found strange, and Rose was careful about which foods she ate in Genine's house. Yet, her mother consoled herself with the fact that Rose was a good student in college and that she still had some of her pre-Orthodox friends.

A week after Rose finished her BA, she went to a seminary in Jerusalem for the summer. The summer soon stretched into an entire year. When Rose was 24, she called home to announce that she was engaged to a young man who looked like a rabbi. They planned to get married three months later in what would look like a scene from Fiddler on the Roof! Genine was beside herself. This was not what she had dreamed of for her daughter's future.

If We Were They Many people in this position would try to do everything they could to talk their beloved child out of such an extreme lifestyle and return to reason. They would also want lots of time to work through their feelings of hurt, fear, and rejection. They might feel that their child has rejected their values, become totally disconnected from them, and shattered their dreams.

It can take many conversations over a period of years for parents to see that such a child still loves them, wants to stay part of the family, and can be "successful" in ways that are different from what the parent once envisioned. Too, there are some parents for whom no amount of time will help them to get used to a child's changes, and no amount of dialogues will heal their rifts. Religious advisors should help *baal teshuvas* anticipate, and prepare for, various kinds of inevitable confrontations.

Ten Commandments for Helping Relatives Adjust

Here are some pointers for *baal teshuvas* who want to help relatives adjust to their changes:

1. Don't overwhelm others with your love for Judaism and how different you have become. Say as little as is necessary to someone who feels threatened or frightened by your changes.

2. Give others time to adjust.

3. Involve a mediator who seems "normal" to your relatives. Choose someone who has successfully explained Jewish practices to secular people and helped create bridges between *baal teshuvas* and their parents.

4. Don't get defensive when others ask you questions about your religiosity.

5. Respond to the emotion behind a question. Ask the questioner what your changes mean to him or her and address their fears when possible.

6. If they are afraid that you won't love them any more or will create great distance, reassure them (if possible) that you still love and respect them and want always to have a relationship with them.

7. Speak to a rabbi about how you should show respect to your parents, and what compromises and leniencies in Jewish law you should use around them.

8. Speak to a mentor who understands family relationships about practical issues of observance when you are with your family.

9. Keep a sense of humor.

10. If your parents are emotionally hurtful to you, and all reasonable efforts fail to get them to treat you respectfully, ask a rav about how to put appropriate distance between you and them.

General Ways of Responding to Hostility

Some people will greet a *baal teshuva's* enthusiasm about Judaism with hostility. They may make sarcastic or nasty comments about the *baal teshuva's* practices or beliefs.

Pointless   It is pointless to explain to anyone who is actively hostile to Torah Judaism why it is not nonsense and to insist that it is true. Until someone has a question about something, or doubts what he or she believes, that person is not open to hearing answers. If someone is fully convinced that his or her beliefs are correct, an opposing view will fall on deaf ears.

Listening   Sometimes, one can address a hostile person by saying, "It looks like it really hurts (upsets) you that I have become religious. What bothers you most about the way I am living now?" Hostility and anger usually mask deeper feelings of sadness or hurt. Empathizing with, or at least truly listening to, some people who are hostile to observant Judaism or to observant Jews can sometimes lead to a productive dialogue with them.

When Under Attack Baal teshuvas who feel that they are under attack, and who aren't expert in responding to religious criticisms, are hardly in a position to do more than try to protect themselves. Leave explanations to rabbis, outreach workers, and Jewish educators. They can address a baal teshuva's relatives' or friends' misconceptions about Torah and observance. Since they are not emotionally involved with the baal teshuva's relatives and friends, they can often be non-defensive and more effective in responding to a non-observant person's criticisms of Judaism than the baal teshuva may be.

Dialogues with hostile parents are best left to an experienced mediator (such as a teacher or the head of a yeshiva or seminary) who is not emotionally involved in the discussion. If the dialogue can address issues and preclude personal attacks, some kind of rapprochement might be reached.

I'll Never Accept This

Some parents stay antagonistic no matter how *baal teshuvas* present their new lives to them. Some will not reconcile with their child because of the parents' negative feelings about Torah Judaism, while others will reconcile with their *baal teshuva* child when the *baal teshuva* has children.

When parents of *baal teshuvas* will never accept their child's becoming religious, the *baal teshuva* has no choice but to make his or her peace with that.

Observant at 80 Elisheva became observant at the end of high school. For years afterward, her mother Donna lamented the tragedy of having a baal teshuva daughter. Thirty years later, Donna still felt angry with Elisheva for "ruining" both of their lives. Every time they spoke, the mother criticized Elisheva for becoming observant. Why did Olivia change her name to Elisheva? Why did she wear such old-fashioned clothes? Why did she live such a restricted life? Why didn't Elisheva have normal children who watched television, ate in normal restaurants, went out on Saturdays, and had a normal relationship with their grandmother? Why did all of this have to happen to Donna?

Finally, when Donna was a great-grandmother, she stayed with Elisheva and her family for a week. Donna saw them observing Shabbos together. She saw how harmonious her daughter's home and family were. She saw the respect that her grandchildren had for their parents and for her, and how emotionally healthy and stable they were.

Donna finally understood that she had been terribly wrong in hurting her daughter all those years. Donna had been so sure that Elisheva had not made the most of her life. Only at the age of 80 did Donna realize that Elisheva had been right all along.

Donna apologized to her daughter and decided that it was time for her to become observant and follow in her daughter's footsteps. Elisheva was only too happy to be her mother's mentor and help Donna to make up for lost time.

It can take years of hard work for *baal teshuvas* to maintain a good relationship with parents and other family members. The good news is that if you are respectful and loving to your parents as they try to come to terms with your new life, many parents will overcome their barriers to your changes. The bad news is that some parents will never accept their child becoming religious. Yet, many parents and children can have a relationship with each other nonetheless. The child can do his or her best to keep open lines of communication and bend when Jewish law permits.

Parents may need to mourn the many losses and dashed hopes that they experience as their child becomes more and more observant— or in the parents' mind, more and more strange and estranged. Empathizing with a parent's feelings sometimes sets the stage for an on-going dialogue that can lead to renewed closeness and acceptance.

Compromises about Food

Most mothers enjoy nurturing their children. When a *baal teshuva* keeps kosher and his or her mother does not, she may feel that he or she has made it impossible for her to nurture the child in the way she would like. Many relatives also feel that the *baal teshuva* has interfered with family socializing. Mothers may feel traumatized when their child won't eat their cooking or use the family's dishes, and think that their child treats the mother's kitchen as if it is contaminated.

Too, Jews love eating so much that comedian Jackie Mason has a routine about how Jews go out to eat and gentiles go out to drink. In many parts of the world, eating is both a social and gastronomic event. In Judaism, eating is also a pleasurable spiritual event. Not only does food allow us to nourish our body so that it can serve our soul, eating reminds us that our Heavenly Parent is constantly nurturing us, just as a loving mother continually nurtures her infant.

All this can make keeping kosher a frequent battleground between parent and child. Unfortunately, many *baal teshuvas* get into fights with parents over "religious" issues that should never have been problematic in the first place. For this and other reasons it is important to know which Jewish laws are based in the Torah, which are rabbinic, and which are customs. We may need to bend over backward using permitted leniencies when necessary to foster domestic harmony. Before imposing one's Judaism on others, such as when going to a relative's house for a meal or a holiday, *baal teshuvas* should first find out from a rabbi what one should or must not do.

Appreciative Seder   Hedi went to a baal teshuva seminary. She loved spending her first and second Passovers as an observant Jew at the principal's home. Her parents were Reform Jews and were not happy that Hedi had become religious, yet they paid her seminary tuition for two years. Meanwhile, Hedi lived away from home, and when she visited her family, she never spent a Shabbos or Jewish holiday with them. Long before Hedi's third Passover, her mother told Hedi that she wanted the family to be together for the Passover seder and that she would do whatever was necessary to make that possible. Hedi didn't want to have her Passover ruined by being in her parents' secular neighborhood, at an "unspiritual" seder, and in a home where her level of Passover kashrut would be compromised. She called the seminary principal and asked if she could come to the principal's Passover seder that year.

The principal replied, "No, you must spend Passover with your parents. They have done so much for you, you have to show them appreciation. I have no doubt that you would enjoy the seder at my table more. Your mother is willing to bend over backward so that you will join them for Passover, and I will tell your mother what she must do to make the house kosher. Don't hurt her feelings by slapping her in the face and going somewhere else."

As one becomes increasingly observant, one must be careful to become increasingly *menschlich* (decent toward people).

Serving Food   Baal teshuvas need to learn practical tips about how to minimize disturbances at meals with their family or other non-observant people.

For example, a *baal teshuva* needn't stick out like a sore thumb at celebrations. He or she can buy beautiful "designer" paper plates and tablecloths, good-quality cutlery, and pretty disposable serving dishes for festive family meals. It needn't cost a lot to buy attractive disposable or inexpensive cookware, flatware, glasses, and porcelain serving dishes if one's family or friends want kosher meals to be served "normally" in a home where the dishes aren't kosher.

One can even put hard, new, clear plastic plates on top of parents' non-kosher china to give the appearance of everyone's eating in the same elegant way.

It is easy to kasher most metal cutlery and to keep some apart for your personal use when visiting family. If a mother has non-kosher sterling silver and you can't kasher it (you don't have time or she doesn't want you to), you can buy nominally priced silver-plated flatware rather than eat with plastic cutlery at a fancy meal.

If need be, many foods can be eaten cold on non-kosher dishes using non-kosher utensils. Consult a rabbi in advance for guidelines as to how to do this.

Preparing Food   A crock pot and electric burner can be great boons. You can make entire meals for many people using them. They are portable, inexpensive, and make up for the lack of kitchen facilities. (The author has made meals for as many as a dozen people using them in hotel rooms.) If need be, they can be plugged into a bathroom or living room electric socket with or without an extension cord and placed safely on a dry sink counter or desk. Keep them away from anything combustible and make sure that their wires will not get wet. A crock pot or burner, an electric skillet, pot, and a few utensils can make a traveling kitchen for observant people.

It is easy to kasher stove burners and (many) microwave and self-cleaning ovens. If you don't know how, ask your rabbi or religious advisor. If you need to cook foods and don't have time to kasher ovens or a stove, foods double-wrapped in foil can be cooked in non-kosher ovens. That's how airlines warm your meals.

Traveling with family members who don't keep kosher can be very easy, especially with in-room refrigerators and portable electric coolers. Easily prepared or ready-to-eat kosher foods are available all over North America and in many other parts of the world. Supermarkets usually stock some brands of kosher fresh, canned, smoked and frozen fish; cottage cheese; yogurt; frozen bagels; pitas; dry or prepared hummus; canned, fresh and frozen vegetables and fruit; canned beans; nuts; and peanut butter and jelly. Most of these need little or no preparation. One can even buy non-perishable, kosher meals that don't need refrigeration.

Websites such as www.kosher.com (1-866-kosherx) sell these products, and some are available in health-food stores. La Briute, sold on this website, makes self-heating meals. Pack them in your suitcase or have them shipped to your destination. For more information, search the Internet using the words "kosher travel meals."

Oneg in Alaska   Shevi and her husband loved to travel to rustic places. They went on a two-week trip where they hiked all over Alaska. After eating mostly salmon, baked potatoes, and vegetables for 10 days, they planned to spend Shabbos in a hotel on a glacier in the middle of nowhere. Shevi went to the only supermarket within a

100-mile radius that Friday morning to stock up on food before they traveled along a pothole-rutted, gravel, 60-mile road to the glacier. As she passed by the freezer case in the store, her eye caught a caramel-and-chocolate cheesecake that was staring at her. Her mouth started to water. For some reason, she went over and picked up the delicacy, knowing full well that it couldn't possibly be kosher. After all, it was manufactured in a small town in Texas, and she was now in the hinterlands of Alaska.

When she turned it over, there was the OU (Orthodox Union's) kosher symbol beaming out at her. She bought it and it greatly contributed to their *oneg* (pleasure) that Shabbos.

Never underestimate how widespread kosher products are today!

Even non-kosher wine stores stock many award-winning kosher wines.

Kiddush in NH   A group of baal teshuva friends went traveling to New England one July. They cycled in Martha's Vineyard, camped out under the stars, and hiked in the mountains of Maine. They planned to spend their first Shabbos in a small town in New Hampshire but forgot to bring wine with them. They went into a local wine store Friday afternoon, thinking that they might find some other alcoholic beverage with which they could make Kiddush that evening. Much to their surprise, there were three bottles of kosher wine on the shelf! It was not a connoisseur's brand, but at least it was perfectly suitable for sanctifying the day.

If it's really important to have a certain kind of kosher wine for an occasion and you can't bring it with you (such as champagne for a celebration), try ordering it from the Internet and having it shipped. The world really has become a global village.

Kosher Bubbly   At the end of four grueling years of graduate school classes and research, Yehudis successfully defended her doctoral dissertation and was congratulated by the (non-Jewish) professors on her committee. Her advisor then surprised her by breaking out a bottle of non-kosher champagne, poured everyone a drink, and toasted her. Everyone waited expectantly for Yehudis to drink. Turning beet red, she quickly raised her glass near her lips and tilted it without tasting a drop. Everyone thought that she was enjoying her champagne along with the others and no one noticed that the bubbly liquid's level only went down as the carbon dioxide dissipated. No one was embarrassed, and Yehudis was able to leave school and her teachers with good feelings all around.

Being caught off-guard then made her think that it would be a good idea to visit a kosher wine store when she went home. Even though Yehudis didn't drink much, she bought a couple of bottles of kosher champagne and stocked them in her secular family's bar. After all, she never knew when she might need them to celebrate with her friends and family.

The next evening, Yehudis' mother surprised her with an elaborate, non-kosher celebration party at their house. Yehudis appreciated her parents' good intentions and drank orange juice and nibbled on baby carrots and fresh fruit throughout the evening. Before dessert, her father poured champagne for all of their relatives and friends. When everyone got ready to toast her, Yehudis was ready with her own bottle of champagne and was able to join in. She appreciated her parents' desire to show their pride in her accomplishments, and their enthusiasm wasn't dampened by any frictions over the food and libations.

Many *baal teshuvas* like Yehudis have discovered that an ounce of prevention is worth a pound of cure. Planning ahead can be invaluable in keeping domestic harmony intact.

Summary

One of the most difficult challenges for *baal teshuvas* is dealing with parents who are opposed to their religious changes. A great deal of empathy and reassurance is necessary to help parents stop worrying that their beloved child has "gone off the deep end," will be emotionally estranged from them forever, has broken up the family, or has ruined his or her life. Knowing what to say, and what not to say, when a child becomes observant can smooth the way for parents to accept their child's religious changes. Involving a religious mentor as a mediator who seems "normal" to the parents can be invaluable.

Some *baal teshuvas* who are respectful and patient may find that their parents eventually accept their religious changes. Some extremely fortunate *baal teshuvas* even have parents who become more observant, either because they find it meaningful or to keep the family together. Unfortunately, some parents of *baal teshuvas* will never agree to amicably disagree. The sting of their parents' ongoing criticism, rejection, or worse may stay with their children for the rest of their lives.

Perhaps that pain is part of why the Talmud says, "In the place that a *baal teshuva* stands, even someone who has always been perfectly righteous cannot stand." The pain is sometimes an inescapable consequence of Jews' choosing to live with greater depth, meaning, and adherence to Torah.

THIRTEEN

Objections to Someone's Becoming Baal Teshuva

Change is not easy, and we don't change in a vacuum. Family therapists know that if you change one person in a family, the other family members will resist and try to reestablish equilibrium. When this happens to *baal teshuvas*, they are rarely prepared to cope with their families' and friends' resistance and opposition. This book will help them to do this.

Families are sometimes opposed to the *baal teshuva's* changes because of what those changes imply. Here are general ides by which people commonly express their objections to a friend's or relative's becoming *baal teshuva*, and some ideas about how one may or may not be able to deal with these ideas and feelings:

1. We are modern, sophisticated people and Orthodox Judaism was developed as a religion for primitive tribes.

Many people are uninformed about the spiritual purposes of Jewish rituals, and the sophisticated morality that Torah brought to the world. Yet, it is rarely productive to immediately correct others' misconceptions. What they know about Judaism is often based on their having read mistranslations of parts of the Torah and/or "scholarly" attacks on traditional Judaism.

They were taught that some men made up the Torah for health and social reasons. Many also have emotional objections to Torah Judaism, feeling that observance keeps them from fully enjoying life, and is both culturally and socially limiting. People in this camp may think, "The originators of Judaism realized that people who ate pork developed trichinosis, so they forbade eating pig. In ancient times, making a fire was a lot of work, so Moses or some other Jewish leader forbade lighting fires one day a week. That way Jews would have a day of rest. Like all primitive people, they celebrated some agricultural holidays to make sure that they had successful crops. They thought that women got impure and were taboo every month so they required women to take a monthly bath and separate themselves from men for hygienic reasons."

Such people think, "We don't need antiquated rituals. After all, we live in the 21st century. We have hygiene and sanitation and are no longer superstitious. We believe in science and don't believe in 'spiritual forces.' We have modern medicine and technology. We don't believe that anyone is 'impure.' The rituals and rules in the Bible served social and legal purposes many centuries ago, but we don't need them any more. We are sophisticated, modern people who can rely on our human reason to decide what is good and bad for us. What's most important is that we are good people."

Parents with these beliefs may try to dissuade their children from becoming more observant, and may not want to facilitate their children keeping kosher or observing Shabbos. If someone's objections are based in ignorance, having others gradually and comfortably expose them to authentic Torah ideas may change their perspectives. If the real objections are emotional, the more a person feels threatened by observance the less productive dialogue may be.

Here is one story that combines elements of both. This resolution was possible only because someone other than the children discussed Judaism with the parent, and the parent was willing to engage in this dialogue:

Chip Removal Marty and Joyce decided to keep kosher shortly after they got married. His parents were devout atheists, hers were modern secularists. Joyce's mother, Cheryl, was so upset at her daughter's decision to keep kosher that Cheryl forbade Joyce to bring kosher food into her home. This made it impossible for Marty and Joyce to visit her parents at their home for more than a few hours, especially once they had children. Although parents often mellow in their opposition to Jewish observances in order to be on good terms with their grandchildren, Cheryl didn't relent. The best that Cheryl would allow was for Joyce to bring wrapped kosher food to Cheryl's house and place it in a special section inside the refrigerator where it wouldn't contaminate the "normal" food.

In time, Marty and Joyce became fully observant. Seven years later, Cheryl was still so hostile to their keeping kosher that their family visits were invariably unpleasant. Cheryl continued to challenge Joyce about why she observed archaic, ridiculous practices.

Joyce finally countered, "Why don't you just go to Jerusalem for one week, take a Discovery seminar, and learn with a private teacher to whom you can address all of your questions? I think that it will help our relationship. I am not the person who can ever lay to rest your negative feelings about Torah observance."

Surprisingly, Cheryl agreed. Joyce arranged a lovely place for Cheryl to stay in Jerusalem, arranged for her to have a private teacher, and booked her to attend a Discovery program. (Discovery is an all-day series of lectures given by speakers affiliated with Aish HaTorah. They logically present why Jews believe in the authenticity of Torah and observant Judaism.)

Cheryl went to Israel with a chip on her shoulder, believing that no religious Jew could say anything that would change her mind about the irrelevance of Torah observance. Yet, her antagonism melted away as she studied Judaism with a special woman. She fell in love with the Old City of Jerusalem and with the Jews whom she met there.

The Discovery program was so convincing that she extended her stay by a week—then by a few more weeks. By the time she left, Cheryl had arranged to continue studying with her teacher by e-mail. That continued for the next two years. During that time, Cheryl kashered her home and became observant.

Some parents will never lose their antagonism to observant Judaism. It takes others lots of time, patience, respect, and, finally, someone other than their child to educate them about observant Judaism in order to view it from a more positive perspective.

2. **Orthodox Jews are so conspicuous. We are Americans who happen to also be Jewish. We don't want to make ourselves stick out.**

Embarrassed Jews Gary's parents were immigrants who had suffered religious persecution and were embarrassed about being Jewish. They wanted to make sure that their children would be all-American. The children attended good public schools, wore the latest American fashions, and lived in a nice neighborhood side by side with gentiles. The parents dreamt that some day their children would be successful professionals.

When Gary was in his last year of high school, a Jewish classmate, Linda, became religious through NCSY (the youth movement of the Orthodox Union, OU). She introduced him to Torah ideas and gave him some Jewish books to read. He felt excited about being Jewish for the first time in his life. One day, he affixed a mezuzah to his door, feeling proud to affirm his connection to Judaism. As soon as his parents noticed it, they took it down, then lectured him about how being too Jewish always leads to trouble. They certainly would not allow such practices in their home. If, tragedy of tragedies, he would ever marry someone like Linda, it would rupture their family forever and they would disown him.

People like Gary's parents can't respect themselves for being Jewish. They have such negative emotional associations with being Jewish that it can be very difficult, and sometimes impossible, to have any reasonable discussions about it.

3. **Orthodox Jews are (pick as many as apply) dirty, uneducated, uncultured, ill-mannered, prejudiced against women,**

have too many children, impose their religious beliefs on others.

When someone has a litany of complaints about something, none of them is usually the real issue. These complaints are often an excuse to distance ourselves from people whom we don't want to be like, or are a reaction to having had some bad emotional experiences with Orthodox Jews.

There are two ways of responding to someone with these complaints. The first is to agree with the truth in them. For example, it is true that some observant Jews are pushy, arrogant, have poor hygiene and grooming, do not treat women with respect, and so on. The fact that secular people also have character defects does not make it okay for us to be less than exemplary. If we are observant Jews, people will hold us to a higher standard of conduct. We shouldn't be so defensive that we can't see our own warts. Everyone has room for improvement.

So, when people voice objections to the conduct of observant Jews, even if they are making sweeping generalizations, admit to the truth of what they are saying.

The second way to respond after validating someone's criticisms is to gently steer the discussion away from black-and-white, sweeping generalizations. Focus on the specifics at hand and show the person that their fears of you becoming that way are unlikely.

Stormy Visit   Anita went to an Orthodox synagogue expecting it to look like the Reform synagogue in which she had prayed a few times. When she entered the Orthodox shul, she was told that she was on the men's side, and that the women's entrance was on the other side. She assumed that they were treating women as second-class citizens, forcing them to enter a place of worship through a side door! The woman sat on one side of a partition, where they could not see what was going on nor participate in the services. She found fault with everything she saw (real or imagined). She noticed that the services were conducted only by men—the rabbi and cantor were men, and women were not called up to the Torah. It was obvious to her that Orthodoxy discriminated against women and didn't think that she, or any women, had worth. She carried this hastily built hatred for all things Orthodox with her for the rest of her life.

Had Anita's daughter heard this, she could say to her mother, "I certainly understand why you feel the way you do about Orthodox synagogues and Orthodox people. Your experience must have felt very humiliating. I would certainly not want to be part of a group that would make me feel that I had little self-worth."

The daughter should not try to "correct" her mother's perceptions or feelings at this point, nor explain how Torah really validates women. Her validating response can open the door to a dialogue about how the daughter could want to be observant and live in the kind of world that Anita found so distasteful. Anita may never want to set foot in an Orthodox shul, and may never understand how her daughter can. Yet, feeling that her daughter understands where she is coming from can allow them to have a better relationship.

Bad Experiences An intense emotional reaction often stems from hurts to someone's self-esteem that preceded their exposure to Orthodoxy by many years. For example, many women are, or were, treated as less worthy than males while growing up, and this denigration often continues into their adult lives. There are plenty of anti-Orthodox writings that disparage traditional Judaism's rituals and its role divisions for men and women. By the time some people meet anyone Orthodox, or confront role divisions in Judaism, they are primed to hate them. The person's preconceived notions of how people should behave and what Jewish rituals mean leads to their condemning any observances or Jews who don't fit their worldview. It is sad how often people who are liberal in their views about all other people are intolerant of observant Jews.

Unfortunately, some people have had bad experiences with Orthodox Jews, and those unpleasant feelings may be bolstered by books, magazines, and newspaper articles that popularize negative misconceptions. Sometimes, people who had bad experiences may end up generalizing from one or a few instances in which their feelings were hurt to feeling angry with, and intolerant of, anyone who is observant.

Good Models   If such a person doesn't have a deep-seated emotional axe to grind, exposing them to exemplary Jewish models with whom they can have a reparative relationship can be helpful. For example, if someone is willing to eat Shabbos or holiday meals with a host family, or meet an observant teacher or rabbi that doesn't fit their stereotypes, it can dispel a lot of negative impressions. Attending a very-carefully chosen class can also be a positive experience for some people.

However, many people who dislike observant Jews have strong emotional issues that are not easily changed. Trying to dispel negative emotions using rational or intellectual arguments is usually a waste of time. The more intense someone's feelings are, the more positive experiences and time he or she will need to work through their negativity.

A True Jew   Sol felt horrified when his son Jonah became observant in his 30s. Among Sol's complaints about religious Jews were that they were dishonest, hypocritical, self-serving, and arrogant. Instead of discounting Sol's opinions by saying that he was mistaken, Jonah partially agreed with him. Because Jonah could accept the truth in what his father told him, Sol was open to accepting the truth in what Jonah told him:

"You know, Dad, you're absolutely right," Jonah admitted. "There's no question that some otherwise observant Jews are all of the things that you say. Maybe that's even true about many of them. I haven't met enough to generalize about hundreds of thousands of people. But I am fortunate to have found some very fine observant Jews who don't fit those stereotypes. I am going to try my best to be like those exemplary Jews, and not be like the ones that both of us find distasteful."

When Sol became observant himself, he told Jonah that it was because he had met a truly righteous, humble, incredibly kind, exemplary Jew whose behavior convinced him that the stereotypes did not—and need not—apply to everyone.

4. (Name) is Orthodox. I hope that you're not going to be like him/her!

Potential Rift When Shelley came home after learning in a Jerusalem seminary for a semester, her mother burst into tears.

"Oh, my goodness, what happened to you?! You look just like your cousin Debbie. She went away to Israel looking normal and came back dressing like a fanatic—long-sleeved shirts, long skirts, stockings—even in the summer. The next thing we knew, Debbie had changed her name to Devorah. Then, she married a guy whom she hardly knew and started wearing a wig.

"Why couldn't she have married someone normal instead of that rabbi? All she does is cook, serve meals, change diapers, and nurse. She just had her fourth child! She's nothing more than a baby machine.

"She won't even eat in her own mother's house. How could any child do that to her mother? My sister cooked for hours so that the family could be together for Rosh Hashana, then Debbie wouldn't eat there because her house wasn't kosher enough! I thought that Judaism teaches that children should respect their parents. What kind of respect is that? I hope that you don't end up like her."

The real fear here is that a child will become so religious that it will cause a rift in the family, and/or that the parent will need to change to accommodate the child's "fanaticism." Part of the antidote is for the child to reassure the parent that they will always want a good relationship with the parent, and that if they both try to resolve their differences respectfully and with love, they will usually be able to find a compromise that will allow them to have a reasonable relationship.

Shabbos-Candle Threat Leslie was from a secular Jewish family. When she was 21, she started learning about Judaism from a friend and then read voraciously. Soon, she was going to Judaism classes. After she heard a talk about the significance of lighting

Shabbos candles, she bought two candlesticks and some candles and set them up in the family's formal dining room. She planned to light the candles that Friday afternoon. When her mother saw what Leslie was doing, the mother became furious.

"Don't you dare light those candles in my house!" her mother yelled.

Leslie was completely taken aback. Her mother wouldn't mind lighting beautiful tapers for a candlelight dinner in her home. Why should she be so upset about lighting plain Shabbos candles?

"But Mom," Leslie protested, "nobody even goes in this room except when you have dinner parties. What's wrong with my lighting these candles?"

Her mother gave her a series of excuses, ranging from it being a fire hazard to how she might influence her brother and sister to want to do Jewish rituals, too.

The real issue was that her mother didn't want her children becoming more observant and expecting her to do the same. Once a child lights Shabbos candles and learns about Judaism, who knows where he or she will end up?

The best that children in such circumstances can do is to try to minimize those behaviors in the parents' home that threaten the parents. Children can also reassure the parents that they will respect the parents' way of life and would never ask the parents to change the way they live.

5. You rejected our values. Where did we go wrong?

Parents tend to feel threatened by what they perceive—often rightly so—as their child's rejection of the parents' beliefs, values, and dreams. It hurts when someone we love rejects our way of life.

Rejecting Liberalism   Roberta's mother was intensely devoted to lots of liberal causes. When Roberta went to an Ivy League college, she and her friends sat around and discussed social and political ideas. One day, a friend convinced Roberta and her friends to attend a talk at the Hillel about how the positive values that Western civilization holds dear were actually first espoused by Jews and were based in the Torah. After the lecture, Roberta decided to attend a weekly class on a Jewish topic.

By the time the school year ended and Roberta came home for the summer, she had decided to keep kosher and traditionally observe Shabbos. She had become more conservative in her political views and was reading a traditional Jewish book about women's issues. Her mother was incensed and frightened that Roberta could reject everything that her mother had worked so hard to inculcate in her daughter for the past 20 years.

This kind of gap can be hard to bridge. It is helpful for baal teshuvas to focus on the general characteristics, values and perspectives that they learned from, and still have in common with, their parents. For example, baal teshuvas can realize for themselves, and tell their parents, that they got the strength to be different due to the strength of conviction that they saw their parents model. Children can note that their parents wanted to make the world a better place, that they were willing to work hard for things that they believed in, that they feel a sense of personal and social responsibility, and the importance of helping others. We may share a vision of world perfection and world peace because we have learned certain ideals from our parents, but have different means of trying to achieve the same goals. Having the parent and child verbalize what they still have in common and emphasizing what the child values about the parent can sometimes ease their frictions.

6. Why isn't my brand of Judaism good enough for you?

One's becoming observant often implies to relatives that their brand of Judaism is not good enough. In their minds, if not in reality, the observant person's choice condemns the family's lack of religiosity.

Too Fanatic Stephanie's parents were members of a Reform synagogue and were very active in Jewish life. Her father donated money to the United Jewish Communities and to Jewish hospitals every year. He worked at annual telethons that raised money for Israel and he had visited Israel on a family mission with a Jewish cultural organization. He and his wife had also sent their children to a Reform Sunday school for several years and had celebrations for their children's bar and bat mitzvahs.

When Stephanie went to college, her lab partner went to Friday night dinners at the local Chabad House. She invited Stephanie to join her and told her about the great food and the nice guys who came. Stephanie came to one dinner for these reasons but was moved by the special feeling of caring and spirituality that pervaded the room. Before the meal was over, the rabbi gave a short talk about making life holy and it struck a chord in Stephanie.

By the end of the school year, Stephanie had become observant, and her family did not understand why she had become so different from them. When she told her parents that she would no longer go on their annual summer family vacation to Cape Cod, her mother was horrified, then angry.

She confronted Stephanie, "What's wrong with going to Cape Cod?"

Stephanie thought about all of the reasons why going to Cape Cod would not be good for her, but there would be no point in detailing them to her mother. The real issue was that her mother was feeling both hurt and rejected and Stephanie needed to address that. Rather than explain all of her changes, Stephanie would do better to try to help her mother feel that each could respect the other's religious choices and see if some kind of compromise were possible that would allow the family to spend some vacation time together in a way that reduced upsets and promoted domestic harmony.

7. How could you reject me? I'm your parent!

Many parents infer that if their child rejected the parents' way of life because it lacked authenticity, their child can't still love them!

Most baal teshuvas still want to be close with the parents who raised, nurtured, love, and support them and with whom they shared much of their lives. The baal teshuva can reject some of the parents' ideas and values and still want a loving relationship with them. Parents may not understand this. The baal teshuva may need to express this point over and over again. We don't have to accept all of someone's beliefs in order to love him or her.

8. How could you reject us after everything that we've sacrificed for you?

Some parents feel loved or validated only if their children live up to their expectations. If parents invest their time, emotions, and money in children who don't fulfill the parents' wishes, some parents take it personally and feel crushed that their child will not live out their dreams.

Pre-Med to Rabbi   Frank was a smart boy, and his parents hoped that some day he would become a doctor like his father.

It certainly seemed that Frank might go into medicine. He was an honors student in high school, and attended a prestigious university where he majored in pre-medicine. In his senior year, he applied to several medical schools and was accepted by his first choice.

Meanwhile, Frank's brother had gone to Israel to study in a yeshiva while Frank finished his BA. Throughout the school year, the brother e-mailed Frank about his studies and referred him to interesting articles and books about Judaism. Frank avidly read them and became more and more intrigued. By the time he got the letter of acceptance to medical school, his parents were thrilled, but Frank was ambivalent. He was burning to know, "Is the Torah really true? Should I be living as an observant Jew? If I become a doctor, should I be a religious Jewish doctor? If so, how do I do that?"

Frank deferred his admission to medical school. A week after college ended, Frank went to a yeshiva and stayed for a year. By the end of the year, he knew that he wanted to be a rabbi and had lost all interest in becoming a doctor.

When he told his parents about his change of heart, they got a triple "whammy." He was never going to medical school, he had decided to become observant, and he had also decided to live in Israel.

His parents were beside themselves. They had invested $120,000 in his college education so that he could be a doctor, and now he wanted to turn his back on medical school? And for what—to be a rabbi?! If he had at least decided to go into some worthwhile career that would be financially remunerative, all of the emotional and financial investment would have been worth it. Not only wasn't he going to become a respectable professional who could comfortably support his family, he wasn't going to make use of years of secular education. He was shunning everything that his parents lived for. He was going to live in what his parents considered to be a crowded religious ghetto. To add salt to their wounds, Frank's living in Israel meant that the parents would rarely see him or their grandchildren. His parents were devastated.

Frank's parents tried to coax him to at least go to medical school and get his degree so that he would have something to fall back on. He told an advisor about his dilemma.

The advisor asked, "Would the talents that you uniquely have be better utilized as a doctor or as a rabbi?"

Frank thought about it for a few minutes, then concluded, "As a rabbi."

The advisor probed, "If you become a rabbi, you may have financial problems. If you lead a congregation, they will be able to tell you what to do and will control your employment. Do you think that you might want to be a doctor for some time, become financially settled, and then become a rabbi much later?

Frank thought this through as well. He thought that his strengths would be as a Jewish outreach worker, where he could innovate ideas and use technology to bring Jews back to their roots. If he did not find a job in outreach that would adequately support his family, he could support himself by working in some medical field and do outreach as a volunteer. If need be, he might even go to medical school some years down the line, but he didn't want to do that now.

With his well-thought-out plan, he let his parents know that he would not be going to medical school.

In situations such as these, the baal teshuva should do his utmost to retain ties to his parents and to express respect, appreciation, and gratitude for their sacrifices. Weekly phone calls that focus on pleasant topics, and visits that include enjoyable activities, can go a long way in emphasizing the positive aspects of the parent and child's relationship and in healing the wounds that can be created by drastic career and life changes.

Baal teshuvas in these circumstances must stress to the parents that the parents' sacrifices weren't wasted, although the rewards didn't take the form that the parents had hoped for. Sometimes an education expands a mind, sometimes it prepares one for a specific career. The value of being trained to think is never wasted.

9. You've become a totally different person. What happened to the person that you used to be?

Becoming religious often seems so black and white. It doesn't help that religious Jews sometimes define themselves, or are defined by others, in terms of some of their observances:

"He's black hat (or yeshivish) now."

"She's going to cover her hair when she gets married."

"He used to be so normal. Now he doesn't speak to girls."

"She doesn't go mixed swimming any more."

We each have temperaments, personalities, character traits, and actions that define and contribute to who we are. If people are creative before they become observant, they hopefully will stay creative afterward, although their forms of creative expression might change. If they were smart, talented, musical, kind, or idealistic before, they will probably stay that way after they become observant. The family of baal teshuvas may need to look past the superficialities and new clothes to uncover the former person who is still there. When this is hard to do, the baal teshuva may need to accent the continuity between who they once were and who they still are. At times, baal teshuvas themselves may need help remembering to take their identity with them.

One-Track Mind Aimee was raised in a suburban neighborhood where art, dance, music, and sports were important. Four days a week, she took gymnastics, ballet, tennis, and piano lessons. Every summer, she went to camps that offered swimming, horseback riding, and drama. When she went to college, she became observant and spent most of her time reading, attending classes, studying, or writing papers. When she came home that summer, she spent half an hour praying every morning, read books about Judaism for the rest of the morning and most of the afternoon, then spent another two hours every evening listening to taped lectures on various Jewish topics.

Her parents invited her to join them at the country club and go to the beach with them, but Aimee refused. Her mother became frustrated by Aimee's lack of interest in any "normal" activities and offered to take her to the ballet or to a concert. Aimee would never have refused those offers before she became observant. Now, Aimee was not interested.

Totally exasperated, her mother insisted, "All work and no play make Jack a dull boy."

Aimee countered, "I don't think that I've become dull. I just find Judaism more fascinating than anything else. I'm not interested in the arts and sports the way I once was."

Her mother retorted, "How can you not have any interest in any of the things that you did for the last 19 years?! Aren't you interested in anything besides Judaism any more?"

Several things are apparent here. First, the mother is doing her utmost to find a way to connect with her daughter, but Aimee doesn't appreciate how important that is. While Aimee may find Judaism fascinating, she should still make time to relate to her mother in a way that the two of them can have a relationship. Juggling her schedule to make time to play tennis with her mother, or going out with her mother once a week to a movie, museum, or concert, would be an easy way to do this. If Aimee doesn't want to sit and read near the swimming pool when her parents are at the country club, she might suggest that they bicycle or go for a walk together.

Second, baal teshuvas sometimes want to make up for lost time. In their quest to learn as much about Judaism as quickly as they can, baal teshuvas may neglect all of their former interests. This often catches up with them if they get lots of intellectual stimulation from books or classes but neglect their relationships, their creativity, emotionally enriching pursuits, and physical health.

It is good to find balance. If someone was always athletic, he or she should continue exercising on a regular basis, even if it takes a different form than before—jogging instead of swimming, power walking instead of going to a mixed gym, same-sex exercise sessions instead of mixed classes, yoga instead of aerobics, and the like. If someone's life was enriched by listening to or playing music, or by dancing, he or she should continue in a way that is religiously acceptable. He or she may want to spend less time in leisure activities or hobbies but shouldn't neglect them altogether. Otherwise, the baal teshuva may burn out (or burn out others) from the intensity of learning and doing little else.

Third, some baal teshuvas have so many demands on their time that they simply don't have enough hours in the day to continue the "extracurricular activities" that they once enjoyed. Studying and practicing Judaism, praying every day, and working or going to school can leave little time for much else. If this lack of time is temporary, they can tell their family, "I would love to spend time doing things with you. I'm going through a lot of changes right now and need a few days to figure out how to rebalance my life." The baal teshuva may need to choose which of their former activities to continue, and do them only a few hours a week, while dropping the less important ones altogether. In the meantime, they should strive to make opportunities for family bonding and emotional enrichment. Continuing some activities that were important to them and their family before becoming observant can help ease the transition to their new way of life.

10. How can you break up the family?

Family members sometimes blame a baal teshuva's Judaism for breaking up the family and for the baal teshuva's lack of participation in family celebrations, events, or rituals. The baal teshuva no longer eats out in restaurants with the family and won't spend most Jewish holidays with them. They don't participate in family outings on Shabbos or Jewish holidays. They don't attend their relatives' intermarriages. The baal teshuva may hear guilt-inducing accusations because he is "breaking up the family." Others may expect him to be "decent" and change back to the person that he used to be.

People may accept many types of eccentric behavior, yet when someone becomes an observant Jew, they may view that form of being different as unacceptable. Imagine that numerous people in a family ate junk food and developed complications of diabetes and heart disease. One day, a granddaughter announces, "I want to live a long and happy life. From now on, I will only eat healthy, vegetarian food at family gatherings, and I will only bring or make healthy food when I am hosting." Some members of the family might respect her choice, some will think she is a bit strange, and a few will be annoyed that her choice pressures them to reconsider their eating habits. Yet, no one would say, "Look at Allison, she's breaking up the family."

If someone does something silly, we don't usually resent him or her. Becoming observant generates more profound reactions because Jews instinctively know that observance touches on core issues of how we should live. It is up to all of the family members to do their utmost not to react in a way that destroys the family. A baal teshuva's changes may threaten others because it impels them to examine their own lifestyles and possibly require them to change.

When a person becomes baal teshuva, some things become non-negotiable. A baal teshuva can't compromise by having the rabbi bless the shrimp cocktail or eat non-kosher meat at the grandparents' 50th wedding anniversary celebration. Nor can a baal teshuva get dispensation and drive to the brother's bar mitzvah on Shabbos which is at a Reform temple ten miles away. It is not fair to expect anyone to compromise principles that are non-negotiable. No one would ask a non-smoker to "smoke just one cigarette" or ask someone to eat a food that makes the person physically ill in order to make other family members happy. If the family members or friends truly care about the baal teshuva, they will do their best to accommodate him or her and accept the baal teshuva's decision not to attend functions that require him or her to make intolerable compromises. Of course, that kind of respect goes both ways, and the baal teshuva should bend over backwards to make allowable compromises when they can further family harmony.

Less-observant family members sometimes extol tolerance for others whose beliefs and lifestyle are different from their own. Yet, they may be intolerant when it comes to respecting a baal teshuva's lifestyle, beliefs, and practices. For example, a family may arrange for a celebration to be held in a venue that is not kosher, precluding the baal teshuva from eating there. If the relatives pressure the baal teshuva to eat there, the baal teshuva can say, "You often speak about how people should be tolerant of others. I don't tell you where to eat, so why do you think that it is okay for you to tell me where to eat? That is not showing tolerance for my beliefs and practices."

Two-Sided Compromise   Elliott felt religious stirrings when he was 14. He started learning about Judaism and decided to observe as much of its rituals as he could. He yearned to go to yeshiva, but his secular parents weren't ready to enroll him in a Jewish school.

One day, Elliott decided to cover his head while saying the prayer before eating bread in the lunchroom of the public school that he attended. His classmates gaped at him, then roared with derisive laughter. They soon humiliated him every day when he said a blessing before eating. He endured it so that he could do what he thought God wanted of him.

One afternoon, a neighbor told his mother what was going on. The mother realized that she must enroll him in a yeshiva so that he wouldn't be publicly humiliated every day, even though she had no intentions of becoming observant.

She took him to a yeshiva, enrolled him, and he flourished. He continued studying in yeshiva in Israel after high school. While there, he wrote his mother a letter pleading with her to make the home kosher and to create an atmosphere conducive to observance so that he could live there when he came home. She decided to do what he asked rather than break up the family. When Elliott came back, the rest of the family welcomed him and lived as observant Jews at home in order to create domestic harmony.

Years later, Elliott and his siblings left home and got married, and their parents lived alone. The parents could have resumed living as secular Jews, but they decided not to. They discovered that observing Judaism was worthwhile in its own right. They exemplified the Jewish saying, "When one does things for ulterior reasons, one comes to do them for their own sake."

11. You've been brainwashed.

Sadly, many Jews are so estranged from healthy Torah observance that they assume that every secular Jew who becomes observant must have been brainwashed. They have heard so much about evangelical sects and cults that they view Torah observance as just one more perversion of religion.

There are many differences between Torah observance and cults. For example, cults prevent adherents from questioning what they are taught and deprive newcomers of sleep and contact with the outside world. Cult members are prevented from reading books that might make them question what they are learning. The cult also does its best to keep outsiders out.

The best approach to non-observant parents who think their child has been brainwashed is to invite them to join the baal teshuva in his or her studies.

Invitation To Learn   Harry, a totally secular Jew in his 30s, went to yeshiva. The classes were intellectually stimulating, fulfilling, and spiritually compelling. He wrote to his father about how exciting his Jewish studies were. His father quickly flew to Israel to rescue his son from what the father assumed was a cult.

Harry told him, "Dad, I'm not going to explain to you what I am learning. Come experience it for yourself. If, after learning with me in yeshiva for a week, you still think that I'm being brainwashed, we'll both leave."

The 68-year-old father agreed. A few months later, the father was still in yeshiva, and he became observant. He studied in a yeshiva every day until he passed away 18 years later.

12. We are Reformed Jews. We don't have to be Orthodox.

Most Jews today have no idea that Reform Judaism began in the 19th century as a way of rejecting traditional Judaism, which had been around for more than 3,000 years.

Many non-observant Jews view the Torah's rituals as burdens that prevent people from enjoying life. They feel perfectly comfortable living the way they are. Observance threatens them because it implies that they should be doing more. Saying, "I am a Reform Jew; we don't have to do these things" is a way of feeling good about the way one is. Such people don't have to examine their values, beliefs, or behaviors in ways that may be uncomfortable or feel compelled to do things that are outside their comfort zone.

If the person is uninterested in knowing more about Torah, the best approach is to accent your respect for the person even though you have chosen a different way of expressing your Jewishness. If someone is potentially interested in learning more, but doesn't want to change the way they live, help them to find a way to learn about Torah in an environment that is warm, accepting and non-judgmental.

Rituals as Love   Many non-observant Jews are Jewishly uneducated, yet they see themselves as very Jewish. They don't know that observing rituals can enhance their emotional and spiritual enjoyment, and they may be open to hearing how this can be true. Invite them to learn in beginners' classes or introductory prayer services according to their interests.

We can also explain to someone who is not hostile to observance that each Jewish ritual we do invests us in our relationship with our Creator. The same way that a loving spouse does loving acts for his or her beloved, Jews do what God asks of them to create a loving bond between them. Rather than thinking of Jewish rituals as mere commandments, it is more accurate to conceptualize them as love letters by which we communicate our love for God, and He communicates His love for us. Simply put, they are the means by which we attach ourselves in loving intimacy to our Partner.

Full Relationship   The more we invest ourselves in a marriage, the more satisfying a marriage we have. The same is true of our relationship with God. We want as full a relationship with Him as possible. Judaism is not a dictatorship in which an absolute Authority figure has nothing better to do than to order us around. Every Jew can benefit from having as deep and as intimate a relationship as possible with the Almighty.

13. This is just a phase you're going through. You'll get over it.

Some parents have seen their child try to find fulfillment and happiness in various ways. The child may have embraced athletics, then followed a rock star, then gotten into adventure travel or extreme sports. In college, he might have switched majors three times, only to realize in his senior year that his most recent choice is not to his liking. He may have an inner restlessness that is never satisfied, as he goes from one relationship to another, he explores different religions, then goes from job to job, never feeling satisfied with any of them for too long. He eventually finds his way to Torah observance. Why should his parents think that this will help him find lasting meaning and inner peace?

Some Jews become observant as just a passing phase as they try to work out an inner void, while others finally come home when they connect to Torah study and its observance.

When people become baal teshuvas due to a drive for spiritual authenticity, some parents still hope for years that their child's becoming observant is just a passing phase. Confronting such denial is usually not productive. Either the parent will realize down the line that the changes are here to stay, or they won't. It is best to try to avoid conversations about religion or observance.

Summary

If a baal teshuva listens carefully to others' objections about his religious transformation, he can learn a lot about how to respond to them. Some concerns are best addressed by giving others information, while some objections will require the baal teshuva to give emotional reassurance to those voicing the concerns. Understanding where people are coming from can often help baal teshuvas to heal relationships that are traumatized by their religious transformation.

It can be helpful to invite some relatives to learn more about Judaism at the right time and in the right place. Some people who object to a relative's observances can benefit from exposure to religious figures who have something in common with the secular person or whose integrity, kindness, and goodness are palpable.

Unfortunately, some people are so emotionally traumatized or hurt that they will never accept their child's becoming observant. When parents and children can't agree to disagree about their life choices, children should speak to a rav or an advisor about what to do.

FOURTEEN

Changed Relationships

It is hard for parents to find the right balance between guiding and letting go of a child, advising while fostering independence, and knowing when to speak versus staying silent. Many parents have good intentions and want the best for their child, but some lack the emotional wherewithal to do what is in their child's best interests, especially when their child becomes observant. Sadly, some parents can even be emotionally toxic to their child.

The Torah says that we must honor and respect our parents. Yet, if they tell us to disobey God, or if they harm us emotionally or physically, we are not supposed to listen to them.

Boundaries Zev became religious against his mother Helen's wishes. She had always been emotionally manipulative and tried to control him. Therapy helped him to put healthy boundaries between them and become more independent and emotionally healthy. To her credit, his mother decided to get professional help and went with Zev to a religious family therapist who helped them improve their relationship. It took about two years, but their emotional work and therapy ultimately allowed them to create a healthy relationship.

The Torah never says that children must love their parents, but children are generally supposed to be respectful to their parents. An exception is if parents are emotionally, physically, or spiritually abusive, in which case it is best to avoid them. Some *baal teshuvas* may need counseling to accept their painful reality. It is hard for many children to distance themselves from parents who harm them. Yet, staying healthy emotionally, mentally, or spiritually supersedes our obligation to honor our parents.

Unfortunately, some parents believe that all of the problems that they have with their children are their children's fault, and they make their children feel bad, worthless, or inappropriately guilty. Other parents are well meaning but mistaken in their attempts to do the right things for their children. Children in either situation can often benefit from psychological and spiritual counseling.

If you and a spiritual advisor have tried to talk to your parents about your religious changes and they are still hostile to you a few months later—don't keep trying to get them to accept you for who you are. If you have made a number of unsuccessful attempts at rapprochement, and you feel sad or guilty after every phone call, or after reading their e-mails to you, stop trying to get them to accept your religious practices. Try to find comfortable ground discussing other matters. If they insist on raising religious issues, and attacking your religious beliefs and practices, ask a rabbi or advisor how to interact with them or set boundaries that allow you to feel safe.

Other Relationships

Family and friends who were important to *baal teshuvas* before they became religious usually remain so because strong emotional connections don't simply disappear. If children and parents had a good relationship before the child became religious, it will usually continue afterward. On the other hand, when children had strained or difficult relationships with relatives, becoming religious will usually be one more source of conflict or tension. In such cases, it is best to find ways to relate that don't involve discussions or conflicts about Judaism. It is okay to disagree about religion, but it is easiest to simply avoid discussing it altogether. Discussing religion, sex, and politics can often lead to flaring tempers.

The same ideas about familial relationships hold true for deep friendships. If the friends treasure something lasting and important about each other, the friendship will survive religious changes and perhaps even deepen as a result of sharing new ideas. Friends who don't share anything lasting are likely to grow apart. The *baal teshuva* needs to have a support system of friends with whom they have much in common.

Superficial Friendships   Vivian had a number of good friends. They ate lunch together once a week, raised their children together, celebrated birthdays and bar and bat mitzvahs together, and supported each other when times were difficult.

Vivian became observant at the age of 40—around the time that some of her friends' children began to marry. Unfortunately, most of the children intermarried, and Vivian didn't attend their weddings. Since there was only one kosher restaurant where Vivian lived, and her friends didn't like to eat there, they also stopped eating lunch together. She felt sad on her 50th birthday when she realized that her becoming observant had pushed away her secular friends, and their relationships were now very superficial.

When she mentioned this to an observant friend, the friend noted that her relationships with her secular friends had always been superficial. They met for lunch, talked about what the kids were doing in school, what movies they had seen, which restaurants had the best food, and the latest novels they had read. Vivian's becoming observant had simply highlighted how she wanted more depth and meaning in her life. Sooner or later, when all of her and her friends' children had moved away, Vivian and her friends would have become more distant anyway. Her becoming observant simply hastened this process and made their differences more apparent.

Drifting Apart   Dara and Cathy were college friends who both became observant their first year in college. Dara later broke up with the boyfriend who had introduced her to Torah observance and began dating a non-Jew. Meanwhile, Cathy became increasingly observant. When the two women vacationed in Maine that summer,

Dara decided to indulge in lobster dinners while Cathy ate tuna fish out of a can in her hotel room. By the time Dara announced her engagement to Preston, it was apparent that the feelings and the experiences that once bonded them were no match for the chasm created by their different ideals and values. By the time Dara got married, their relationship was already over.

Growing Together   On the other hand, Alisha and Martha met and became friends at an infertility support group. They discovered that they had a lot in common. They both came from suburban, upper-class, Jewish neighborhoods. They had attended similar public schools and universities. Both had masters' degrees in science and teaching. Each wanted their children to have good values and strong ethics. They both were analytical, capable, organized, thoughtful, and caring.

Their friendship was continually strengthened through their infertility ordeals and the support they gave each other through their challenges. During this time, Alisha became observant and Martha did not. Yet, they felt such a strong bond and enjoyed each other's company so much that their religious differences never separated them. When each finally had children, they took their children to the playground together, spent time at each other's houses, and discussed the challenges and joys of parenting. They shared their professional knowledge as well as their ideas about parenting. They had similar views about many issues, including politics, holistic medicine, being working mothers, and how to deal with their aging parents. Although their religious practices were very different, they respected each other greatly and learned from each other. Since their relationship was so deep, Alisha's becoming observant only changed the logistics of how they ate together. Martha's lack of observance gave Alisha an opportunity to teach her children that there are many kinds of Jews. Her children learned that we can get along with, love, and respect those who are different from us, without compromising our beliefs and practices.

The Pain and the Gain

There is a common misconception in the Western world that we are supposed to live comfortable lives, striving for ease and pleasure. The lives of most *baal teshuvas* turn out to be very challenging. This is especially true in the area of relationships.

Baal teshuvas can be comforted by the fact that every difficulty that we go through has a spiritual purpose and affects our soul for the better. For reasons unknown to us, the pain of changed relationships is something that most of us will undergo as we metamorphosize from secular to observant Jews.

Summary

Baal teshuvas sometimes stay friends with former friends and family, although they might need to do so by relating on a superficial level. In other instances, we prefer to develop new friendships to replace the old ones. Many times, becoming religious simply accentuates the differences that we had with others all along. Inevitably, many *baal teshuvas* will mourn the loss of closeness that they once felt with certain relatives or friends, and some of those relationships may be irreplaceable.

An advisor, therapist and rabbi can help *baal teshuvas* to reduce contact with people who cause them pain, find common ground with former friends and loving relatives, and develop a support system with other observant Jews who share their religious perspectives, life goals and interests.

FIFTEEN

Staying in Seminary
or Yeshiva

When parents watch a child became increasingly observant, they shouldn't be surprised if the child takes the next step and decides to learn in a yeshiva or seminary. The child may want to make up for lost time by intensively studying Judaism in a religious environment, and such opportunities may be lacking in his or her home city.

Some young adults take off a year between high school and college to learn in a seminary or yeshiva. Others take a brief leave of absence from university or from work to do the same. Still others come to Israel, New York, or other cities for a vacation or a summer to learn what being Jewish is all about

Parental Reactions

Parents have very different reactions to their child's wanting to study in a yeshiva or seminary. Many Orthodox parents assume that their child will study in Israel after graduating from religious high schools because that is common practice. Yet, some modern Orthodox parents worry that children's plans to stay one year may stretch out indefinitely, with a consequent scrapping of a career or college plans. So many graduates of Jewish high schools come to Israel for a year of learning and never leave that a major Jewish organization held a seminar about how their distressed parents can deal with this.

For many secular parents, though, a child's decision to study Torah far away is a bombshell that takes them by surprise. Many wonder if their child has gone off the "deep end" or if this is just a phase he or she is going through. Many parents hope that once the child finishes a few months of study, he or she will come back to his or her senses, return home much the way they left, and go on with his or her former life.

In recent years, many teenage secular Israelis have become *baal teshuvas* and have left public school to enroll in yeshivas. Half of the Israeli teens from upscale suburbs of Tel Aviv who start learning in yeshiva become observant. Some horrified (and often angry) parents have organized support groups and legal organizations to close down yeshivas that attract their teenage sons because of the threat that religious values pose to the parents' secular hopes for their children. Their parents feel that they have lost their children and the dreams that they had for them to be athletes, "normal" kids who hang out, and university students who get into prestigious careers where they can earn a lot of money. The parents of many Israeli females who become observant in seminary will not allow their daughters to come home.

Anxious Feelings   When their child is in yeshiva or seminary, some parents worry and feel out of control. Where will this process take their child? How frum will their child become? Will their son decide to leave the modern world and study in yeshiva for the rest of his life? Will the daughter become chareidi and marry a man who appears to be the antithesis of everything the parents believe in?

At some point, many students will have that long-feared conversation with their parents:

"Guess what, Mom and Dad? I love it here in Jerusalem (or New York, or in yeshiva/seminary). I've finally found my place. I love being religious and I want to stay in this school longer than I had originally planned. I realize now how much more I need to learn about Judaism in order to practice it properly."

The Timeframe   The parent may catch his or her breath and ask, "Does that mean that you're not planning to come home—ever?!"

At this point, different children will give different answers. Some will say that they want to stay a few more months, or even a year or two, but they will give an approximate date by which they plan to end their full-time Jewish studies. Others won't know how much longer they want to stay, but they do want to come home eventually. They want to study in a university, have a career, and earn a living in the foreseeable future. Still others want to forego the next school year and perhaps study Judaism indefinitely.

The worst answers for most parents is when their child doesn't give a finite end date for the Jewish studies, or indicate that the child is no longer interested in university or the "real" world.

The speechless parent may have many intense feelings at this time. Being happy for their child may not be one of them. It is not easy for a parent to invest 18 years or more in a child, only to hear that a child has rejected their values, beliefs, way of life, and hopes for the child's future. Parents can certainly feel anxious, depressed, or devastated if their child thinks that going to college isn't a good idea and has no future plans to ever come home or to become self-supporting in the way that the parents envisioned.

Five Stages of Catastrophe   People who face a catastrophic illness typically go through five emotional stages: shock, denial, anger, bargaining, and (hopefully) acceptance. Parents of baal teshuvas may do the same:

Shock

"What do you mean, you're planning to stay for the next school year? You just spent six months sending in applications for university and you got a full scholarship to Yale!"

Denial

"You don't really plan to stay in yeshiva instead of going into finance, do you? You just spent four years in college and two years getting your MBA so that you could work as a business consultant. Of course you'll come back and work. Otherwise, how will you pay back your $80,000 in student loans? You can't be serious about staying and learning for a few years."

Anger

"After everything we've done for you, how can you go to seminary, destroy the family, and not want to go to college?"

Bargaining

"I'll tell you what. We'll pay your tuition at the religious school for another three months, but that's it. After that, you have to come home and get a job or finish your degree."

Of course, many *baal teshuvas* will also hear some of the objections to observant Judaism that were mentioned earlier in this book. Rarely does the child hear the response they dream of:

(Acceptance*)* "I'm so happy for you, sweetheart. You learn as long as you like. I'm glad that you've made a choice that's so right for you."

Productive Dialogue

Career & Financial Plans   Even if baal teshuvas believe they are doing the right thing by staying in yeshiva or seminary and learning about Judaism, they can only dialogue productively with parents if they can see matters from their parents' point of view. Most parents sincerely want what is best for their child, even when they are misguided about what that is. Some parents believe that observance is always bad, and they want to protect their child from all bad things. Most parents believe that having a college degree and getting a well-paying job are keys to future success. After all, yeshivas and seminaries only exist because of donors and parents who work and earn money. If a child blithely dismisses their parents' concerns, it is likely to harm their relationship, not to mention jeopardizing continuing their studies at the Jewish school. The baal teshuva should acknowledge the parents' feelings and concerns and show appreciation for whatever support the parents have given:

In Your Shoes   "You know, Mom and Dad, I really appreciate your giving me the wherewithal to study in yeshiva these past few months. I'm sure that it hasn't been easy for you to spend so much money for me to learn things that you don't believe in. You have given me the opportunity to broaden my knowledge of what it means to be Jewish. I have met lots of people from all walks of life and I have wonderful teachers and special friends here. I feel that I am developing the tools to be a better person, expand my knowledge, and get along with others.

"I don't know how I would feel if I were in your shoes. I don't know what I would say if my child asked me to help him continue in a path that seemed so unhealthy to me. I can only imagine that I would have the same strong feelings and internal struggle that you must be having now."

After the parent has had a chance to respond, the *baal teshuva* might say, "I certainly appreciate your fears that if I don't leave yeshiva soon, I will never move on with my life. You are sure that if I don't get an academic degree, I won't get a good job, and you may have to financially support my future family and me. My future must seem pretty bleak to you if I continue on this path."

The *baal teshuva* doesn't have to agree with their parent's assessment of their future in order to empathize with him or her. Yet, they should consider the merits of the parents' arguments and discuss them with an objective advisor.

Parents who give their children an ultimatum about staying in yeshiva or seminary are really saying that they want the child to know that there is a finite amount of time that they will get financial help. At a certain point, they want their child to pay his or her own way and to become financially independent.

They are right in wanting this. When a child is living off parents' funds, it is easy for children to minimize the importance of working and making money. The child needs to feel and express that financial self-sufficiency is important to him or her, although the child may want to defer that longer than the parents want. That may set the stage for a compromise that will be acceptable to both of them.

Religious Plans   Some parents are as concerned about where the child will end up religiously as with the career and financial implications of staying in yeshiva. Some also fear that the child will reject the parents and will no longer love them.

A child can respond, "I am very grateful for everything that you've done for me. You have been wonderful parents. Parenting is similar to a mother bird raising her babies. She does it with love, yet expects that her little ones will become independent some day. You also gave me the wings to leave your nest and fly. Thank you for giving me the tools to think about what I really want out of life. You taught me to have the self-confidence to make choices without worrying what everyone else will think of them, and the strength to follow my convictions. I could never reject you. I've incorporated so many wonderful traits that you've taught me. I carry some of your ideas, nurturing, and values with me wherever I go."

Most *baal teshuvas* need to anticipate how such discussions will go and to prepare how to best respond to their parents' feelings and objections.

For example, a parent might say, "You've been in seminary (or yeshiva) for three months already. How long do you plan to stay there instead of getting on with your life?"

The parent is not only asking for a projected date of departure from seminary. She is wondering, "Are you ever going to be a responsible person who will be self-supporting? Am I going to have to pay your way forever? How 'fanatic' and divorced from the real world are you going to become? Will you come back to your senses any time soon?"

If one can't give a concrete response, such as, "I'm planning to stay until the end of August," one should at least respond in a way that acknowledges the parent's feelings:

"You know, I'm not really sure how long I'll be here, and I know that it must be hard for you not to have an answer right now. I want you to know that whatever amount of time I decide to stay, it will be a responsible decision that will take into account the fact that you are supporting me. I never want to take your financial support for granted. Right now, I'm learning how to be a better person and that includes having a good relationship with you."

Validate Feelings   If a parent expresses frustrations or other upset feelings, the baal teshuva should validate his or her feelings. This is not the time for the baal teshuva to tell how he or she feels and defend what they want to do. Even though it is natural to respond to an emotional barrage or "attack" by defending ourselves, this is not the time to challenge parents' presentation of "facts." It is a time to try to appreciate their feelings.

For example, if a parent says, "You are breaking up the family by staying in yeshiva and staying away from us," don't explain how you really are not breaking up the family. Try, "I hear how upsetting this is for you."

A rule of thumb in relationships is that remarks that express people's feelings should be responded to on a feeling level. Even if you aren't breaking up the family, insisting that you aren't as a first response won't get you anywhere. Your parent is telling how he or she feels and you should respond to them as such.

A *baal teshuva* can say, "It must be very hard on everyone that I am here and have become so different." If the parent then elaborates on that, the *baal teshuva* can listen. Being non-defensive and empathizing as much as possible is the best path for diffusing emotional upset. Hopefully, over time, the *baal teshuva* might be able to have a dialogue where others want to hear what he or she has to say!

Feeling Secure   The more secure we feel with ourselves and with our decisions, the easier it is not to get defensive when people attack our choices. It can take years, though, for many baal teshuvas to feel secure with their religious choices. Until that happens, it is important to get a lot of support before and after intense interactions with parents. It can be very helpful to do role plays and practice responding in a calm manner before potentially unpleasant conversations occur. Invoking the help of, or mediation by, a sensitive rabbi or advisor can also be invaluable.

Summary

A seminary or yeshiva education can give *baal teshuvas* a firm religious foundation and wonderful support system that will serve them well for the rest of their lives. Yet, that choice may be very hard for parents to swallow—and even harder for them to support emotionally or financially. It is important for *baal teshuvas* and their parents to keep open lines of communication about this, with each appreciating where the other is coming from. Often, the head of the seminary or yeshiva that the *baal teshuva* is attending can help mediate these discussions.

Parents are neither required to support their adult children nor pay for their religious education (the obligation to teach one's sons Torah only applies to minor children.) Those who do support children who become observant share in the eternal reward that their children, and their children's descendants, will earn by living according to the Torah.

Nevertheless, *baal teshuvas* should acknowledge and appreciate the sacrifices that their parents make for them and the financial support that they provide. Empathizing with a parent's unspoken concerns and being respectful can help reassure parents that you, and they, have made a good choice by having you study Torah full time.

SIXTEEN

Intermarriage in the Family

A scant 50 years ago, many Jewish parents would sit shiva and formally mourn if one of their children married someone who wasn't Jewish. Today, it is a rare *baal teshuva* who does not have at least one sibling, cousin, aunt, uncle, or even a parent who (re)marries a non-Jew and expects the *baal teshuva* to attend the wedding.

Many rabbis forbid Jews to attend an intermarriage, especially at a church ceremony. What to do in individual instances should be discussed with a rav or spiritual mentor. There are sometimes ways to minimize the family's animosity toward a religious relative who won't share the family's "joy" when their Jewish member marries a gentile. Unfortunately, it is not uncommon for some family members to be furious with a *baal teshuva* relative who doesn't come to their intermarriage and cut their ties with that person forever.

30-Year Freeze   Brenda became observant five years before her brother decided to marry his Catholic girlfriend in a church wedding. Brenda, now Bryna, informed her family as sensitively as she could that she would be unable to attend. Her parents and three siblings were outraged, and her brother and his wife never spoke to her again. Thirty years later, when Bryna attended her father's funeral, her siblings and mother were still angry with her. Bryna endured many painful events in her life, but her rejection by her family over this issue was the worst.

Intermarriages have so many possible variations that it is impossible to address them all here. This discussion will be limited to two general situations—one, where the *baal teshuva* is close to the person who is marrying out, and two, where that is not the case.

When a *baal teshuva* is close to the person who is intermarrying, the *baal teshuva* usually knows long before the wedding that their relative is dating or living with a non-Jew. There may be opportunities for heart-to-heart talks with that relative about why he or she may be unable to attend the wedding. In some cases, the observant relative can even convince the one who is planning to get married to explore why Judaism is important and why marrying out is a problem or to take a few classes to learn why being Jewish is important.

Books   The baal teshuva may give them the book, Why Marry Jewish? by Doron Kornbluth, the introductory pages of my Guide for the Romantically Perplexed, or the first few pages of Made in Heaven, by Aryeh Kaplan, as a springboard for discussion.

Principles   When relatives criticize or pressure the baal teshuva to attend the wedding, the baal teshuva can say, "You admire other people who live by their principles and who are willing to die for them. You admire Martin Luther King and Abraham Lincoln. They stood up for, and even died for, unpopular ideas that had great value. You admire soldiers who fought, and sometimes died, to protect democracy. I am trying to live by the Jewish values that have made the world a place worth living in. If you want to learn more about why being Jewish is so important, I can help you to do that. But please don't pressure me into compromising myself and don't force me to give up my values."

Non-Defusible Animosity   Many families will ratchet up the criticism and guilt unless the baal teshuva capitulates. Some won't take "no" for an answer. To keep some semblance of family harmony, some baal teshuvas invent excuses or take a trip to avoid being in town when the wedding is scheduled. Neither approach will diffuse the family's animosity. It just postpones the inevitable.

Meal Invitations   After the deed is done, some baal teshuvas try to invite the intermarried couple to their house for Shabbos or holiday meals to teach them about the positive aspects of Judaism and draw them closer to it. Maintaining a relationship with a Jewish relative who marries out can have a positive effect on the relationship and their connection to Judaism regardless of who they married.

Waiting Out the Marriage   Meira became a baal teshuva in college. Two years after her sister Tara married Dwight in an interfaith ceremony, Meira married Nosson. Meira invited her parents and sister's family to join them for every Passover seder and for Rosh Hashana meals. They all came, yet Dwight always felt uncomfortable. He invariably insisted that his family leave before dessert was served. He wanted nothing to do with Judaism. Seven years and two children later, he also wanted nothing to do with Tara, and they got divorced. Meira invited Tara for Friday night dinners every week, and Tara admired the wholesomeness and warmth of Meira's family, now blessed with three children. She enjoyed the beauty of their Shabbos meals, the serenity, and the peace that she felt there. Tara became interested in learning more about observant Judaism and started keeping kosher. She enrolled her children in an observant after-school program as well.

Several years after her divorce, Tara started dating. This time, she only went out with Jewish men.

Guilt

Relatives can make *baal teshuvas* feel guilty for putting their allegiance to God and observance of Torah above all else. When *baal teshuvas* refuse to attend an intermarriage, they might hear:

"You're ruining your sister's wedding."

"Look at how you are breaking up the family with your fanaticism."

"How can you do this to your mother?"

How does a *baal teshuva* deal with such painful comments, which often continue unabated for months?

First, you have to believe that what you are doing is right. You must speak to a rav about whether not attending a specific intermarriage is the right thing to do. Second, you must get a lot of support if you are told not to attend.

Internalizing Judaism   It takes a lot of religious conviction to believe that God is running the world and that Jewish law is right when others keep telling you that it is wrong. Our emotions may tell us that we should attend an intermarriage, and we can easily rationalize doing so. After all, our relatives don't know any better, and it will hurt them so much if we don't attend. Also, the non-Jewish partner is so nice, and the Jewish partner is so happy. How could this marriage be wrong?

It is hard to believe that what we feel is not absolutely real or right, and that what we can't see is very real. We may relate more to loving our family and friends and not causing them pain then we do to the idea that we have a relationship with God no matter where we are and what we are doing. We don't always see how bad it can be to follow our emotions instead of following Jewish law when our hearts hurt. We can be expert at convincing ourselves that Jewish law needs to be "flexible" under circumstances when it isn't.

It's All Good   Some baal teshuvas attend intermarriages to make their relatives happy when Jewish law forbids doing so. Yet our making a small compromise in Jewish law to please others (or ourselves) sometimes results in our losing our spiritual compass more intensely than we could have imagined.

When *baal teshuvas* try to please friends and family by compromising what their rabbi tells them Jewish law requires them to do, they may think that what they are doing is benign. The *baal teshuva* can't see where such small steps are going to lead. That is why a rav or advisor is so necessary. Such people can keep us from taking small missteps that can lead us off-track.

What To Do

When a *baal teshuva* is invited to an intermarriage, what should he or she do?

First, speak to a rav or spiritual mentor and find out what Jewish law permits or advises you to do in your circumstances.

If the rav tells you not to attend, ask him what to tell people who ask why you're not coming. Decide if people who ask you to attend really care to hear why you won't be there. Asking, "Why won't you come?" doesn't mean that they really want to know your reasons. Making a rhetorical statement that is followed by a question mark means that it is better not to give reasons. Simply say, "I'm sorry, but I can't attend." If someone repeatedly asks why you are not attending a relative's intermarriage, and you've already explained why you can't, try repeating a brief response such as, "I don't want to discuss this."

Summary

Dealing with a family intermarriage is a difficult challenge for many *baal teshuvas*. It is important to get rabbinical advice to know what to say and do. This can minimize guilt later if one wonders if a different course of behavior would have had less drastic repercussions. It can also be useful to prepare responses to antagonistic conversations that you anticipate will occur with family members.

It is usually a good idea to try, whenever possible, to keep open lines of communication with a sibling before and after the intermarriage. Invite them to your Shabbos and Jewish holiday meals if they are interested in joining you. It is possible that your sibling will eventually be closer to you again. Maintaining a relationship with him or her may help the sibling stay connected to Judaism and stay on good terms with your family.

Whatever happens, know that you have done the right thing if you follow your rabbi's advice. Sometimes doing the right thing feels very bad. Call a good friend or spiritual advisor and get some emotional support. You'll need it.

Part Four:
Spouses and Children

SEVENTEEN

Non-Observant Spouses

Many Jews are married when they start their religious journeys. In the ideal world, spouses grow together and become interested in greater observance around the same time. They may attend the same seminar, class, or Shabbaton, or meet an inspiring religious teacher or neighbor. They can share their enthusiasm and reinforce each other's growth.

In the real world, though, many spouses go on a religious path while their partner is indifferent or even opposed to becoming observant. The more abrupt or intense a *baal teshuva's* changes are, the less opportunity their spouse has to adapt and the more friction there may be between them. Sometimes, their differences become so divisive that they lead to divorce.

In general, how the religious changes of one spouse affect a partner depend on the overall quality of their relationship. If the couple has a good marriage, good communication, a helpful rabbi, and an insightful religious mentor, most marriages involving a *baal teshuva* will thrive. Some marriages will become even stronger as they work through their differences. If the marriage already has big cracks in it, though, one spouse's religious changes may catalyze the fissures to become a chasm that tears them apart. Their religious differences are likely to become insurmountable.

There are countless couples in which one spouse becomes a religious Jew while the other does not. Often, a less-observant partner will become more observant if exposed to positive, religious experiences and role models and if given time to grow at his or her own speed. This process is enhanced when the *baal teshuva* spouse gives lots of support, respect, reassurance, and love that is not conditional on their partner's becoming observant.

Delayed Response   Marian became an observant Jew after she and her husband Jerry had three children. They loved each other very much and had a good marriage. Jerry had no interest in becoming more observant. After much soul-searching, they decided that they wanted to stay married despite their differences. She made the home kosher, strictly observed Shabbos and Jewish festivals, sent the children to religious school, and kept the laws of family holiness. Jerry went along with it all but never became observant. He did, however, respect her beliefs and practices and backed her when he was around the children.

Throughout their years together, Marian was extremely respectful of her husband and sincerely admired him despite their religious differences. One day, 16 years after she had become observant, her husband turned to her and said, "You are right, I am wrong. I am going to be an observant Jew from now on."

Of course, this kind of scenario is extremely rare. It is unusual for a spouse to start becoming observant so many years after a partner does. It shows, however, that even when one spouse is religious and the other isn't, some marriages can survive if the partners show each other much love and respect.

There are many couples where one spouse becomes observant and the non-observant spouse feels pressured into observance long before he or she is ready for it. It is unrealistic, and often counterproductive, to expect a non-observant spouse to quickly be on the same page as the now-religious partner. Every Jew must find his or her way to Judaism at a pace that works for himself or herself.

Traumatic Observance Stephen decided, after hearing just one lecture on Torah Judaism, to become totally observant. He started studying basic Judaism several hours a day. Such a drastic change often fades as quickly as it begins, but Stephen's changes lasted. There was just one problem—his wife Elizabeth didn't share his religious idealism. While he didn't expect his wife to observe Shabbos immediately, he did ask her to keep kosher and the laws of family holiness as soon as possible. He presented both in such an abrupt, insensitive way that it traumatized Elizabeth for years. He couldn't understand why, years later, she observed Shabbos and kept kosher but resented him and observant Judaism. Had he followed the recommendations in this chapter, she might have embraced Judaism wholeheartedly and without reservation, albeit a few years later than when he pressured her into becoming observant.

Ideally, the observant spouse should help the partner feel secure in the marriage and be supportive in choosing, at the partner's pace, whether or not to join the first partner in their religious odyssey. That way, the less-observant spouse can feel in control of whatever Jewish commitments he or she does make.

Slowly But Surely Gail and Adam liked the humanistic and cultural aspects of Judaism. They did not like the Reform temple in their neighborhood. They wanted to pray in a place with more Jewish content, but didn't know where to find it. There was an Orthodox synagogue about 10 miles away, but neither was interested in what they had been raised to believe was religious "extremism." So, they searched to no avail for an "authentic" form of Judaism.

Years later, Gail saw a flier advertising a Jewish seminar and she convinced Adam to go with her. They were both excited about what they heard and one of the presenters arranged a Torah study partner for her. Adam did not think that he had time to study since he barely had enough time to work and see his family. So, Gail studied Torah with a phone partner twice a week. Soon, she was going to several classes each week at an Orthodox synagogue, as well as having telephone study sessions. It didn't take long before the Orthodox synagogue was no longer intimidating to her.

The Orthodox synagogue offered beginner's services on Saturday mornings and she went by herself every week. Adam preferred to catch up on his sleep and spend time with their children. Within a few months, she convinced Adam to try out her place of worship. He enjoyed the services and the explanations and accepted the rebbetzin's invitation for their family to have lunch at her home.

A year later, Gail decided to keep a kosher home. By then, Adam was enjoying his weekly hour of Torah study with a partner but he wasn't ready to give up eating non-kosher food. Gail told him that she wanted him to eat whatever he felt like outside the house, but that it would be good for the children if they kept only kosher at home. He agreed. As he learned more about Judaism, she always expressed interest in his studies and encouraged him to share his ideas with her. When he expressed doubts and questions, she was happy that he was thoughtful about what he was learning. She encouraged him to ask questions of his teacher and share the answers with her. This allowed them to grow together and gave Adam time to resolve his doubts at his own pace.

Gail invited Adam to take on some family rituals, such as making Kiddush on Friday night, ritually washing hands, and saying the blessing over the bread before eating. She started observing commandments and rituals that were easy and comfortable and hoped that he would see how pleasant becoming more traditional could be. Gail's teacher told her that the key to encouraging people to become more observant was to make it as comfortable, enjoyable, and familiar as possible. Gail discovered how true that was.

Five years after Gail started learning about Judaism, and seven years after Adam started learning, each was fully observant. This gradual process led to a strengthening of their marriage and their family. Their children benefited from their parents' changes, and learned invaluable life skills by watching how their parents dealt with their differences.

What's Your Motivation?

Actors who play various characters typically ask themselves, "What's my motivation?" Some people are motivated by truth, others by pleasure; some by comfort, others by avoiding discomfort. Some of us are motivated by emotional connection and intimacy, others by feeling competent and independent. Some people are more motivated by approval, others by power; some by love, others by fear. Some are motivated by emotions, others by logic, yet others by a sense of responsibility.

People tend to think that others value what we value, but that isn't necessarily the case. When we appreciate what motivates someone else and we speak their language, we maximize our chances of drawing them closer to Torah study or toward observance.

Emotional If one spouse is emotional and the other logical, what convinces the former to become observant may be irrelevant to their spouse. By understanding what motivates a spouse, the more observant one can describe Judaism in ways that speak to the partner. For example, Manny became observant because he believed that the Torah is true. Yet, when discussing observance with his emotional wife Betty, he emphasized how Torah Judaism can enrich their family life, bond them with their children, heighten their marital intimacy, and help them to get along better with others.

Approval If someone values approval, a partner should give them lots of compliments, reinforce their changes, and introduce them to other observant people who will do the same.

Meaning People who value meaning will appreciate hearing that Torah Judaism gives eternal meaning to every thought, word, and action and that we create an afterlife for our soul from how we think, speak, and act. They may want to learn more about how and what rituals spiritualize our lives and how we can think and speak with greater meaning.

Responsibility People who are motivated by responsibility, self-discipline, and self-improvement can be shown Judaism through those lenses. They can be inspired by stories of people such as Rabbi Akiva who became great. He decided at age 40 that he didn't want to be ignorant of Judaism any more and began studying Judaism in a class of young children. By applying himself to his studies for many years, he became one of Judaism's greatest rabbis. Accepting the responsibility to learn about, and live up to our covenant with God and the Jewish people, is important to people who value responsibility.

Pleasure A person who values pleasure will want to see how Judaism makes life more enjoyable and will avoid that which makes him or her feel deprived. Such a person should be taught how God made a world only so that we could get pleasure from it. By studying and following His owner's manual—the Torah—we learn how to maximize and spiritualize pleasures that are permitted to us.

Spirituality Someone who values Far Eastern thought can be taught about Jewish meditation and the mystical ideas that come from Judaism, including how we find spirituality in every aspect of life and spiritualize pleasures such as eating and intimacy.

Truth Courting Comfort Larry spent a few weeks studying in a yeshiva. During that short time, he decided to become observant because he saw that Torah was truth. When he came home and told his wife Rachelle what he had learned, and that he wanted to observe the Torah, she was horrified, not impressed. She was not going to give up her seafood and cheeseburgers and stop eating out in her favorite Chinese restaurant and steak house. She couldn't imagine not shopping at the mall on Saturdays, let alone following a million other restrictions.

Larry is motivated by truth while his wife is motivated by comfort and pleasure. The only way that she might become more observant is if she finds religiously acceptable substitutes that are as good as, if not better than, the pleasures that she gives up. If Larry can help make that happen, Rachelle might be willing to make gradual changes over a period of months or years and become more observant.

For example, Larry could get some recipes for tasty kosher foods and make them for her at home. (If he's not a good cook, he could pay someone to do it or buy delicious kosher take-out if available). He can surprise Rachelle at home once a week with a romantic candlelit dinner and/or take her out to a nice kosher restaurant (nice by her standards, not by his) if there is one in their city.

He can shop for groceries and try to find kosher substitutes for some of the non-kosher foods that she loves. Shopping for her so that she has less work to do, and bringing her home a special kosher treat every week, will help her associate positive feelings with keeping kosher.

If Rachelle agrees, Larry can accept invitations for them to be hosted for Shabbos or holiday meals and take her to beautiful (and delicious) catered kosher affairs where Rachelle will enjoy the food and the socializing. Larry has to keep in mind that the people whom she likes are not necessarily those whom he likes. If she likes people who enjoy shopping, the performing arts, and tennis and he loves listening to people who mostly speak about Torah and business, he will need (with the help of a teacher, rabbi, or advisor) to find people who share her interests with whom she can socialize.

Once she sees that religious people can be "normal," warm, and nice, he can suggest going together to a beginner's service for not more than 45 minutes on a Saturday morning. If that conflicts with her tennis or shopping, he can suggest that she reschedule her usual activities and even join her if she does them on a different day.

Alternatively, he might say, "It would mean the world to me if you would come to services with me just once. There are lots of people there like us and the rabbi is very nice. If you don't like it after half an hour, we can leave." He might offer to spend time with her afterward to make the offer more appealing. Limiting the number of times that he asks her to join him in what might be intimidating circumstances for her, and letting her know that she can leave after a brief try-out, will make it more comfortable for her.

Inspiring Models In general, it is very important for women who are becoming baal teshuvas to connect with other women whom they find "normal," accepting and with whom they can easily converse. Both men and women who are new to observance tend to be impressed if they see healthy, stable, "good" families. If someone has negative stereotypes about religious people, such as believing that they are dirty, noisy, poor, have no knowledge of the "real" world, or have too many children, find models who don't fit those stereotypes. If a partner's career or interests are important to him or her, introduce them to observant Jews who share similar interests and/ or who are successful in their careers. If a woman values mothering, introduce her to religious women who are great mothers.

If a less-observant spouse is afraid of being judged, make sure a host family is accepting and down to earth. If approval, honor, and feeling successful are important to someone, introduce him or her to observant Jews who will value what they are and not make them feel inadequate for what they aren't.

Poor Match   Howard was insecure after losing his third job in five years. He was not having much luck finding other employment. Valerie was eager for Howard to use his time between jobs to learn more about Judaism, and she accepted an invitation from an observant family for Shabbos lunch. Howard was reluctant to go, but Valerie convinced him that it would be fun.

Unfortunately, Valerie did not do her homework. Other people would have enjoyed the host's opulent home with beautiful furnishings, but Howard felt embarrassed that he lived in a small, run-down apartment. To make matters worse, the hosts had invited three financially successful Yuppie couples who talked about work, money matters, vacations, new cars, and their high-tech gadgets during the meal. When Howard was asked what he did, he admitted that he was between jobs and an embarrassing silence ensued. He felt so humiliated listening to everyone else's successes that he never wanted to go to a Shabbos meal again.

Howard would have done very well with a different kind of family. The Diskins were Torah teachers who lived in a modest home. Rather than discuss career, finances, and material things, the Diskins ask their children to tell what they learned in their classes that week. They sing Shabbos songs together, eat simple food, and are down-to-earth people. If Howard had felt that Shabbos is a time when we focus on spirituality and who we are in God's eyes, he would have had better feelings about becoming observant.

Make It Familiar, Comfortable, Enjoyable

Explaining Values   People can feel more comfortable with religious change if they see how similar Jewish ideas and rituals are to ideas and behaviors with which they are already familiar. For example, less-observant Jews can be taught how the great values of Western society have their roots in the Torah, or how the humanistic ideas that they already embrace encompass many mitzvahs (being kind, giving charity, social welfare, creating harmony and peace, honoring parents). It is important not to focus people with little Jewish knowledge on the minutia of Jewish rituals. Instead, show them the beauty of Jewish ideas and how they are generally put into practice.

Explaining Rituals   If we discuss the general meaning of rituals in terms that someone can relate to, doing such rituals will make sense. For example, few Westerners like the idea of animal sacrifice. If we reframe it as a barbecue with the Almighty as our host, most secular Jews find it comprehensible and reasonable. Telling someone who isn't observant that Jews are supposed to observe 613 commandments, or mentioning the myriad details of what one can't do on Shabbos, might be overwhelming. Instead, discuss the Torah's commandments as ways that we can show our love for God, just as we like to have many ways to show our love for a spouse. We can describe Shabbos as a gift that the Almighty gave us. We have one day a week for spiritual contemplation, when we especially enjoy physical pleasures with God present. We can also stress how Shabbos encourages us to spend quality time with our family. If we want our spouse to be receptive to the laws that govern physical intimacy, we should present them in a framework of how they intensify the various pleasures of marriage.

The Way to a Man's Heart... Shaindy and Jason got married when he was starting medical school. She worked in an office to support them. He was busy studying most evenings, so Shaindy decided to take a few classes after work in a nearby Jewish outreach center. One was a course in basic Judaism and she enjoyed it. She continued learning about Torah and slowly became more observant.

Meanwhile, Jason was very busy for the next seven years. He had no interest in attending Judaism classes that would only make more demands on his precious time.

During those years, Shaindy slowly brought Jewish rituals into their home and explained to him what she was learning and doing. Jason never shopped or cooked and didn't care what he ate as long as it tasted good and was readily available. As the years went by, they had children. Shaindy took their children to a synagogue that had children's groups on Shabbos while she prayed in the learner's service, thus giving Jason a chance to rest on Saturday mornings. By the time she and the children came home at noon, Jason was awake and looked forward to spending quality time with them and having delicious meals together. He didn't mind honoring Shaindy's request that he not watch television when they were home on Shabbos because he had such enjoyable substitutes.

When the children grew older, Shaindy enrolled them in the local Jewish day school. She countered Jason's financial concerns by telling him that any private school would cost more than the Jewish school's tuition and they both wanted their children to get a good education. When Jason saw that the school stressed being respectful and kind, and that the children were happy and learning a lot there, he felt that their tuition money was well spent.

When Shaindy started keeping a kosher home, she spent an hour every week making Jason delicious pastries that were tastier than what she once bought for him from the non-kosher bakery. She put one in his lunch bag with a love note before he went to work every morning. He never missed the non-kosher food because what he got was so much better.

By the time Jason finished his residency, he saw the value of the life that his family was living, and he also became observant.

Working through Issues

Just because a spouse conforms to Jewish rituals, it doesn't mean that he or she has resolved his or her underlying emotional issues about becoming observant. There are also some spouses of *baal teshuvas* who don't ever want to become observant. Such couples may eventually get to the "make it or-break it" point over their religious differences. They have to decide if they will both become observant, agree to live with their differences, or end the marriage. Counseling by a religiously sensitive and competent therapist, and/or by a rabbi who has experience with such couples, can help people work through the issues involved and decide what they want to do.

Counseling To Remedy Trauma   Henry and Jackie were happily married for four years. He was a sales rep and she worked in an advertising agency. They each had fulfilling careers and adored their two-year old son, Eddie.

Jackie welcomed weekends, when she had a chance to relax and spend time with her family and friends. She spent Saturday mornings and all day Sunday with Eddie and Henry. She spent Saturday afternoons with her mother, sister, and girl friends who lived a 20-minute drive away. They typically had lunch together in their favorite restaurants.

One day, Henry planned to take a new client, Moshe, to lunch, but Moshe declined. Moshe kept kosher and there were no kosher restaurants nearby. Henry was amazed that such a worldly businessman could look like a rabbi. After they finished discussing business, Moshe asked Henry if he wanted to know the key to his financial success.

Henry said, "Sure."

Moshe told Henry about the importance of giving 10 percent of one's income to charity, and the eight possible levels of charitable giving. Moshe said that God promised Jews that if we tithe our money, we will gain more than we give away, and that giving to Jewish charities had been his key to wealth. He ended by saying, "Our only real wealth is that which we give away."

Henry was intrigued. If this is what Judaism had to say about money, he wanted to learn more. Moshe offered to study Judaism with him every week and invited Henry to come to his house for a Shabbos meal. Moshe lived nearly an hour's drive away but Henry figured it would be worth going.

When Henry told Jackie about this conversation, she was unimpressed. Nor did she have any interest in going to a stranger's house for a meal. So, he went without her. He continued to learn about Judaism with Moshe once a week and took Eddie with him to Moshe's house on Friday nights. They went to Moshe's synagogue (where Eddie's favorite part was drinking the grape juice and singing) and then walked a few minutes to Moshe's house. Moshe and his wife made their guests feel most welcome. Henry and Moshe spent hours discussing Judaism while Eddie ate to his heart's content, then played with their hosts' grandchildren and toys until it was time to leave.

Henry had lots of questions. One night he queried, "How do we know that the Torah is from God? How do we know that the Torah that we have now is authentic? How do we know what God's will is? Where did the Talmud come from?" Although he didn't agree with everything he heard, Henry's questions were met with sensible answers and Henry was very pleased to hear them.

Within a month, Henry decided to become an observant Jew. Moshe helped Henry find a rabbi in Henry's neighborhood with whom Henry could study Torah and spend Shabbos and holidays. Moshe also recommended that Henry read a few books on basic Torah Judaism, and Henry did.

By this time, Henry and his wife were living in two different universes. He didn't expect Jackie to change with the lightning speed that he had, although he was already keeping kosher at home. He gave Jackie lists of foods that he could eat, and she did her best to accommodate him when she bought their groceries.

Over the next two years, Jackie enrolled Eddie in a religious Jewish preschool. She made their home kosher so that Henry could be comfortable eating the way that he wanted. She lit Shabbos candles on Friday nights (when she got home from work in time) and on the Jewish holidays. She had family dinners with Eddie and Henry after they came back from the synagogue on Friday nights. And, she followed the laws of family holiness. Meanwhile, she continued to work at her job, getting home after Shabbos in the winter, and she drove to visit her mother and sister on Saturday afternoons.

When Jackie had to decide if she would keep Shabbos for her son's sake, she and Henry sought the help of a sensitive, observant counselor. The counselor helped Henry understand how traumatic it was to his wife that he became observant so suddenly. He needed to acknowledge how much she had done for him, and how many more sacrifices she would need to make for them to be on the same page. She would have to give up her job because she could not leave early on Friday afternoons. She would have to forego the wonderful Saturdays with her mother, sister, and friends. The latter would pressure her to eat with them in non-kosher restaurants and in their non-kosher homes. Although these sacrifices were no big deal for Henry, they were for Jackie.

The counselor taught Henry how to listen to his wife and support her while allowing her to grow at her own pace. Telling Jackie that he understood how difficult it must have been for her to start going to a mikvah and keeping kosher allowed them to have a rapprochement. He made it clear that he loved her no matter what and that she could take as much time as she needed to learn about Judaism. He felt that it would be good for Eddie if she would observe more, but he only wanted her to do it if and when she felt ready.

It took Jackie five years to decide that she wanted to observe Shabbos. Only then was she ready to give up her job, which she no longer found emotionally fulfilling. By that time, she wanted to have another baby and be a full-time mother for a while. When she gave up her Saturday outings with her mother, sister, and friends, they were ready to come to her house for Shabbos lunches. She had met some wonderful observant families in her neighborhood and some of them were amazing cooks. That took away the sting of giving up eating out in non-kosher restaurants. Best of all, she discovered that she really loved being observant, now that she had accepted it at her own pace. She also realized that its prescriptions for how to live were the best way to raise her children.

Divorce

While some couples will grow religiously, others will not bridge the differences that ensue when one partner becomes a *baal teshuva*. Some non-Jewish spouses do not want to convert, and some non-observant spouses don't want to become observant. The resulting gaps may be too wide to bridge, especially if a couple has, or expects to have, children. Often, one spouse's religious metamorphosis highlights problematic differences that have always been part of the marriage, such as poor communication or problem-solving skills, or having incompatible life goals. When one spouse becomes observant, they can no longer live with their differences and the marriage falls apart.

Couples may divorce when one spouse resents or disdains Judaism or the other partner's becoming observant. When this happens, children may be caught in a tug-of-war between two parents whom the children love and want to please. Nasty custody battles and bad feelings between ex-spouses may cause the children to be victims of their parents' hurt and power struggles with each other. For instance, some children spend five days a week in a religious school and live with an observant parent, then spend weekends with a secular or non-Jewish parent who tries to destroy the child's connection to Judaism and to the other parent. Battles over children's souls have even come to family courts when one ex-spouse wants his or her children to be removed from a religious environment or school and placed in a secular or non-Jewish parent's custody and compatible school. Sadly, children usually lose, thanks to overburdened judges who have little appreciation for Torah Judaism, who often side with the non-Jewish or secular parent's point of view.

Lowering the level of hostility between the parents is in everyone's best interests. If a rabbi, advisor, or professional therapist can help the parents work out their conflicts, children might get the security and religious foundation that they need when the parents have such differences.

Non-Jewish Spouses

If a Jewish man marries a gentile spouse and they have children, their children are not Jewish, yet the parents and children may believe that they are. If the father becomes a *baal teshuva*, the children and spouse may have an identity crisis that can take years to resolve. As one woman put it, "My father is Jewish and my mother is Catholic. Jews say that the mother determines the child's religion, and Catholics say that the father determines the child's religion. I guess that makes me a spiritual zero."

Some Jewish men become observant after fathering non-Jewish children. If they get divorced and remarry religious Jewish women, the fathers should not reject their non-Jewish children.

Some *baal teshuvas* fathers urge their gentile children to learn about Judaism, hoping that the children will convert to the father's religion, yet this may not be in the children's best interest. It is worthwhile helping non-Jewish children to learn about and appreciate the seven Noahide laws that all non-Jews are required to observe. These form the foundation of becoming a moral human being. A sensitive rabbi can help the father to do this.

It is important for children to know that both parents love them regardless of whether or not they become Jewish or observant. The complexities that arise when there are (religious) Jewish and non-Jewish spouses and children in the same family are best addressed by a competent family therapist who is sensitive to observant Judaism or by rabbis who are experienced counselors, trained to work with such families.

When a gentile spouse erroneously thinks that he or she is Jewish (due to non-halachic conversion, for example) and then finds out he or she is not Jewish, it can throw the family into emotional disarray. These families can all benefit from help from a competent observant therapist in consultation with a rabbi who is an expert in such matters. Such situations are too complex for rabbis alone to deal with if they are not trained therapists.

The bottom line in all cases is that acting with decency toward one's spouse and children is always best for everybody involved. Doing so sets the stage to resolve the very complex issues of personal and religious identity, custody, and children's education and upbringing.

Summary

How a non-observant spouse reacts to the other spouse's becoming more observant is often a barometer of the health of the marriage. Loving couples with strong marriages, good communication, and excellent problem-solving abilities will usually find a way to stay married and work out, or live with, their differences. Couples who want to stay together may need, and benefit from, professional help with halachic guidance. This can aid couples to develop better communication skills, identify areas of commonality, highlight where they need to compromise, and make room for differences. This is especially important when they have minor children.

In some cases, the increasing observance of one spouse simply widens a chasm that grows over time. When divorce is necessary, parents may need to bend over backward to ensure that children are not made into the victims of their parents' unresolved emotional issues.

Putting the children's needs into the picture can make sure that when divorce is necessary, the children can still get the emotional security, good values and love they need from both parents.

EIGHTEEN

Child Rearing

When parents become baal teshuvas, the psychological and religious issues that affect their children can be simple to mind-boggling. Whether or not children will become observant often depends upon how old they are when the parents become observant, the quality of the relationship with the parents, the child's personality, and how the parents present and practice Judaism. It cannot be stressed enough that the best way to encourage children to be observant is for them to experience Judaism as a joyful, positive way of life that creates a harmonious home. Children should be taught Judaism in a way that is appropriate for the child's age and personality and that considers motivations discussed earlier in this book.

Parents bring their personalities into how they raise their children. People who generally help children to feel good about themselves are more likely to create an atmosphere in which being observant is viewed positively. Parents who criticize more than praise need to notice positive traits in their children and make them feel good about their steps toward observance. Parents should encourage their children to feel proud, rather than feel burdened, as they take on more and more Jewish responsibilities.

For example, a father can criticize his teenage son for waking up Saturday morning at eleven o'clock and praying at home in his pajamas for 10 minutes. Or he could say, "Wow, Alvin, I am so impressed! When I was your age, I slept until noon on Saturdays. And I never even prayed until I was almost 30. When you come down for lunch, would you like hear some of the interesting ideas that I heard in synagogue today?"

Imagine how Alvin will feel if instead he hears, "Too bad that you were too lazy to get out of bed in time to make it to synagogue this morning."

As the saying goes, we get more with honey than with vinegar.

There is a Yiddish expression, "It is hard to be a Jew." When parents adopt this attitude, it doesn't make children embrace Judaism with enthusiasm. Or, as one teen put it, "If the only reason to identify as a Jew is because six million Jews were killed in the Holocaust, I'm not interested." Rabbi Moshe Feinstein, z"tl, once said that parents should stress the positive aspects of being an observant Jew rather than what we *can't* do, and how it feels fulfilling and pleasurable rather than restrictive and uncomfortable. For example, instead of stressing the "thou shalt nots" of Shabbos, we can focus on how fortunate we are to spend quality time with our families, friends, and Creator. We should make the Shabbos meals, singing, and family time so pleasurable that the child will love it.

Instead of threatening children with the punishments that lie in store for doing the wrong things, parents should stress how God loves us and wants to reward us for loving Him back. This isn't to say that we never mention punishment, but that it should be in the context of, and take a back seat to, the love and rewards of being in a relationship with our Creator.

The more parents make their children feel loved, the more the children can appreciate that God loves them. If children really love their parents, they won't want to let their parents down. That also applies to how we should feel about God. He is disappointed in us when we behave in ways that are beneath us. We should miss our closeness with Him when we act in ways that harm that relationship.

Honey vs... Batya was three years old. On Fridays, her mother asked, "Who wants to have the mitzvah of setting the Shabbos table?" Batya took great pride in setting the napkins and silverware and her mother would exclaim afterward, "What a wonderful mitzvah girl you are! You did a great job. Our guests and I are so proud of you."

When her mother lit Shabbos candles, Batya lit her special candle next to her mother's, and got a warm hug after saying the blessing. Shabbos was a special time when her parents blessed her. She got to eat yummy bread and pick a favorite food that her mother would make for each Shabbos meal. When Batya grew older, she personally prepared her favorite foods for Shabbos.

Batya loved the Jewish holidays. It was such a treat for her to attend the synagogue's children's group where she joined other children who sang, drank grape juice, played games, and heard Torah stories. When the group was over, she joined her parents and they ate more yummy food at kiddush—food that she never ate the rest of the week. At Shabbos lunch, her parents always gave her extra attention, despite their having guests over. Whenever she finished eating, she played with toys, games, and other children while the adults chatted. Her parents tried to invite guests who had children Batya's age so that she would enjoy Shabbos and have friends to play with rather than feeling that the meals deprived her of attention and fun. Batya could not understand how anyone would not want to observe Shabbos!

When Batya woke up every morning, her mother sang *Modeh Ani* (a short prayer thanking God for giving us back our soul and life every morning) with her and gave her a hug and kiss. Before Batya ate, her mother would say a blessing with her over the food that God gave them. When they left the house, Batya and her mother would kiss the mezuzah. Her mother explained to her that there was writing inside the mezuzah that was like a special love letter between *Hashem* (God) and the Jewish people. When Batya went to bed every night, her mother told her a bedtime story and tucked her into bed. They sang the Shema prayer together and her mother told her how much she and Hashem loved Batya. Batya's day was filled with God's and her mother's love for her.

Vinegar   Seven-year-old Baruch was not so fortunate. His parents were so concerned with doing the right thing that being observant was very unpleasant for him. He went to a religious school where the boys didn't have much time to play or run around. They had to sit still or the teacher yelled at them. The teachers made them daven (pray) for half an hour every morning, long after he and many of his classmates lost interest. He wanted to color, paint, and draw but his teachers wanted him to listen to boring subjects instead. When Baruch came home with a less-than-stellar report card, his parents were angry that he hadn't done better in his classes.

Shabbos was especially unpleasant. When he dirtied his clothes, as invariably happened, his mother was angry with him. He had lots of potential time to play, but if he ran around the way that he liked, his father told him that he wasn't acting in the spirit of the Shabbos. His father took him to a *shul* where there were no children's services or playgroups for Baruch. When he couldn't sit still in shul, his father scolded him for not davening or following the Torah reading. When they got home, Baruch's parents invited boring adults over and the grown-ups spent hours at the table talking about boring things. The worst part was when his father went on and on with *divrei Torah* (words of Torah) that Baruch couldn't understand and to which Baruch was expected to listen.

On Shabbos, no one ever asked Baruch what he learned in school. He would have felt so proud showing everybody how well he knew the answers to his Torah review questions. By the time the guests left, Baruch hoped that his parents would play with him. Instead, they took naps and left him alone. Being religious was a terrible experience for him. It should not have surprised his parents when he dropped out of Judaism before he finished high school.

Many *baal teshuvas* don't have a model of how to raise normal, religious children. It is very helpful if they find parents of well-adjusted children in their community whom the *baal teshuvas* can ask for advice and whom they can observe raising children. Seeing how normal, religious people relate to their children and deal with everyday issues is a great way to learn how to do both.

Respecting the Child   Yisrael's mother Ahuva called him in from playing outside one Shabbos afternoon. He had gotten dirt on his pants, and his formerly white shirt was stained with the grape juice from lunch. Lisa, the family's Shabbos guest, was impressed that Ahuva didn't mind.

"Yisrael," Ahuva reminded him, "I arranged for you to go play with Shimi at four o'clock today."

Nine-year-old Yisrael was not pleased. "But *Imma* (Mom), I don't like Shimi."

"I'm sorry," Ahuva responded, tucking in his shirt, "I thought that you did. The two of you were good friends last year."

"That was last year, *Imma*. He tries to hang around me but I don't really like him any more."

"I made a mistake, Yisrael. I didn't realize that things had changed, and I thought that you would enjoy the chance to play with him. Please go today, because otherwise his feelings will be hurt. If you really don't enjoy being there, you can leave after an hour, and I won't ever ask you to go back again."

Yisrael accepted this and went with his mother to Shimi's house.

Lisa learned from this brief exchange that she had unrealistic expectations that religious children always want to do what their parents want them to do. She also learned how to balance a child's feelings with honoring parents and not shaming others.

Being observant doesn't mean that children should stop wanting to play and be children. They still want their parents' approval, love, and attention, and need joy and love to balance an environment that is filled with lots of structure and restrictions.

Age Differences

Young Children   Children until the age of 10 or so will generally follow their parents' lead. If they see their parents observing Jewish rituals, praying, lighting Shabbos candles, giving charity, keeping kosher, observing Shabbos and holidays, and not speaking badly about others, children will probably do likewise. If parents make Judaism enjoyable and part of their daily lives, young children will usually embrace it as well.

Secular Peer Groups   Once children reach third or fourth grade, their peer group may be as strong as, if not stronger than, their parents' influence on them. This can create problems if children of baal teshuvas are in secular schools and have secular friends whose values clash with those of the parents. Children want to be like their peers. Thus, children of baal teshuvas usually do best living in a religious neighborhood and attending religious schools where other families have good character traits and similar values.

Transitioning to Religious School   However, a recently observant family may need a transitional period of a year or two before it is ready to move to a religious environment. One way of bridging this gap is for the children of baal teshuvas who are still in public school to get private tutoring or attend a Hebrew/Sunday school until they are ready to enroll in a religious school that is appropriate for the family's level of observance.

Before children change schools, parents need to prepare them emotionally and practically to lose good friends, make new ones, fit into a new environment, adjust to new school hours, and so on. Children may resent being tutored until they catch up in Hebrew studies, so it is important to make the process interesting and fun.

It is helpful before the school year begins if the child can make friends with religious children who will be in their class. Ideally, parents should listen to their children's concerns and preferences before deciding when to change schools and which religious school is best for each child. The more the child feels that he is in control of what is happening to him, the easier the adjustment will be.

Minimizing Stress

Parents sometimes stress their children by the way they practice Judaism. For example, as soon as some children adjust to their parents' religious changes, the parents become stricter, move to a different community, and/or enroll their children in new schools. Their children feel out-of-control and can't feel comfortable. Just as the children get used to becoming more observant, they have to make new friends, lose old ones, and find a new way to fit in. Parents should strive to keep open the lines of communication as they go on their religious journeys and take into account the effects that their changes have on their children.

While children are flexible, they also need stability and consistency. Parents need to carefully investigate which schools, peer group, community, and level of Jewish observance will be right for themselves and for their children. They should find out not just how well the students do academically, but whether they are nice, have good character traits, and accept newcomers who are different from themselves. Will people in a new community expect the *baal teshuva's* children to act, dress, think, and talk the way children in their community do? Will it be good for your child to fit in that way? Do teachers in the new schools have teaching styles from which your children will learn well? Will the teachers be good role models for the children?

Taunted and Bullied Gil and Sharon heard from several advisors and parents that a religious elementary school and a certain small Jewish community were wonderful. They visited the school and met with the principal during the summer. They spent a few Shabboses in the community and were welcomed by its families. Based on these positive experiences, they enrolled their eight-year-old daughter Shira in the school's third grade and moved to a new home nearby.

The first week of school, Shira was taunted by her classmates and was bullied by an older girl. During recess, no one wanted to play with Shira because she was a newcomer. Her teacher screamed at some of the children in the class when they misbehaved. Shira came home in tears. When Sharon called the teacher and asked what happened, the teacher corroborated what Shira had said. When Sharon discreetly observed what went on in the school the following week, she was very upset. The teacher was oblivious to children's negative interactions and felt that they should work out their problems themselves. When Sharon spoke to the principal about the teacher's screaming and her inability to control the class, the principal agreed that that teacher was problematic, but they had not been able to find a replacement for her.

When Sharon discussed this with the other mothers in her new community, they agreed that there were problems at the school. They hadn't mentioned it to Sharon earlier because it was the only religious school in town and they had to overlook what they didn't like. Sharon learned to ask more questions the next time she investigated a school. She inquired about class discipline, how nice the children were to newcomers, and specific questions about the teachers of the class that Shira would attend. When she found a school that seemed to better suit her child's needs, she sent her daughter there with the realization that, although it had its downsides, its positives outweighed the negatives.

Preteens and Older

Introducing observant Judaism to children who are preteen and older can be tricky. By these ages, they have formed strong peer connections and are used to certain activities. Children who were raised in a secular environment may spend lots of time watching or listening to entertainment that isn't conducive to good values or to spirituality. Their ways of having fun may violate Shabbos or Jewish holidays and involve drinking, drug use and inappropriate relationships with the opposite sex. Telling children at this age not to dress, talk, or date like their peers may be akin to telling them to commit social suicide.

Older children are likely to resist changes that separate them from their peer group. They will be loathe to give up pleasures such as television, racy movies, shopping, going to the beach on Shabbos, and eating out in non-kosher restaurants unless and until they have something better with which to replace these activities. While children still want parental approval at this age, their desire for peer approval and social connection may be stronger. This makes it important for parents to make Judaism fulfilling before weaning children from the non-spiritual pleasures that they are used to. Introducing religious changes takes careful planning and timing.

Since having like-minded friends is so important, parents need to make it easy for their children to meet desirable observant peers. Teen outreach organizations such as NCSY and synagogue religious groups can help bridge the gap between not-yet-observant teens and observant peers. Such organizations offer activities that meet teens' emotional, social, and religious needs in an atmosphere that is appealing to many high school students. Teen Shabbatons and youth groups have amazing leaders who inspire children to be religious in ways that most parents cannot.

Parents should find out where there are charismatic observant families and ask if their children can join them on Shabbos and holidays. Some religious families practically adopt less-observant and *baal teshuva* kids into their families. This is a great way for everyone in a *baal teshuva* family to eventually get onto the same page.

NCSY and other outreach organizations also offer weekend retreats, Shabbatons, and week-long summer camps that introduce not-yet-observant kids to observant peers in warm, enjoyable, and accepting environments. The emotional pluses of a Shabbos with singing, dancing, good (or at least lots of) food, friendship, *kumsitzes* (people come and sit down in a circle, sometimes around a campfire, while someone tells stories), and emotional storytelling make Shabbos-observance a wonderful experience. Watching spiritually-destructive movies, television, and shopping on Saturdays pale by comparison.

Relationship with Parents

The Torah requires fathers to teach their sons Torah. When learning and practicing Judaism is enriched by a parent's love for their child, it is a deeper and more meaningful Judaism. If parents can teach their children Torah in a way that the children enjoy, it enriches their bond with one another. When parents can't do this, they should arrange for a teacher who has great rapport with their kids to inculcate knowledge and love of Judaism in them.

Good Relationships   Children who have a good relationship with their parents are likely to adopt their parents' values and religious behavior. Parents who become observant should make time to listen carefully to their children and share their thoughts, feelings, and values with their children without preaching. They can help children to think critically and logically by learning bits of Torah, raising questions about what they have learned, and discussing how to deal with moral and ethical dilemmas. Spending time together on Shabbos can create a framework for good communication and bonding since many of the weekday distractions are not present.

As children associate Judaism with healthy rules and emotional goodies such as parental love, attention, and listening, chances are that the child will learn and do more. Parents should expose their children to information and experiences that help the children see that observance is good for them rather than lecturing children about it. If the children feel that the parents are imposing Judaism on them, or are trying to manipulate and control them for their own needs, children will oppose it.

Poor Relationships   When children have a poor relationship with, or feel angry with, their parents, disdaining Torah Judaism is a way to get back at them. Parents should try to heal their relationship before encouraging a rebellious child to become more observant. Modeling Judaism as a positive way to live is the best way to transmit Judaism under such circumstances.

Back Door   Some baal teshuva parents whose children seem uninterested in Judaism may help their children to learn about Judaism "through the back door." They may converse with friends about Jewish topics that they think will interest their children, knowing that the children are within earshot. They can also leave books about Judaism with intriguing titles around the house in the hope that their teens will read them.

Ambivalent   Max was a 14-year-old who was ambivalent about being observant. The rest of his family was becoming observant, and he could see that it had great value. On the other hand, his father Bob wanted Max to be observant for his own reasons rather than because it was really good for Max. It embarrassed Bob that Max stood out like a sore thumb while the rest of the family was observant. Yet when Max finally put on a yarmulke at home, Bob expressed annoyance that it had a baseball logo on it rather than being solid black. Praise would have gone a long way to encouraging Max. His father's disapproval and criticism of Max' steps toward observance made Max decide that observance was not for him.

Judaism became a battleground for who was going to control Max, and Max was determined to win. If he couldn't get his father's approval, love, and attention in healthy ways, he would get Dad's attention in negative ways. Max' observing some things was akin to his doing nothing in Bob's book. By the time Max was 15, he started hanging out with non-Jewish girls and blatantly violated Shabbos. Bob was unwilling to praise him for the good things that he did and love him unconditionally, so Max got attention in ways that upset his father instead.

How Judaism Is Presented

We need to present Judaism to children in ways that speak to their interests and concerns, while modeling Judaism as vibrant, interesting, and enjoyable from the child's perspective.

Parents who lack the tools to appropriately convey and discuss Judaism with their children need ongoing guidance from a rabbi who is expert in such issues. He can help them to incorporate Judaism into the family in a way that suits each child.

Psychologically Healthy   Walter and Renee became observant over a period spanning 10 years. They had one child before becoming observant, and three more along the way. Lindsay was five when the family started keeping kosher, Nathan was four when they started keeping Shabbos, Aryeh was three when they started sending the children to day school, and Sima was two when the parents became chareidi. Renee was keenly aware of her children's differences and the need for each to march to his or her own religious drummer. Nathan didn't do well in yeshiva, so Renee put him in a day school where he thrived. Sima had a learning disability and didn't do well in a pressured school environment, so Renee sent her part-time to a Bais Yaakov school and home-schooled her part-time.

As adults, Lindsay and Aryeh were chareidi, Nathan was modern Orthodox, and Sima was a religious Zionist. Walter and Renee were delighted that each child ended up psychologically healthy and found a way to be observant that suited their personality. Although they had hoped that their children would all become chareidi, they realized that what was most important was that their children love being Jewish and follow the Torah. Their ability to see the forest for the trees allowed their children to find each's unique path to Torah observance.

Summary

Becoming observant is rarely a process that affects the *baal teshuva* alone. If one is married, a *baal teshuva* needs to carefully consider how each of his or her changes will affect not only his spouse but also his children. An advisor can recommend how to pace religious changes so that they don't adversely affect family members' stability, self-esteem, sense of belonging, and love of Judaism.

Preparing children for religious changes can enhance their appreciation of, and excitement with, Judaism instead of making them feel overwhelmed. When becoming observant is associated with positive experiences and a happy family environment, children are most likely to adopt an observant lifestyle. Recognizing the uniqueness of each family member and encouraging each person to relate to Judaism and God on their wavelength is a critical foundation of religious growth.

Integrating Children into a Religious Community

This chapter will address how *baal teshuva* families can successfully integrate into a religious community. Each has unique circumstances, such as the children's ages when the parents become *baal
teshuvas* (the younger, the easier it is), the rapidity with which the
family becomes observant (the more gradual, the better), the parents' parenting skills, the complexity of their family situation, the
personalities and needs of each child, and their community's openness. Getting good advice from a rabbi, advisor, other families in the
neighborhood, and, if necessary, a religiously sensitive and competent therapist, are all helpful in this process.

Networking Networking with other parents can ease the
way for children of baal teshuvas to fit into a religious community.
The "old-timers" can give information about Jewish schools, camps,
neighborhoods, synagogues, and more. These parents can also help
newcomers connect to other families who will invite them for Shabbos and Jewish holidays and whose children will befriend the baal
teshuva children. The established families can apprise the newcom-

ers of religious norms in various schools, synagogues, and neighborhoods so that the newcomers can fit in.

It helps to join a synagogue that has children's groups or children who socialize together. Parents can invite families with children their children's ages for Shabbos meals and arrange play dates for their younger children. Some synagogues are good places for *baal teshuva* parents to meet other parents who have children their kids' ages and to learn about schools and social groups that might be appropriate for their family.

Summer Friends   One way for children of a baal teshuva family to meet other children their age is to go to a religious summer camp. If it is attended by other children in the neighborhood they can become friendly with their neighbors at the same time.

Researching the Schools   Since every child and family has different circumstances, religious schools should be chosen with that family's specific needs in mind. Before enrolling their children in a religious school, parents should speak to other parents about its pros and cons. Ideally, parents should visit the school while it is in session and meet the teachers who will teach their children.

Since children can be cliquish, it can be hard for new children to integrate into some schools or communities. *Baal teshuvas* should try to meet parents and teachers who will encourage a popular child in each of their children's classes to take the newcomer under his or her wing and help him or her adapt to new surroundings.

Invitation to Fun   Beth saw that her 10-year-old daughter Mimi was shunned by the children in the religious school in which she had enrolled her. The other girls had all been together since first grade and they had no interest in Mimi's joining them. Beth had a brilliant idea. After asking the school's principal if her kashrut would be acceptable, Beth invited the 18 girls in Mimi's class, six at a time, to her house for an afternoon of jewelry-making, followed by homemade pizza. This gave all of the children a chance to get to know Mimi without the usual clique issues interfering, as well as associating Mimi with having a fun time. By the end of the week, Mimi had several new friends and was better liked by her classmates.

Help from Hosts   Amy and Stan started becoming observant shortly after their son Ricky was born. Their rebbetzin asked a wonderful woman, Roz, who lived near Amy and Stan, to invite the couple to her house for a Friday night dinner. When they came, they expressed their concerns about sending Ricky, now four years old, to a very religious school. Roz's children attended chareidi schools, and she agreed that a very religious school might initially be too intense for their family. Roz told them about a Jewish preschool in the neighborhood that had children from both non-observant and religious homes. It was warm, the teachers were loving, the children were happy there, and they learned Jewish songs and rituals in a very nice way. Roz called them after Shabbos and gave them names and phone numbers of parents whose children were enrolled there.

Those parents gave glowing reports about the school. Amy then went to visit the school with Ricky. She was so pleased to see that the children were happy, well supervised, and stimulated. The school provided a nice environment where the children joyfully played and learned about Judaism. Ricky immediately made himself at home among the books and toys. Amy was so impressed that she enrolled him that day. Over the course of the year, Amy and Stan saw that they had made a good choice.

As they became more observant, they widened their circle of friends. They spoke to other parents whose level of Jewish observance was close to theirs and asked where they sent their first graders to school. Based on those reports and a visit to another school, they found a religious day school that was appropriate for Ricky when he entered first grade.

Differences   Children sometimes make fun of children who are different, so it is important for newcomers to dress and act like their peers wherever they are. Baal teshuva parents should not give their children strange names, clothes, shoes, belongings, or haircuts that make them stick out. They should also prepare their children to handle comments about their differences from other children.

Dress Code   Steve and Shari didn't know that yarmulkes are not simply head coverings but are also statements of religious and political affiliation. When they became observant, Steve went to a religious bookstore and bought a few embroidered hats for his sons that he thought looked nice. When the boys attended religious school their first day, the boys in their school made fun of them. The family had no idea that the other boys all wore black yarmulkes and some had payos tucked behind their ears. The new boys felt so relieved when their parents bought them yarmulkes that looked like those of their peers. They also grew their payos to look like those of the boys around them.

Summer Camps

Children should not go to a religious summer camp unprepared for what it will be like. Other campers can shun them if they are different or are not part of their clique, and others who are more knowledgeable about Judaism may make fun of their ignorance or lack of observance.

Misfit   Emma had been a baal teshuva for a year when her parents sent her to a religious summer camp in upstate New York. When she arrived, it seemed that all of the other girls in her bunk already knew each other, and there were several cliques—none of which welcomed her. When she prayed slowly and deliberately every morning, she arrived late for breakfast and no one wanted her to sit next to them. She didn't know about washing negel vasser (ritually washing the hands with a cup in the morning) and the girls made fun of her behind her back for not doing so. When the girls asked if she liked cholent, the hot stew traditionally served at lunch on Saturdays, she had no idea what they were talking about. When it was brought to the table, she couldn't fathom how they could eat hot soup on a steamy summer morning. When the girls learned Torah every morning, she was placed in a class with younger girls because she couldn't read Hebrew well, yet she had already learned the content of what they were learning. All in all, camp was a dreadful experience for her because she never fit in. Had she only gone with a friend, or had one camper befriended her and helped her fit in, she would have had a very different summer.

Unprepared Adelle's parents were in the process of becoming baal teshuvas. Their rabbi thought that it would be good if 14-year-old Adelle went to a religious sleep-away summer camp. There, girls learned Torah for a couple of hours every day, and the rest of the day was filled with sports, arts and crafts, swimming, and typical camp activities. After hearing recommendations from several parents, Adelle's parents enrolled her for a month.

Nobody thought to tell Adelle's parents that the girls there all wore modest clothing. Adelle had never been to a camp before that had a dress code, and her mother bought her clothes that did not meet the camp's standards. When she arrived at camp with short-sleeved shirts and too-short skirts, the other girls made her feel so humiliated that she wanted to die.

Nor was that the only humiliation that she suffered. She was still in public school and had mostly learned about Judaism from watching what her parents did or from what she learned in Hebrew school classes. While her bunkmates prayed every morning, she sat around feeling bored. She didn't have a prayer book. When her counselor gave her a Hebrew one, it took Adelle nearly 10 minutes just to read the morning blessings. When the girls learned Torah, the teacher asked her to read, and she burst into tears when a girl snickered at her mistakes. When Adelle squeezed out toothpaste and brushed her teeth on Friday night, her bunkmates were aghast.

Adelle's camp experiences were the worst social fiascoes that she had ever endured. She begged her parents to let her come home her first week.

These terrible experiences could have been avoided with some advance planning. Someone could have apprised the camp director of Adelle's lack of knowledge. She (or a counselor) could have discussed dress code, morning prayers, and classes with Adelle and with her parents in advance. The camp could have made adjustments for Adelle's lack of knowledge and paired her with a caring bunkmate or older girl who could have helped her.

Friends from the Start Claire was so excited about going to summer camp for the first time. A week before camp, she got a phone call from Yehudis, her counselor-to-be. Yehudis spent 10 minutes telling Claire about herself and what their bunk and camp would be like, and asked Claire what she thought she would most enjoy about camp. By the time camp started, Claire already felt that she had some connection with her counselor. Yehudis spent five to 10 minutes the first day of camp getting to know each child so that each would feel welcome and would feel comfortable letting her know if things weren't going right. Claire loved the camp and was so fond of Yehudis that she couldn't wait to go back the next year.

Children are likely to have a positive experience in religious summer camp if they have friends there, if they fit in socially, and if the camp offers activities that suit them. Today, parents can choose from a bewildering array of religious camps, including Outward Bound-type experiences; Torah tours that travel around the United States, Eastern Europe and Israel; and music, drama, horse riding and conventional camps.

Outreach organizations such as NCSY have summer touring trips in the United States, Eastern Europe, and Israel, as well as weeklong camps attended by *baal teshuva* and non-observant teens. By the end of camp, the not-yet-religious teens are likely to be excited by Judaism, will have had a good time, made new religious friends, and will feel close to some caring advisors.

Shot in the Arm Micha became observant in 10th grade but he continued to attend public school. Spending Shabbos with his secular family was very unpleasant. To make matters worse, they lived in a town that had few observant teens. An advisor recommended that Micha attend a religious summer camp, and he did. Although he had just been observant for several months, he had the time of his life there! There were 15 other boys in his bunk, and he formed close friendships with two of them. Many Torah classes were offered and he could pick those that interested him most. There were opportunities to swim and play sports without pressure to do either. He did not enjoy athletics and was relieved that he didn't have to be a misfit engaging in activities that he hated. He loved to sing and learn Torah and there were plenty of opportunities to do both. When the summer was over, he couldn't wait to go back the following year. Although he had two more years of public school ahead of him, the camp and the friends that he made gave him a tremendous shot in the arm to stay religious until he finished high school. As soon as he graduated, he spent the following year in yeshiva in Israel.

Parents of already-observant teens should learn from other parents or advisors about religious youth organizations in or near their neighborhood. Many observant communities have youth groups that meet on Saturday afternoons. These have a variety of flavors and may be under the auspices of a local synagogue, Bnai Akiva, or Agudas Israel. It is important to choose a group that is suitable for the child and not simply send them to a group because it is the only one in town. Not socializing at all is usually better than a humiliating or hurtful social experience.

Surrogate Friends   Elise became observant as a teenager and was desperately lonely. Her family did not live in a religious neighborhood and there were no other religious children where she lived. She walked three miles to the nearest religious community every Saturday afternoon in an attempt to try to find religious friends. Unfortunately, all of the teens whom she met had been friends since childhood and she didn't fit in with them. She tried going on an outing with Bnai Akiva, but she was an outsider to them and she never felt like she belonged.

One day, a religious teacher introduced her to a *baal teshuva* couple who lived a few miles from Elise's house. The couple invited Elise and her family to spend Shabbos with them any time they wanted. Elise gratefully accepted. She couldn't find religious friends her age, but at long last she had found religious people with whom she could have a nice experience on Shabbos. Such families have been instrumental in helping many teens to stay observant until they are old enough to establish their own place in a religious community.

Thinking Outside the Box

Baal teshuva parents may have to think creatively about how to integrate their child into a religious community.

"His Path"   Shaya went to a religious school with a strict dress code, where some of the Jewish studies bored him. The best time of the day was the half-hour that he played during recess. He longed to learn more about science, history, and language. He was fascinated by the rare lab experiments they did in school, and he loved the elegance of mathematics. He was intrigued by some of the philosophy, literature, and science books that he found on his father's bookshelf, but his teachers never taught such stimulating topics in school.

When the summer came, he couldn't wait to be outdoors instead of cooped up inside a sterile classroom.

When he was 16, Shaya told his *baal teshuva* father, "I don't want to go to my school any more. I don't want to wear those clothes, I don't want to sit all day in a classroom, and I don't want to study Talmud."

His father Yaakov was horrified at first, and thought, "Where did I go wrong? I sent my son to the finest Jewish school in our city." The father had wanted so much to fit into what he considered the "mainstream frum world" that he hadn't considered the unique needs of his children. Yaakov thought about how Shaya's younger brother Gershon was thriving in the same school that Shaya hated.

Thankfully, Yaakov got beyond worrying what others would think about him if his son didn't do what everyone else in his community did. He told Shaya, "I'm glad that we have the kind of relationship where you can tell me these things. I want to hear what you want and what you don't like, and together we'll try to find a solution."

Shaya was so relieved that his father loved him enough to listen to him. He had been so afraid to tell his father what he really felt because he thought that his father might be angry or disappointed in him. He told his father what was in his heart and his father took his concerns very seriously. Yaakov then went to his rav, a man who was experienced with *baal teshuvas*, and asked him what to do.

The rav advised Yaakov to follow King Solomon's proverb, "Educate the child according to his path. Even when he becomes old, he won't deviate from it." Shaya's path was not to sit and learn Talmud for hours every day, but that didn't mean that he wasn't a wonderful, religious boy who could enjoy learning many other subjects.

The rabbi advised Yaakov to see if the school would allow Shaya to attend Jewish studies only in the mornings. If so, the father could get Shaya private tutors, homeschool him, or do guided independent study in the afternoons about topics that interested him. When Shaya wasn't in school, he should wear casual clothes that were comfortable for him. Yaakov should be proud, not embarrassed, that he had such a great son.

When Shaya turned up in the synagogue the following Saturday wearing navy blue slacks and a colored dress shirt, some congregants made negative comments about him behind Yaakov's back. One of them later approached Yaakov and told him that he should insist that his son wear more formal Shabbos clothes.

Yaakov just smiled at the man, put an arm around Shaya, and replied, "Rainbows have many beautiful colors in them. There's room enough in God's world for each Jew to sparkle differently and still be beloved in our Father's eyes."

Raising observant children is not about forcing them to do whatever the parents want. If a child is to stay emotionally healthy and religious, parents and teachers must sometimes give up their hopes for what their child will be like and change their plans. Yaakov knew that if Shaya felt his father's love and support, he would probably stay normal and religious, even if he did so in ways that met with their neighbors' disapproval. There was nothing *halachically* wrong with the path that Shaya wanted to follow, even though it was different from the boys around him.

Thanks to Yaakov's ability to see what was really important in rais-ing a Jewish child, and his not being overly concerned about what others would think, Shaya is religious today. He has a special talent helping Jews from a variety of backgrounds to come closer to Torah and observance. It's obvious where he got that from.

Extra-Curricular Activities

Baal teshuvas often enjoy activities that aren't part of the main-stream religious world. These may include martial arts, horseback riding, art, drama, voice, music, team sports, gymnastics, skiing, wa-ter sports, and nature outings. Jews shouldn't have to automatically give these up when they become religious. There are now teachers or classes in many communities that offer children and adults oppor-tunities to participate in these activities in a way that is compatible with observance. In Israel, for example, there are separate courses and groups for men and women, as well as teens, to learn and enjoy scuba diving! Many communities, including in Jerusalem, even offer separate martial arts classes for observant girls and boys from age six and up, as well as for adults!

Home schooling and private teachers offer *baal teshuvas'* children opportunities to study subjects that religious Jewish schools don't teach. Children can also pursue special areas of interest using CDs and Internet programs. These can be followed up with family field trips to museums, nature reserves, and exhibitions.

Built-In Exercise   A yeshiva had baal teshuva students who were frustrated by the lack of daily exercise, and many of these stu-dents didn't learn well. A wise advisor insisted that the boys play basketball or run every day for at least half an hour during recess. He knew that exercising in the middle of day would result in their learning more efficiently and enjoying their studies far more.

After instituting this change, they discovered what research has shown: many children, including some who were "hyperactive," were able to focus much better for the rest of the day. Some yeshivas in Israel with American students now offer exercise rooms onsite. They recognize that having a healthy body facilitates having a healthy mind.

Missing Horses   Sol's uncle had a farm with horses and he loved riding there every Saturday. When his family became religious, they stayed home on Shabbos, and he missed the horses. Before he became religious, he had attended public school 30 hours a week. After his family became religious, he was in school 45 hours a week and had a lot of homework as well. He couldn't concentrate and lost his motivation to learn. So, his wise parents arranged for him to ride several times a week and took him out of school early to do so. They understood that a happy child will learn far better in whatever time he studies than a child who is miserable and hates school. This setup gave Sol the exercise and fresh air that he needed to be able to stay in yeshiva and do well in the classes that he did attend. Reducing the number of hours that he sat in a classroom changed school from being a miserable experience to one that he enjoyed.

Summary

Children of *baal teshuvas* have needs of which their parents aren't always aware. Children want to fit in with their peers, they want to feel successful in school, they want to have fun, and they also want to feel that they can be themselves. *Baal teshuva* parents need guidance from religious mentors about which community, schools, and summer camps will be best for their children and how to help their children fit in and be "normal." A child is more likely to be a happy, religious child if the parents are sensitive to his or her emotional, educational, and social needs. At the end of the day, a child who is emotionally well-adjusted and who enjoys learning is more likely to continue doing so for the rest of his or her life. One who associates observance and learning with misery is unlikely to continue either as soon as he or she has an opportunity to live otherwise.

TWENTY

Remarriage with Children

It is very difficult these days to have a successful marriage. Divorce rates for Americans are higher than 50 percent. Observant Jews usually have more successful marriages than the general public does, but their divorce rates are also higher than is desirable. Some of the most challenging marriages among *baal teshuvas* occur when they marry each other and have minor children from their prior marriage(s). Such marriages potentially have many hurdles to be surmounted.

Religious remarriages are not immune to the same problems that affect many marriages—inability to resolve conflicts, difficulties dealing with anger, poor communication, unrealistic expectations, control issues, lack of love and intimacy, and so on. However, issues of religious observance bring their own challenges. Even when two very nice people marry each other, the complexities of remarriage between *baal teshuvas* can be mind-boggling. Consider Rona's and Phil's circumstances:

Unresolved Issues Rona became a baal teshuva two years after getting divorced, when her daughters were six and eight years old. Rona got custody of the children, and her ex-husband has the girls every Sunday. He is a secular Jew who does not see eye-to-eye with

Rona on many matters. He no longer objects to his daughters attending religious school, but he doesn't want them to be "too religious."

Phil, a *baal teshuva* for three years, met Rona when her girls were 13 and 15 years old. The girls had been living in a modern Orthodox community where they attended a modern Orthodox day school. Phil was a bit more observant than they were, but he had two non-Jewish sons, ages 12 and 14. The boys lived with their mother three days a week and with Phil four days a week.

Phil and Rona got married after six months of dating and many discussions about how to blend their families. Yet, they never resolved in advance some serious issues that nearly destroyed their marriage. They discovered, much to their chagrin, that blending their families had all of the usual challenges, and then some. Their children didn't like each other. Even though Phil was good to Rona and contributed financially to her daughters' Jewish education, the girls resented him. They didn't care that he took a financial load off of Rona. All that mattered to them was that they had had to move into his more-spacious house and leave their home, friends, and school. Meanwhile, Phil's boys brought offensive books, posters, and music into his house and used language that shocked and offended Rona's girls—exactly the effect that the boys hoped it would have.

The boys resented Rona and her girls for taking their father away from them. Before "the females" invaded their home, Phil and his boys had been a great family. Now "the females" were ruining it all. The girls left their female stuff in the bathroom and talked endlessly on the phone. The boys had to listen to the girls' dumb music and chatter and were furious that Rona insisted that their mess downstairs get cleaned up every Friday. They could never find their things any more, thanks to Rona! To add insult to injury, she had convinced their father not to let them put up their posters anywhere but in their rooms. Rona's and Phil's marriage barely survived with the help of many hours of family and individual therapy, rabbinic counseling, and fortitude on their parts.

Some potential remarriages are recipes for disaster, which, with proper planning and forethought, could be minimized or avoided.

Ideally, single *baal teshuva* parents should think about the details of their family life before they decide who could be a potential spouse. It is so easy to be excited about meeting someone special and having a happy marriage that *baal teshuvas* may not consider the repercussions of each potential relationship on their children.

Energy Drain Shulamis was an older baal teshuva who had never been married. She found everything that she was looking for in Hersch. He was kind, yeshivish, interesting, caring, and attractive. There was just one problem—his three children from his first marriage. He had become observant four years earlier, but his teenage children had not. They alternated between living with his ex-wife and spending most weekends with him. Shulamis didn't particularly like his children, but figured that if she loved Hersch, how bad could things be if his children only came around on weekends?

Eight years later, she could write a book about what could be so terrible. She loved her husband but rued, "I wouldn't wish this marriage on anybody." Hersch loved his children and constantly felt torn between making Shulamis happy and keeping his children happy. Since those goals were often mutually exclusive, he usually chose not to alienate his children rather than to create the home atmosphere that Shulamis craved.

When the children visited on Saturdays, they wore their usual clothing—everything from torn blue jeans and shirts with offensive captions on them, to clothes that left little to the imagination. Shulamis didn't know how they found so many body parts to pierce with rings. Their language was coarse and the topics they discussed offended Shulamis. The stepchildren were disrespectful to Shulamis and invariably disturbed the atmosphere of holiness that Shulamis relished, especially when the two daughters were there with their boyfriends. The son used such coarse language and fought so much with his father that Shulamis often ate quickly and beat a hasty retreat into the bedroom. She spent many hours on Saturdays alone so as not to be around them.

While Hersch loved Shulamis, much of his emotional energy was drained by his children's problems and the continual battles that he fought with his ex-wife. Shulamis felt that he had little nurturing left for her.

While *baal teshuvas* want to be happily married, they must be realistic about when, and with whom, that is possible. When one or both people have minor children, putting the children's needs first may make remarriage to an otherwise-wonderful spouse a bad idea.

Here are a few points for single parents with children to consider:

1. **Do the children still have any emotional traumas due to their parents' divorce (or one's death)? What emotional issues still need to be resolved?**

Children need time and, sometimes, professional help to work through their feelings about their parents' divorce. They may still hope that their parents will reconcile. They may be grieving the loss of an intact family. Some fear that their parents will abandon them. They may worry about finances or about their future. They may feel a lack of stability and no longer trust adults. Some feel unloved and don't get the nurturing and attention they desperately need.

2. **How is each child's relationship with each parent?**

Children and parents may not communicate well. Children may manipulate their parents to get what they want or play one parent against the other. They may feel angry and/or be rebellious or destructive. These kinds of problems usually intensify with a remarriage unless they are worked out ahead of time.

3. **What kind of relationship do the divorced spouses have? How does this affect the children? How will it affect a remarriage?**

Only a minority of ex-spouses get along well with each other. Many divorced couples continue to have discord that affects the children, including using the children as pawns in a vendetta against the other parent. Some ex's will go to great lengths to hurt each other, such as by withholding child support, sabotaging visitation, taking the ex-spouse to court, or suing for custody in the event of remarriage.

4. How do a potential partner's children feel about you?

Some, especially younger children, may welcome a new parent or parent's spouse in the home. Other children may not like the stranger who they feel is invading their family, especially if this newcomer takes their parent away from them or wrecks their fantasy that their parents will reconcile. They especially don't like someone who changes the order in their lives and imposes new rules on them.

5. What will remarriage do to, or for, the children?

Single parents should contemplate before dating what kinds of remarriage will destabilize, or be positive, for their children. What ingredients will help a child feel secure, loved, taken care of, and given enough attention? If children were living in chaos, amidst lots of fighting, or in poverty, remarriage to the right person may bring stability, warmth, and security. On the other hand, some ex-spouses with an acrimonious relationship respond to the other's remarriage by making new tensions. They sue for different custodial arrangements and changes in child support, use the remarriage as an opportunity to woo their children to live with them, try to get back at their ex-spouse by destabilizing the remarriage, and worse.

6. How do potential spouses deal with each other's children? How do their children relate to one another and to the potential stepparent? How does the new couple handle discord between the various blended family members?

These issues are so complicated that almost every couple with children from a prior marriage should get premarital counseling from a therapist who is experienced with such matters. Possible issues to be addressed include how stepparents or step-siblings don't get along with, or even hurt, one another; anger that isn't handled constructively; how to handle discipline and disrespect; and how to reallocate time and resources fairly and in ways that don't cause strife.

7. How old are the children?

Blending families with teenagers, especially of both sexes, can be difficult. Sometimes, older children who resent newcomers may bully and attack their new siblings verbally, if not physically. Very young children may also become aggressive or regress when they have to share their parent, toys, and space with newcomers. On the other hand, some children welcome having an older sibling who loves them. They love having new playmates. Others are very excited that they can dote on younger children.

8. Is a potential spouse aware of how little time they might have with their new mate?

Children have needs. The amount of time that a couple spends dating isn't necessarily a good predictor of how much time spouses will spend together after remarriage. People often make more time to be with each other when they date because they assume that it is a temporary situation. After they get married, they reduce their time with a spouse in order to take care of their children's ongoing needs.

9. Have both people considered how much upheaval their marriage might engender for their children? How will that be remedied?

Will one family have to move away from their friends, family, support systems, school, and the children's other parent? How will those losses or changes be handled? Will people move from one end of the country to the other, or from one country to another?

10. How intense are the problems that other family members already experience?

Do any of the children have problems in school? Does anyone suffer from depression, alcohol or drug use, or serious frictions with parents? Are there ongoing custody battles or unfinished divorce issues? Are any children rebelling or in crisis? Do any of the children have special emotional or physical needs? Are there financial stresses that will intensify with remarriage?

11. Will the children have the security and support that they need with a remarriage, or will a remarriage destabilize them more?

Children may feel rejected or supplanted by the love that their parent feels for a new spouse or for stepchildren. A remarrying parent may need to give their children extra time and reassurance in order for them to feel secure.

Some parents never give their children enough quality time in the first place, and remarriage cuts the children adrift in a sea of tumultuous relationships and feelings. Sometimes the parent must walk a fine line between making sure that their child gets what he or she needs, yet not be manipulated by a child who wants things to stay the same.

12. Is the timing of the remarriage appropriate?

Some children have emotional, school, or social problems that need attention. They may also have experienced so much turmoil due to separation or divorce that it is wise not to stress them by more changes for a long time.

In addition, baal teshuvas need to consider the following:

13. How compatible are the religious lifestyles, goals, and attitudes of the two families?

Although people date only one person, they marry the person's family. Each child will impact the blended family and be impacted by them.

14. Can family members live religiously as they want without harming others in the family who are not as observant?

When Meryl married Dovid, her two sons, 8 and 16, moved in with him. Dovid and Meryl were *baal teshuvas* but her children and ex-husband were not observant. The eight-year-old became observant due to his good relationship with Dovid while the 16-year-old did not. Thanks to the mutual respect that Dovid and both sons had toward one another, they could all live with house rules that allowed them to get along together.

15. Is it possible that someone (such as an ex-spouse) will negatively affect the blended family in ways that can't be totally foreseen?

For example, an ex-husband may not like the fact that his ex-wife became observant. In the meantime, their 15-year-old son is not sure as to whether or not he wants to be observant. If the ex-wife remarries an observant man who tries to enroll the boy in a Jewish school, it may trigger the ex-husband into going to court to get custody. Or, if the new husband sets rules that the boy dislikes, the boy may decide to live with his father. Such scenarios are not uncommon and should always be considered.

16. If a new couple has children together, how will that affect their children from prior marriages? How will the other children relate to these new children? How will new children affect the blended family's emotional and religious dynamics?

Better Family   Shalom shared custody of his three well-adjusted children ages three, five, and seven with his ex-wife. They had a great relationship and lived in the same community. When he met Faige, a divorcee without children, they spent three months getting to know one another and another three months allowing the children and Faige to get to know each other. The children told Shalom how excited they would be to have more brothers and sisters, and how much they wanted Faige to marry their father.

When the couple got married and later had children, it created an even better family for everyone involved. Such are the possibilities of remarriage under the right circumstances.

Growing on Each Other   Gary was a baal teshuva divorce with two teenage boys. Sandra was a widowed baal teshuva with two young girls. After dating for a few months, they wanted to marry each other, but they needed to give their children time to see if the children could adjust to their remarriage.

One Sunday, Sandra met Gary's boys as they enjoyed a Red Sox game, which they followed by eating pizza in a nearby restaurant.

They all hit it off. The next Sunday, Gary met Sandra's girls and the four of them had a picnic in a park. They also had a wonderful time together. The third week, the children met each other and had a barbecue together. Over time, Gary's neighbor hosted Sandra's family for Shabbos, and the families had a pleasant experience together. The boys actually liked having little sisters and couldn't wait for Gary to get remarried.

Soon after Gary and Sandra got married, he adopted her children, and they had another baby girl together. Thanks to their being well adjusted, and carefully preparing for remarriage, theirs has been a match made in Heaven.

Summary

This chapter does not give an exhaustive list of everything that Jewish parents should think about before they remarry. It does raise issues that single parents should consider and how they might deal with them.

Single parents don't have the liberty to date someone only three times, then get engaged. Remarriage requires tremendous thought, months of getting to know a partner and his or her children, and, ideally, premarital counseling. Single parents need excellent communication, problem-solving, and child-rearing skills to have good remarriages. When partners are properly equipped and properly chosen, remarriage with blended families can be a richly rewarding experience.

Part Five:
Practical Advice

Religious Dating and Marriage

When singles become *baal teshuvas*, they have to learn about religious dating and marriage and how it differs from the secular counterparts. In my book, *Guide for the Romantically Perplexed*, I discuss what singles should know about a potential partner, what issues are important when deciding who to marry, how to assess compatibility, what tools are needed for a successful marriage, and how to know if someone is ready for marriage. That information is beyond the scope of the present book and will not be repeated here.

Fun vs. Marriage-Oriented The change from secular dating to dating in the Torah-observant world is enormous. Secular singles typically start dating in their teens, with the purpose of having a good time. Only much later do singles date with an eye toward marriage. Rather than meeting through a matchmaker or through religious functions, secular singles may meet at school, sports events, parties, singles events, in bars, in clubs, in classes, at work, or by being introduced by friends.

Generally, religious singles only date when they are ready to get married, and they do so as means of assessing their compatibility with a potential marriage partner. They are often set up on dates by a rabbi, rebbetzin, friend, or *shadchan* (professional matchmaker), in addition to meeting at weddings, Shabbos meals, charity or singles' events, and so on. The process of dating usually lasts only a few weeks or months rather than dragging on for years. Most religious couples get engaged and married in the space of six months or less. One reason for this is that observant couples have no premarital physical contact. If two people know that they want to spend the rest of their lives together, there is little point in waiting any longer than is necessary to get started.

Attitudes & Intermediaries   Making the attitudinal shifts necessary for religious dating can be difficult for baal teshuvas. They are suddenly expected to date without touching, to assess their feelings for someone after just a few meetings, and to decide if they want to spend the rest of their lives with someone they barely know. Dating with a third-party acting as intermediary can also be uncomfortable, if not daunting. Some people feel that it is an invasion of their privacy having to report back to a third party about how their dates were.

Dating Coach   Baal teshuvas may need a coach to help them date successfully. A coach can explain what to say and not say to shadchans and on dates, when to divulge personal information, and how to "pace" their dates.

Discretion   Zoe grew up in a secular family in California. Her parents divorced when she was seven, and by the time she was in college, her father was married to his third wife. She and her friends experimented with drugs in high school but she stopped using them by the time she finished college. She started dating at 15. By the time that she became baal teshuva at age 25, she had already had relationships with many men. As was the case with many of her friends, Zoe had spent several years in psychotherapy and was taking Prozac. She never thought twice about disclosing these facts to others because everyone she knew had similar situations. However, when she became observant, religious people were not comfortable hearing most of these details about her life.

A Shabbos hostess, Mina, heard about Zoe's difficulties dating and offered to coach her. Mina advised her that, although Zoe was comfortable with the facts of her life, religious people would find them jarring. Dating would go smoother if she only offered this information if a shadchan or date asked her about these aspects of her life. Of course, if she was seriously dating a man, it would be appropriate to share this basic information with him, but not on the first few dates.

Now knowing to be more discreet, Zoe met a lovely *baal teshuva* man. After a few dates in which they discovered that they were very compatible, she slowly divulged some of the "unpleasant" aspects of her past, and he was able to accept them. They got married seven months after their first date.

Marrying a Cohen   Baal teshuvas are often surprised to hear that the Torah restricts which Jews they can date. They may not know with whom they can discuss such delicate matters. For example, a cohen is forbidden to marry a convert to Judaism, a divorcee, or a Jewess who has had a sexual relationship with certain people. A baal teshuva who has had a sexual relationship(s) and who may be interested in dating a cohen should discuss with a posek whether her circumstances bar her from marrying one.

Many *baal teshuvas* have lived with a partner or have had premarital sex with partners whose halachic religion they don't know, or who are mistaken about their halachic religion. Consequently, they don't know if they are permitted to marry a cohen or not.

Some Jewish women live with a Jewish man long enough to constitute being a common-law wife, thus invalidating them for marriage to a cohen. Although the women don't think of themselves as "divorcees" after such relationships end, some rabbis advocate that these women get a Jewish divorce if possible.

Who's a Cohen?   Just because a man has a last name that is associated with cohanim (plural of cohen) doesn't mean that he is one.

For instance, almost all Jewish men whose last names are Rappoport or Katz are cohanim, but most whose last names are Cohen are not! How does a baal teshuva know if he is indeed a cohen if his own father isn't sure? The rabbi may ask the man to look at his father's circumcision/baby naming papers, bar mitzvah certificate, or Jewish wedding document to ascertain if his Hebrew name or lineage indicate that he is a Jewish priest. Unfortunately, a secular Jewish father may not have any of these.

Sometimes, a man will visit his father's or father's male relative's (such as paternal uncle or grandfather) grave and see two hands engraved on the headstone. The two raised hands symbolize Jewish priests blessing the Jews and are a sign that the person buried there was a cohen. The converse, though, is not necessarily true—that if there are no hands, the person was not a cohen.

Mamzerut Another complication for baal teshuvas is their personal status as Jews. Sadly, the high divorce rates in America and Europe mean that many Jewish spouses divorce, then remarry other Jewish partners. If a baal teshuva's mother was previously married according to Jewish law and never got a Jewish divorce, any children resulting from subsequent relationships are mamzerim (children of an adulterous relationship). A child born out-of-wedlock is illegitimate in the secular world, but that is not the case in Jewish law. However, a mamzer, a Jew born of an adulterous relationship, may only marry a convert to Judaism or another mamzer. Thankfully, since few non-observant Jews get married according to Jewish law, mamzerut today is rare.

Note: What constitutes marriage according to Jewish law? Among other things, two fully observant Jewish men who are unrelated to one another or to the bride and groom must witness the groom's giving a ring to the bride. In addition, a proper *ketubah* (Jewish marriage document) must be prepared and given by the husband to the wife before the marriage can be consummated.

Many ketubahs today are beautiful works of art but are invalid according to Jewish law because they do not contain the proper information for a valid marriage contract.

Many *baal teshuvas* are surprised to discover that they, or their "Jewish" spouse, are not Jewish according to Jewish law. If they want to stay married, the non-Jewish spouse must convert according to Jewish law and the couple then needs a proper Jewish marriage.

Not Valid Marriage Ephraim's mother had been previously married to a Jewish man before she married Ephraim's father. She and her first husband had a civil, but not Jewish, divorce. Since his mother's first marriage took place on a Saturday afternoon and was conducted by a Reform rabbi, Ephraim's posek knew the marriage could not have been valid according to Jewish law. (Even though the couple was common-law married, they are not considered married for purposes of determining if a child is a mamzer.) The posek declared Ephraim not a mamzer.

Baal teshuvas who may be affected by these Jewish laws should never decide for themselves what their status is. They should consult an expert posek when sensitive religious decisions must be made.

Cohen Records Bernie Cohen was a miracle. His parents and grandparents were secular Jews, yet instead of disappearing into the American melting pot, Bernie found his way back to Torah Judaism at the age of 30. After studying in yeshiva for two years, he wanted to get married. He consulted a well-known posek about his status as a cohen, since many of the *baal teshuvas* that he could potentially meet would not be suitable dates if he was a Jewish priest. When Bernie tried, but was unable to locate any evidence that he was a cohen from any family records, memories, or cemeteries, the rabbi told him that he could assume that he was not a cohen.

Get from Boyfriend Leora became a baal teshuva when she was 24. Before she started religious dating, she mentioned to the principal of her seminary that she had once lived with a Jewish man for six months. The principal told her not to divulge that information to others and took her to a posek with experience dealing with baal teshuvas. After hearing the details of Leora's circumstances, the rabbi asked if she knew how to contact her former boyfriend. She did. The rabbi advised her to ask him to give her a get (Jewish divorce document). Her boyfriend was surprisingly agreeable, and Leora's advisor helped arrange all of the details. She got her get, then met her future husband a month later.

Being Ready for Marriage

While marriage is wonderful for those who have the tools to sustain a healthy marriage, singles of marriageable age don't always have these tools. Going out just because someone is "too old" to be single, is the "right age," or is lonely does not remedy the lack of marriage skills and necessary attitudes. If people get married without adequate preparation, they will simply bring all of the problems they had as singles into their marriage. Adults do not simply "grow out" of emotional problems when they get married. Someone who has emotional problems or who lacks the tools to have a good marriage typically needs, and deserves, coaching or professional therapy. The good news is that coaching, therapy, and hard work can do a great deal to equip singles to have great marriages. The bad news is that faulty character traits tend to stay that way unless a person works hard for a long time to change them.

Baal teshuvas-in-process should be able to answer the following questions before they start dating:

Know Your Life Goals   What are your life goals? Which goals are negotiable and which are not?

Qualities of Mate   Which qualities do you seek in a mate? Which of these are essential and which are simply preferences?

Flavor of Judaism   Singles need to decide which level of religious observance to adopt, or have an idea of which religious orientations they could comfortably live with. Do you see yourself fitting into a modern Orthodox, chareidi, or Chassidic environment? Are you flexible about marrying someone more, less, or differently observant than you are? Do you have strong feelings about the religious requirements you would like in a spouse? Where do you see yourself religiously in 10 years?

Location   Will you live in the United States, Israel, or some other country? Are you prepared to move to a Jewish community elsewhere?

Many *baal teshuva* singles want to live near a parent, a specific Jewish community, or in Israel. This can limit one's potential marriage partners. Singles should discuss with a wise religious mentor or advisor how flexible to be with these matters.

Yeshiva/Seminary   Singles should have an idea of whether or not, and for how long, they would like to study in a yeshiva or seminary. Many *baal teshuva* couples are fortunate in being able to learn in yeshiva and/or seminary for their first year of marriage.

Finances   Singles who are trying to get married should have an idea of how they will earn a living. Will you need further education? Who will support you until you are able to support yourself?

Children   In what kind of community, and in what kind of schools, do you want to raise your children? Where will you and your future family best be able to grow religiously?

Giving the Process Time   These are not the kinds of questions that baal teshuvas can answer after just a few months of study or observance. They need time to formulate realistic answers based on knowledge, experience, and conferring with an advisor. Some baal teshuvas start dating and marry before they have thought through where they are headed and where their choice of spouse will lead them.

It can be risky for *baal teshuvas* to get married when they, or a potential partner, have been religious for less than a year. Being *baal teshuva* for less than a year simply isn't enough time to know where one wants to end up and what it feels like to be religious. Young adult *baal teshuvas* are still "trying on" identities to see which ones fit. It takes time to see if those changes will last.

Clear Compromises Abby was from an assimilated Jewish family. In the city where she grew up in California, the definition of a religious Jew was someone who married another Jew.

One night at a party, she met a very religious Jewish businessman from another city. He asked her if she was Jewish. She thought about it for a minute and replied, "Yeah, I guess so."

They spent a couple of hours in conversation and he was very taken with her. He flew back and forth to see her several times during the next six months and they had phone conversations in-between. Before he proposed to her, he asked her, "Do you understand what it means to live as a religious Jew?"

"Sure," she said.

Actually, she didn't have a clue. She spent the next year learning with a rebbetzin and finally decided that she could do most, but not everything, that observant Jews are supposed to do.

They decided to get married, after being very clear with each other about what compromises each would need to make in order to make their marriage work. This allowed them to have a good marriage for the past 25 years.

It is important to know what compromises a person thinks that they can and can't make in marriage. These must be clearly expressed to a potential partner who expects a spouse to be different than the person they are dating. Some people want so much to be married that they choose a partner who is so different religiously (and in other ways) that both end up miserable. Despite wanting very much to be married, neither may be able to compromise enough to make it work.

Conflict-Resolution Skills Today, many people marry because they find each other attractive, have good chemistry, have fun together, or have similar goals. While these might seem to be important ingredients for a good marriage, they have little to do with the likelihood that a couple will stay happily married.

Two of the most important ingredients in a successful marriage are a couple's ability to handle conflicts and to continually create feelings that they love and like one another. Many couples do their utmost to avoid conflicts while dating, or they seek someone with whom they have no conflicts. Invariably, they discover after their wedding that their "perfect" spouse has lots of shortcomings and that the couple doesn't have the tools to deal with their differences or disappointed expectations. Dating should allow conflicts and differences to arise so that couples can see how they deal with them.

Emotional Work Dassy and Dov were introduced by one of her seminary teachers. They dated for two months, during which time they had good chemistry and good conversations, but some troubling issues also arose. Dassy expressed to Dov her concerns that he seemed to be too religiously stringent for her, and that he tended to shut down emotionally when she did things that upset him. When this didn't get resolved, she mentioned these issues to Dov's religious counselor. Meanwhile, Dov told Dassy that her insecurity and need for reassurance might overwhelm him, and he shared his concerns with her spiritual advisor. After a few meetings with a couples' therapist and both advisors, the couple learned to communicate in ways that resolved these issues. They got married six months after they first met and have had a very strong marriage as a result of the emotional work that they did before they got married.

Compatible Expectations

Another important ingredient for a successful marriage is compatible expectations. What does each person expect will happen in marriage and what role will each partner play? It is very important to discuss *in detail* what it means to be a husband and wife, to build a Jewish home, and to raise children.

While many couples think that they will marry for life, they don't date in a way that prepares for that. A research study asked wives and husbands why they married their spouses. The men replied, "I married my wife hoping that she wouldn't change." The women said, "I married my husband hoping that he would change!" The first rule of marriage should be, "If you can't accept the person the way he or she is, don't marry the person!"

Singles should think about, and discuss, how they expect to change as they grow older and how their spouse-to-be might change. Predicating a marriage on the hope that neither will change, or that one partner will change in the ways that only the other wants, is always risky.

Change/No Change   Yoni was a divorced baal teshuva who lamented, "When I got married, I was going in a certain direction. My ex-wife was going in a different direction. Our paths happened to intersect when we dated. We never thought about the fact that we were going in totally opposite directions. I had left a very turbulent family and expected marriage to bring me peace from all of the conflicts that I had experienced. I didn't want to grow in marriage; I didn't want to change; I just wanted to stay exactly as I was. My ex-wife wanted me to grow just as she was growing. She wanted me to study Torah every day, to work on my immaturity and become more responsible, to communicate better, and to try new experiences. She did all of that in her life, so she assumed that I would do the same. I just wanted to stay where I was and be accepted for being me. We got divorced because I didn't want either of us to change and she wanted both of us to change."

Individual and Premarital Counseling

The system of rapid religious dating and marriage can work quite well when people grow up in comparable environments, have similar expectations of marriage, and grew up in loving homes where their parents had good marriages. Such singles hopefully learned at home how each parent fulfills their role, how couples communicate, and how they solve problems and parent as a team.

Lack of Role Models   None of this can be taken for granted any more. Jewish singles may not come from stable families and may not have healthy relationships with their parents. Their parents may not have had good marriages to serve as models from which the children could learn how to have their own marriages.

Incongruent Expectations   In addition, single males and females often have incongruent expectations of marriage, based on a combination of what they have seen in secular movies and read in secular books, what they have learned in their Judaism classes, and what they saw or found lacking in their parents' marriages.

Fantasy Spouse   Hannah and Yossi were in their late 20s. Each had dated a lot before becoming baal teshuvas. After college, each studied in a religious school for a year, and then a shadchan introduced them to each other. On their first date, they felt instant chemistry with each other. Each talked about their likes and dislikes, their general hopes and dreams about getting married and raising a family, and their love of Judaism. During the next month, they went on another four dates, and they spoke twice each week for an hour on the telephone. Hannah felt good that Yossi was a good listener who cared about her.

On the other hand, Yossi had never had a deep relationship with a woman before. His relationships had always been superficial, even though some lasted for a year or two. This was the first time he had known a woman with whom he could envision raising a family. He proposed to her on their sixth date. She accepted soon afterward, and then began having second thoughts. Some of her teachers and married friends advised her that it was normal to have cold feet before a wedding and urged her to just get married. They reassured her that it would all work out. After all, Yossi was kind, attractive, religious, and had similar goals to hers. What more could she want?

Hannah and Yossi started to argue almost every time they spoke. After confiding their misgivings to psychologically attuned teachers, they were advised to get couple's counseling.

The therapist pointed out that neither Hannah nor Yossi actually admired nor loved who the other was. Each hoped the other would be different. They had fallen in love with their fantasy of a perfect spouse. Hannah wanted Yossi to be a spiritual giant whom she could put on a pedestal. He wanted Hannah to be a warm, stay-at-home Mom that he had never had, despite the fact that she hated to cook and expected him to share domestic responsibilities with her.

Fortunately, they broke off their engagement and got psychother-apy to work out their individual emotional issues. By the time they resumed dating other people, they were older and wiser. Each later married someone who was far better suited to them than Hannah and Yossi were to each other.

Emotional Maturity   The world is much more complex than it used to be. Many singles today have lots of emotional baggage and it takes time to get to really know someone's strengths and challenges. Some baal teshuvas need to date for six months or more before de-ciding if they should get engaged, while some religious singles need only a few dates to believe that they have found the right person to marry. It is better to spend more time getting to know someone and creating a firm foundation for a marriage than it is to marry hastily and spend a lifetime regretting it.

Baal teshuvas often make many religious changes, but they do not necessarily grow emotionally at the same pace at which they become observant. Getting married because it's the frum thing to do, or because one's biological clock is ticking, doesn't repair the underly-ing emotional obstacles to a healthy marriage. Some need emotional healing and help overcoming emotional problems before they can have good marriages and/or be good parents. Getting psychothera-py and doing the emotional work necessary to have a healthy mar-riage also impacts positively on one's religious observance. Overall, getting therapy for depression, anxiety, poor self-esteem, unhealthy anger, authority problems, and decision-making difficulties, and learning how to be organized, manage time well, and set and reach goals, can have very positive effects on one's life.

Vague and Unsure   Ralph was a man who got infatuated with ideas, new situations, and new people, and soon became un-infat-uated. Surprisingly, he became observant in his early 20s and stuck with it. By age 30, he had dated about 50 religious women, but none went out with him for long. He was attractive but vague and unsure about his future plans. After attending three universities, he finally earned a master's degree in a field in which he could not get work.

He moved from job to job, working for six different employers between high school and age 32. After leaving his last dead-end job, he enrolled in a full-time yeshiva. He assured his dates that he would leave yeshiva and work full time when he got married, but women sensed that he was not very stable. It wasn't until Ralph's spiritual advisor told him to get professional help that he understood that his problems would not simply go away with age or by talking to friends and mentors.

Therapy helped him understand why he had bounced around so much in his life, and why he got infatuated with ideas, jobs, and women and then lost interest. The reality of those people or situations never lived up to his fantasies. Therapy helped him learn to tolerate some "boredom" and to develop realistic expectations and meaningful long-term goals. It also helped him to grow up and prepare for marriage. Two years after starting therapy, Ralph had set realistic goals for his future and got happily married.

Wise people recognize when they have emotional issues to work through and then get the help they need. Or as one patient, Sally, put it, "Right now, I feel burdened by all of my emotional baggage. My goal is to get it down to a carry-on!"

Sally spent the next year working out her emotional issues and it made all the difference in the world—her self-esteem improved, she got a job that she loved, her relationship with God became more fulfilling, she had fewer conflicts with her parents and friends, and she was able to date in a way that led to getting married.

Matchmakers

Baal teshuvas sometimes expect that friends or matchmakers who set them up on dates will have almost magical powers. Some singles hope that after a shadchan (matchmaker) meets them for 5-45 minutes that the matchmaker will find them their mate. Amazingly enough, that does sometimes happen. On the other hand, singles sometimes expect too much of shadchans, including that the latter should know everything about the people whom they introduce to one another or that they should know people who don't exist.

Matchmakers are only human. Some are much better at making matches and understanding singles' pluses and minuses than others are. Many are quite altruistic, really try to help, and are very successful at putting appropriate people together, while others are not.

Check It Out   No one should depend on others to find out everything they need to know about a potential mate. Shadchans or other referring people may hear, and may say, misleading or inaccurate information about the people they set up. Singles should always do their own background searches and get references about someone whom they will consider marrying.

Nasty Temper   Erica was a 30-year-old baal teshuva. She was happy, emotionally stable, and financially secure. She wanted to find a husband who would be attentive and warm like her own father had been. She went to a shadchan who suggested a "great guy" for her. He had a lucrative job and seemed open and warm. He was divorced, but was a terrific father to his son. He was attractive and solidly religious—in short, he was a great catch.

After Erica dated Jonathan for two months, he divulged to her that he had been abused as a child and that he had been clinically depressed for years. He had taken medication since his divorce but had been "fine" ever since. Erica researched the medication that he took and read that it had some disturbing side effects. When she asked him about it, Jonathan admitted that he experienced those complications. Erica also found out that Jonathan had a nasty temper with women—which was why his ex-wife had divorced him.

Erica went back to the shadchan and asked if she knew that Jonathan took medication, that he saw a psychiatrist every week, and that he had a bad temper. The shadchan admitted that she did. Erica asked why she had never mentioned it to her.

The shadchan replied, "Those things wouldn't be important to some women. They would only care about the fact that he is frum, a good provider, and a good father."

What a sad comment on how some people view marriage!

Some singles get angry at matchmakers for setting them up on dates with people who are clearly inappropriate for them. While singles should be appreciative of volunteers who work hard to do a thankless job, it is best not to go back to individuals who can't help them.

Serious Flaws   If a date has serious flaws (which may only be apparent on a date), the person who was set up should mention those to the shadchan. Otherwise, the shadchan may not know about these problems.

When a shadchan hears that someone has a serious problem, she should either not set that person up, or she should inform the person she is trying to set up and offer the option to decline. Ideally, a shadchan who hears that a person has serious issues should use that knowledge to help the person improve when possible, or recommend someone who can help them if the person is open to changing. Interviewing someone for all of 20 to 30 minutes, when the interviewee is on his or her best behavior, does not allow most shadchans to know someone well.

Own Preferences   A shadchan's recommendations sometimes say more about their own preferences than about what the single person is seeking. A single woman complained to a shadchan that the man she set her up with was obese and unattractive. When the single woman met the shadchan's husband, who looked unkempt and was 60 pounds overweight, she understood why the shadchan didn't think that the date's obesity and grooming were problems!

Discussing Religious Dating with Parents

Baal teshuvas have the opportunity to learn about, and adjust to, religious dating. Their parents often know nothing about what this entails. Unless parents are overly controlling or hate Judaism, *baal teshuvas* should generally explain to their parents the process and rationale of religious dating when the *baal teshuva* first starts going out.

Don't tell parents in your first conversations about religious dating that you will not touch the person whom you marry until after the wedding ceremony.

Don't tell parents (or anyone else) about every date you go on. Be vague about details until the right person comes along.

Don't give more information about your dating than your parents can handle. Otherwise, you may unnecessarily upset them, or they may give you unwanted advice.

Someone dating one person seriously should update parents a few times along the way. If a couple is moving toward engagement, they should let their parents know that they are serious about someone they are dating. They can give a few details about what the person is like and what they cherish about them.

Parents will want to be the first to know when their child gets engaged, even though one's rabbi or religious advisors might actually know earlier. It hurts parents to find out that their child told rabbis, teachers, and friends before the parents. When a couple gets engaged, they should keep it as private as possible until the parents are informed.

Parents normally want to meet the fiancé before their child announces their engagement. Making the effort to respect parents' feelings in this area can set the stage for family harmony in the future.

Parental Disapproval of a Spouse

Jewish law says that children may marry their desired spouse if their parents disapprove. Children may also move to Israel over their parents' objections.

Legitimate Concerns   Still, it is worth thinking about, and discussing with a spiritual advisor and/or a couples' therapist, whether parents have valid objections to a child's marital plans. A parent may be concerned that the fiancé is unable to support a family, is unstable, has a mean streak, or has traits that aren't compatible with their child's personality—or that the couple doesn't know each other well. The parent could also believe that his or her own child is too immature, unstable, or irresponsible to get married. Worries that an intended spouse is abusive, has emotional problems, is not responsible, doesn't relate to their child with warmth and respect, has no direction or goals in life, or lacks maturity should be taken seriously and given due consideration.

Less-Legitimate Concerns Some objections are not as legitimate.

Observant for Life For example, some parents will say that their child is too young to be married because he or she is in his or her early 20s, yet the child may be quite mature and responsible. It is important to know if the parents' real objections are that their child is marrying someone who is observant. Their objections about age, maturity, career plans, personality, and so on may merely be covering up their true concerns. The fact that a baal teshuva is going to stay observant for the rest of his or her life and this choice will be sealed by marrying another equally "fanatic" Jew is not a good reason for the couple not to get married.

"Right" Some parents object to one's choice of partner because no one will ever be good enough for their child. Others object because the spouse-to-be doesn't fit the parents' image of "the right" son- or daughter-in-law. Some parents will only welcome an academic, a doctor, a professional, a wealthy person, and so on into the family. Anyone who does not fit that bill is regarded as inappropriate for his or her child.

Longer Dating/Earlier Earning Secular parents sometimes expect their child to date a lot of people and to date their future spouse for at least a year or two before getting engaged. Some believe that studying in a yeshiva or seminary for the first year or two of marriage is irresponsible because that is when a couple should start building a career or a nest egg. A wise advisor may be able to reassure the parents, mediate between them and their child, or do reality testing as needed to allay their fears.

Negligence   Some parents object to their child's choice of spouse because the parents were not involved in the process of selecting him or her. Such parents are understandably hurt. They may wonder why their child didn't think enough of them to ask their opinion and consult with them along the way. There are times when children are negligent in not generally apprising their parents about the fact that they are dating. However, such omissions can be necessary and appropriate with overly intrusive and manipulative parents who might devise ways of trying to delay or sabotage plans to get engaged.

Abruptness   Baal teshuvas need to be sensitive to how shocking it can be for a secular American parent to hear that their child has decided to spend the rest of their life with someone they have dated for only a few weeks or months! Many parents, though, will warm up to the marriage if they have time to come to terms with this abrupt, life-changing decision.

Although it is difficult for engaged, observant couples to wait to get married, extending the engagement period by a few weeks can sometimes buy enough time to mitigate the parents' objections and help them adjust to their child's seemingly abrupt decision. This is especially true when their child gets engaged to someone whom the parents have never seen. The parents may want time to meet their future son- or daughter-in-law and his or her family and get used to the idea that this person will be their child's life-long partner. It is sometimes important to get married later than one wants in order to accommodate a parent's prior plans, work, or vacation schedule. A religious advisor's guidance in such matters can be very helpful.

Future Gains   Orly and Art were baal teshuvas living in Jerusalem for five years. Orly's mother Lillian lived in New York and was very intrusive. Lillian felt hurt that Orly had decided to put boundaries between them and would only discuss superficial topics with her. When Orly dated Art, she only told her mother general information about him—that she was dating someone who was religious, 28 years old, attractive, and in a graduate program for Jewish studies. When they were ready to get engaged after nearly five months of dating, Orly asked her parents to visit her in Jerusalem. The second day of their visit, Orly invited her parents to join Art and her for dinner at a kosher restaurant. The evening went reasonably well. As they ate dessert, Orly told her parents that she and Art planned to get married.

Lillian asked if they had a date in mind, expecting Orly to have at least a year-long engagement. It was three weeks before Passover, and Orly announced that she hoped that they would get married on Lag B'Omer, a holiday that was a mere eight weeks away.

Her mother nearly choked on her dessert. Two months wasn't enough time to plan a wedding!

Orly indicated that if they didn't get married on Lag B'Omer, they would have to wait until after Shavuot (a holiday seven weeks after Passover that celebrates the Jews' receiving the Torah) to get married. That wouldn't work because Art's parents had booked a trip in June that they had waited two years to take. It had been difficult for Art's mother to arrange to take off that much time from work and to find someone to take care of her infirm mother. If Art's parents cancelled this vacation, they would lose thousands of dollars and the opportunity to take their dream trip for the foreseeable future.

Orly's father could not get away from work in July. He was an architect who covered for his partners during the summer. The partners worked out their vacations and holiday schedules a year in advance.

Orly and Art couldn't get married for the first half of August because of the Three Weeks, a time of mourning when weddings aren't held. They didn't want to wait nearly five months to get married, yet it was clear that getting married when they wanted would cause terrible frictions with someone's parents. Meanwhile, the couple hadn't even discussed with her parents setting a convenient wedding date! Rather than argue over dinner, Orly decided to discuss this with her religious advisor.

Her advisor spoke to both sets of parents, and then told Orly her opinion. Much to Orly's surprise, her advisor urged the couple to get married in late August. That compromise set the stage for both sets of parents' feeling good about their children's marriage. Taking the parents' feelings into consideration led to more harmonious relationships in the long run for everyone involved.

Have In-Laws, Not Outlaws

Appearance of Normalcy   Since parents' first impressions of a future son- or daughter-in-law are very important, it can be wise to plan the first meeting. A fiancé should look and sound as "normal" as possible and act in ways that make a good impression. Choose a comfortable venue in which to meet and wear clean, attractive clothes. It may be better for a man to wear a cap instead of a yarmulke at a casual venue. If the parents are meeting the prospective son-in-law at a fancy restaurant, he should wear a nice suit with an unobtrusive yarmulke and leave the hat at home if it's not cold weather.

Parents want to see that their child is marrying someone who looks normal, talks normally, and dresses normally. Peppering the conversation with Hebrew or Yiddish words does not go over well. (This same advice applies to any conversation between observant and non-observant people.) Try to make sure that you use English equivalents of words like *chasunah* (wedding), *chupah* (wedding canopy), *chassan* (groom), *kallah* (bride), *frum* (observant), *sheva brachas* (nightly celebrations after the wedding), and other foreign terms when you speak to your parents.

Appreciation   Although children often worry about making a good impression on their parents, parents may be just as anxious to make a good impression on the new addition to their family! Let your future in-laws know that you like and admire them and that they have made a good impression on you. Also let them know what a great job they did raising their child.

Warmth   Parents will want to see that, despite not touching each other, there is great warmth between their child and the future spouse, and they seem happy and comfortable with each other.

Good Husband/Wife Most parents will want to know that a daughter-in-law will nurture their son, be able to run a household, and be a good mother. They will want to know that a future son-in-law will treat their daughter well and earn a living. Saying vague things to parents such as, "Well, we think that we should learn more Torah and then we're sure that some kind of job will come along" will not reassure parents. If the son-in-law doesn't have a realistic means of making a living, nor plans to work soon, the couple should discuss before they get engaged when and how this will change after they get married! Parents are sure to ask about it.

Conversation Try not to let the tenor of the conversation get too heavy. You can break the ice by sharing a few jokes or funny stories.

Apprise your fiance about what topics can be discussed and which topics may be touchy. Don't let the conversation just be about the fiancé. We tend to think that others are scintillating conversationalists when they ask us about ourselves, so make sure to show interest in your future in-laws—their interests, what they do, how they met, and so on. Talk about the mother-in-law's gourmet cooking, her career, and her good taste in home decorating. Ask the father-in-law what he thinks will happen with the stock market, about his job, and who he's rooting for in sports this season.

It never hurts for a man to say to his future mother-in-law, "Now I see where your daughter gets her good looks from!"

Avoid discussing politics or religion. If a parent persists in asking about something controversial, it is best not to talk about it. For example, you might say, "Dad, I really don't know enough about that topic to discuss it. I'd prefer to talk about some of the wonderful experiences that we had. Ken loves to hear stories about our family and me. Remember that amazing summer when we went to Bear Lake? Tell Ken the story of our hiking along that trail when we ran into that moose…" Or, "We'll have plenty of time to talk about Judaism after we've all had a chance to get to know each other." Don't get baited into discussing hot topics such as whether you will have children immediately, whether you and your children will spend Jewish holidays in your parents' home, how religious Jews treat women like second-class citizens, and whether or not Aunt Joelle will do her famous belly-dancing at your wedding. These topics will only lead to conflict. There will be time enough in the future for those discussions.

If parents keep pressing a couple for details about how religious they plan to be, a vague and reassuring response is best: "We want to be religious in a normal, healthy way. As we work out the details, we'll keep you posted. It's important for us to have as good a relationship as possible with everyone in our families."

Religious Mentors   Around this time it is good if your rav and/ or rebbetzin meet the parents. These experts can help allay the parents' concerns and explain what will happen from the time of engagement until the sheva brachas. They can also make sure that the parents participate in as much of the planning process as is feasible so that they don't feel like outsiders during this very special time. Children, and their religious advisors, have to make sure that parents don't feel supplanted by religious figures in their relationship with their children, even if the children spend much more time with their religious mentors and have closer relationships with them than they do with their parents.

Wedding Clashes

Perfect Wedding   Mothers and daughters dream for years about having a perfect wedding. Yet, parents and their baal teshuva children may have very different ideas about the kind of wedding each wants. Religious or not, almost every couple has to compromise with parents about these issues. Even though society stresses having "the perfect wedding," couples must not lose sight of the fact that the next 50 years of marriage will be much more important than whether the chupah was decorated with white roses or with chrysanthemums and whether the guests were served prime rib or chicken. It can be worthwhile giving in about issues such as esthetics, or how many guests are invited, in order to have greater harmony with your parents. Choosing your battles well and compromising now will set the stage for the many compromises that every couple needs to make for each other and with their parents later.

Pre-Wedding Soon after they get engaged, couples should meet with their rav or mesader kiddushin (the rabbi marrying them). They should ask him how he recommends that they carry out the pre-wedding and wedding rituals. These begin with a vort, or engagement party, attended by the couple's close relatives and friends. The men will "toast" the new couple and share Torah ideas. On Shabbos before the wedding, the bride has a Shabbos Kallah: Her friends keep her company and enjoy refreshments or a third Shabbos meal together. Shabbos morning before the wedding, the groom has an aufruf (he is honored by being called up to the Torah and attendees at the service throw candy at him). He or his family usually sponsor a kiddush afterward.

Observant couples have a formal betrothal ceremony called *tannaim*, which is usually held just prior to the wedding ceremony. Since the people involved may have different ideas about how to conduct various rituals, and who should participate, the rabbi should advise the couple about what to do.

The following are some of the questions that couples should ask their rabbi:

Seating Can men and women sit next to each other at the wedding ceremony? At the reception? Some weddings have three areas at the reception—men on one side of a physical divider (mechitzah), women on the other side, and the remaining guests at tables with both men and women. Some weddings have men and women seated together throughout, with separate dancing for men and women. Many weddings have separate seating for the wedding and the reception.

Dress Should the couple urge the women who will attend or be in the procession to dress modestly?

Walk Down the Aisle   Who should walk the bride and groom down to the wedding canopy? Sometimes, both fathers walk with the groom and both mothers walk with the bride. At other weddings, the parents walk with their child. A *baal teshuva* whose parents have no relationship with him or her may have a rabbi, rebbetzin, or religious advisors walk with them.

Honors   Which family members and friends can recite blessings under the chupah, recite blessings for the sheva brachas at the end of the meal, or be witnesses to the marriage? Which honors can be given to family members who are non-observant or non-Jewish, including the bride's or groom's parents, close uncles, or half-siblings?

Non-Jewish Participants   How should they handle a relative who expects to be called up to the Torah at the aufruf who wasn't born Jewish and who had a Reform conversion? Can non-Jewish relatives be part of the wedding procession?

Excluding a Parent   Can, or should, a parent who is mentally unstable or who is abusive to the child be excluded from the wedding?

Mixed Dancing   How should a couple handle a parent's insistence that there be mixed dancing and disco music?

Social Touching   How can the couple preempt, or minimize, the social hugging and kissing that normally occurs at such a family celebration?

Consulting a rav before planning a wedding or discussing the wedding details with parents can avoid a great deal of grief.

Catholic Mom   A Catholic young man decided to convert to Judaism. He studied at a baal teshuva yeshiva, became Jewish, and got engaged to a baal teshuva. They planned to get married in Israel and made their wedding arrangements without notifying his mother. Since she was a devout Catholic, the couple's teachers assumed that it would be inappropriate to invite her to participate in his wedding ceremony.

When his mother received a wedding invitation in the mail, she was humiliated and outraged. She flew to Israel and announced to him, "I didn't fly 7,000 miles to be a guest at my son's wedding."

The teachers didn't quite know how to handle her. She dressed in flamboyant, immodest clothes and wore a huge crucifix around her neck. They finally asked a renowned posek what to do.

"Where does it say in the *Code of Jewish Law* that a gentile mother may not walk her son down to the wedding canopy?" he responded.

It had never occurred to any of the teachers to allow this. It took someone who was a Torah giant and objective about the situation to give this advice.

The humbled teachers relayed the news to the son. Someone convinced the mother not to wear her crucifix that day and she ecstatically walked her beloved son down the aisle on his way to getting married.

After the Wedding

Unanticipated Changes   Baal teshuvas almost invariably marry other baal teshuvas. They often have much in common with each other, including the same frame of reference. They are familiar with the pluses and minuses of the secular world; have similar backgrounds, families, and religious journeys; and share a special enthusiasm for Judaism.

At the same time, they are more likely than people who have always been observant to change in ways that a partner can't anticipate. That can be healthy if it is done in the right way, but it can also be done in unhealthy ways that can lead to marital problems. Proper rabbinic guidance should be sought in meshing a married person's path to Yiddishkeit with that of their spouse.

Stringencies   Some baal teshuvas take on more religious stringencies after marriage. Some specifically choose a partner who is more stringent than they are to make sure they will grow. This can be fine if each partner is aware of expectations and is comfortable with the stringencies and the customs that will impact on their marriage.

There can be many motivations for choosing the most stringent way of life possible. Some want to serve God without compromise. Others view life as all or nothing, black and white. Others are afraid of making mistakes and don't know enough to choose appropriate boundaries and rules. Others have reached an intense level of religious commitment where only the most stringent level of observance allows them to reach their spiritual pinnacle.

Adopting stringencies must be balanced against a concept in Judaism called "religious arrogance." Some stringencies and practices are inappropriate for people who are not at that level of observance. Too, there are times when someone "grows" at their partner's or children's expense. This can lead to marital conflict, and in such cases domestic harmony requires *not* unilaterally adopting customs or stringencies. In general, married people should adopt stringencies that affect their spouse only after discussing it with their spouse and their rabbi.

Stringent Instead of Sensitive   Avi and Ettie got married. He was starting a business and she was supporting them on her librarian's salary. When they dated, he never told her that he expected after marriage to become more stringent in his religious observances.

When they moved into their first apartment, he asked his rabbi if they had to throw out the oven that had been used by prior tenants. Avi (who was normally very frugal) was pleased when his rav said that it would be best to buy a new oven. Avi never mentioned to the rav that Ettie was supporting them and that she would have to pay for it out of her savings.

When Ettie mistakenly cooked chicken in a dairy baking dish, Avi asked the rav what to do. The rav told Avi that they could eat the food and use the dish under certain circumstances. Avi decided that the rav was too lenient and he refused to eat his wife's cooking. This upset her greatly.

He frequently arrived home minutes before Shabbos began. This made Ettie nervous. She wanted a calm atmosphere when she lit the Shabbos candles and needed help getting everything ready in time.

Avi's "stringencies" were misplaced. He should have been less focused on creating his own standards of kashrut and more concerned with being sensitive to his wife, listening to his rabbi, and working out his emotional problems that interfered with his marriage. Were he as scrupulous in creating harmony with his wife as he was in keeping kosher, Ettie would have been happy to support his stringencies.

Jews should parallel adopting ritual stringencies with improving their character, working on their emotional problems, relating better to people, and developing healthy attitudes toward God and their fellow Jew. Adopting religious stringencies should never be an excuse to think of oneself as "holier than thou" or to treat others who are less stringent as beneath us.

Supervising Jonathan and Miriam got married a few months before Passover. As the holiday approached, Jonathan supervised as Miriam cleaned. He checked up after she finished cleaning each room to see that everything was spotless. After Miriam spent all day shopping in a kosher-for-Passover store, Jonathan checked each food item to make sure that it had acceptable rabbinic supervision. When he found three products that did not have the stringent supervision that he preferred, he gave them back to Miriam and told her to return them.

Miriam was very upset by Jonathan's holier-than-thou attitude and asked his rav to speak to him. The rav told Jonathan that he should be cleaning along with his wife, not supervising her. If he didn't want to eat certain products, he should exchange them at the store himself.

Marrying a More (or Less) Observant Spouse

Less-Observant Spouse Sometimes religious singles are introduced to potential mates who are not as observant as they are, yet they are compatible in many other ways. They then wonder if their religious differences are too big to bridge or if they can have a successful marriage despite these differences.

Singles have to be realistic about how their religious differences will affect their marriage and their children. It is possible to have a good marriage with someone who is good marriage material, who is less observant than the other person, provided that he or she respects their partner's religious observance, and is willing to keep kosher, observe Shabbos and holidays, and follow the laws of family holiness. The couple also needs to agree about how the children will be raised and how each parent will present their religious outlook to their children.

More-Observant Spouse   Some baal teshuvas believe that an observant life with great self-discipline will help them on their path to spiritual self-actualization. Some become chareidi or Chassidic and try to find a spouse who shares that ideal. But it is one thing to admire how people live in theory and another matter to live the way they live. The only way to know if someone will be comfortable living a more observant lifestyle is to try it for a few months.

Chassidic Fit   Phyllis was a baal teshuva who studied at a modern Orthodox seminary for two years. Much of that time she felt that something was missing in her Yiddishkeit. When she started spending Shabbos in chareidi communities, she felt a depth to Judaism that she lacked elsewhere. She began to observe chareidi stringencies and attended classes in a chareidi seminary. When she went on shidduchim, she only dated chareidi men.

One day, a shadchan introduced her to a Chassidic *baal teshuva*. They had good communication, rapport, and chemistry; similar family backgrounds; and compatible goals. After dating each other for three months, her only reservation about marrying him was whether she could fit into the Chassidic world. She was advised to spend as much time as possible in his community, go to classes and spend Shabbos there, and meet other married *baal teshuvas* her age. She followed this advice and it laid to rest most of her concerns. Two months later, they got engaged. After they got married, it was clear that she had made a good choice and she fit in beautifully in her new community.

Stifled & Devalued   Masha became observant in NCSY at the age of 16. She attended college, then law school, all the while taking Judaism classes wherever she could find them.

In her mid-20s, she met Shmuel. She was "right-wing modern Orthodox" while he was a chareidi FFB who had rabbinical ordination from a well-known yeshiva. He was intrigued by her depth of knowledge about Judaism, albeit disturbed that she was so involved with the secular world. He did not understand, let alone appreciate, how she could listen to secular music, banter with male co-workers, and enjoy romantic novels and secular plays. She loved to hike and camp outdoors, while the closest he got to the great outdoors was sanctifying the new moon once a month. She had a sense of adventure while he preferred predictability and familiarity. Yet, each appreciated that the other was a good listener, could be a trusted friend, had integrity, and would be a good parent.

They dated for a few months and then decided that they needed to spend time in each other's communities. Masha spent a few Shabboses with Shmuel's friends and family and he did the same with hers. Only then did it become apparent how uncomfortable each felt in the other's world. She felt stifled among chareidim while he felt looked-down-upon in her milieu. They realized that their religious differences reflected deeper parts of themselves that neither wanted to change. They decided to break up and seek partners who were more like themselves.

Summary

Deciding whom we will marry is one of the most important decisions that we will ever make. It requires much thoughtful preparation.

Marriage Goals   A baal teshuva should consider why he or she wants to get married, what his or her primary goals are in getting married, and how various potential spouses would or wouldn't complement him or her in achieving these goals.

Building Blocks   Baal teshuvas should not think marriage is easy, or that it "just happens" when the right person comes along. The best preparation for marriage is understanding the building blocks of a successful marriage and practicing them while one is still single. These include good communication, conflict resolution, compromise, and delayed gratification. These issues are discussed in detail in my Guide for the Romantically Perplexed.

Right Age   There is no "right" age to get married. It depends on when one is ready for the responsibilities of marriage and has worked out any detrimental emotional baggage that can interfere with creating harmony and intimacy with a spouse.

Right Person   Secular movies and books often help singles formulate unrealistic ideas about what marriage and the "right" partner should look and be like. There is not one "right" person to marry. Every potential spouse has his or her positives and negatives.

Singles often construct "wish lists" of a spouse based on their emotional wants that were never met. Yet, since no one can make up for the pain or lacks that one suffered in one's childhood, singles should never expect that a spouse will do so.

Finally, the world of religious dating is very foreign to newcomers to observance and to their parents. Taking the time necessary to be comfortable with one's choice of spouse, and helping parents feel comfortable with this choice, may reap benefits that last a lifetime.

TWENTY-TWO

How To Be and Not To Be a Shabbos Guest

One side-benefit of becoming observant is the openness and hospitality of observant Jews to strangers. Non-observant Jews who attend a beginner's service, a religious retreat, or a class on Judaism—or who pray at the Western Wall in Jerusalem—may be asked by a rabbi or teacher, "Would you like to eat a Shabbos meal with a Jewish family?" It is hard for many non-observant Jews to believe that total strangers would want to host them, and that hosts actually enjoy having extra guests for their Shabbos or holiday meals. After all, many Westerners view cooking and cleaning up as a chore. They think that inviting oneself for a meal is imposing on a host.

Finding Hosts Ironically, many observant Jews feel that they can only fully celebrate Shabbos or Jewish holidays if they have guests. Most baal teshuvas studying in yeshivas or seminaries soon discover that many people are happy to host them for meals and even have them sleep over. All students need to do is to ask their school's principal or their teachers for referrals and they are likely to walk away with a list of names and phone numbers of potential hosts.

Many *baal teshuva* schools have people who routinely place students for Shabbos and holiday meals. Some synagogues do the same for Jews who want to experience Shabbos or Jewish holidays in their community. One can always call the synagogue office or the rabbi of a community and ask.

Some hosts make it known that they are always open to newcomers and don't mind prior guests sharing their phone number with fellow students or friends. Some synagogues' members or rabbi greet every newcomer after Friday night and Saturday morning services and make sure that each person has a place to eat. If you are new to a synagogue and no one has greeted you, make sure to introduce yourself to the rabbi. If you haven't done so during the week, ask if the synagogue has families that host guests for Shabbos or holiday meals if you would like to experience that. He might even be delighted to host you and your family himself.

Not-yet-observant Jews who want to experience Shabbos or holiday meals with a host family in Jerusalem can call Jeff Seidel's Jewish Student Information Center (02-628-2634). They can also show up near the water fountain at the back of the men's section at the Kotel about an hour after candle-lighting on Friday nights and holiday evenings, or at 11 am on Saturday mornings and get placed.

A Jerusalem hostel called Heritage House has a prime location in the Old City, with separate quarters for men and women, and the price can't be beat. It is free.

Accommodating Guests   At first, it is uncomfortable for Jews who are becoming observant to call hosts out of the blue and ask if they can come for a meal and/or to sleep over. It takes time to get used to this. Eventually, though, not-yet-observant Jews learn that it is a great pleasure for religious families to host them and that even large religious families regularly host strangers. Some children willingly give up their rooms or double-up with siblings so that they can participate in the wonderful commandment of offering hospitality to guests.

While every Jew is obligated to be hospitable to other Jews, that doesn't mean that *baal teshuvas* should take this for granted. Many hostesses have large families and spend two or more days every week shopping, cooking, serving, and cleaning up after festival, Shabbos, and High Holiday meals. If guests sleep over, there are also extra linens and towels to wash. Being a guest should always be done with sensitivity and appreciation for the great effort involved on the part of the host family. Here are some guidelines about how to be a guest whom host families will enjoy having over:

Do's

1. **Call**   Call a potential host early in the week and ask if it is convenient for them to have you that Friday night, Saturday lunch, or upcoming holiday. Most religious women have prepared their menus, invited their guests, and shopped by Wednesday or Thursday for Shabbos.

2. **Help Cook**   Find out if your hostess has someone to help her cook. If not, ask if there is a time when it would be convenient for you to come and help her.

3. **Food/Gifts**   Ask what you can bring. If the hostess says "Nothing," you can ask the person who gave you her number what the family likes and bring it over Friday afternoon. It is forbidden to carry on Shabbos in an area that is not enclosed by an eruv. If there is no eruv, or you do not live within your host's eruv (you can ask her), do not bring anything to them on Shabbos. One may carry some objects on Jewish holidays in an area that does not have an eruv, but not phones, wallets, money, or items whose use is forbidden on holy days. If you want to bring your host's children presents of battery-operated toys, paints, pencils, or art kits, you must bring them before or after, but not on, Shabbos or Jewish holidays.

Before bringing hosts a gift, ask them if what you plan to bring is okay. Do not bring your host homemade foods, desserts, snacks, or wine that lack acceptable rabbinical supervision. If you don't know which supervision is acceptable to your host, ask.

Some families do not drink wine or alcoholic beverages, and others may not like the kinds that you like. Ask about their preferences, or if they would prefer kosher sparkling or regular grape juice instead.

Always ask before assuming that it would be nice to give a book as a thank-you present. Your taste in books may not suit the family.

Personal Art   An artist brought host families beautiful greeting cards that she had made. Her hosts were touched that she had shared something so personal with them. They appreciated that more than if she had brought a bottle of wine or flowers.

Organic Snacks   A guest showed that she appreciated her host's tastes when she bought them some organic snacks. Before doing so, she made sure that the rabbinical supervision on the package was acceptable to them. The guest knew that the mother didn't like feeding her family junk food, and the gift was much appreciated.

Don't just bring the cheapest bottle of kosher wine that you can find—put a little thought into what you bring, just as the family is putting thought and effort into hosting you.

4. **Arrival Time**   Ask the hostess when she would like you to arrive. Be on time. Don't come earlier than the time she recommends because religious homes are usually very hectic as families prepare for Shabbos or Jewish holidays.

5. **Linens**   If you are staying over someone's house in Israel, ask the hostess if you should bring your own linens and towel. If your bed isn't made up when you arrive, ask if you can make it yourself.

6. **Help**   When you arrive, ask the hostess how you can best be of help—keeping the children occupied, helping set the table, working in the kitchen, (for women) keeping the hostess company, or keeping out of the way.

7. **Home & Play** If the hostess has young children and doesn't ask you to help, play with the children if the parents are too busy or too tired to give them attention.

8. **Park & Play** If you are with a family Saturday afternoon, offer to take the children to a park or play with them after lunch so that the parents can take a nap. That is the only time that many parents have a chance to catch up on their rest.

9. **Listener** Be a good listener at the table.

10. **Family First** Be sensitive to your hosts. If they seem tired or the hour is late, don't keep talking or asking questions. Shabbos is the only time when many families can spend time together and parents can get a good night's sleep.

Religious parents normally value Shabbos as an opportunity to spend special time with their children. Even though many families are hospitable, they still need to juggle giving their (many) children individual attention and interacting with their guests. This can be very difficult, especially when children are not well-behaved, parents are exhausted, a child is not feeling well or has special needs, and so on. Don't expect that you will be the focus of the meal. Some hosts are more able to give guests attention than others. Above all, don't criticize the way that your hosts are raising their family or running their home. If you aren't happy there, don't go back again.

Host families should put their family first and may not have as much time to focus on guests as some would like. Hopefully, you will learn from host families how difficult it can be to be a great host, parent, spouse, religious Jew—all at the same time. Also notice how people do this well. You can learn from what you like and don't like how to prepare yourself to do a good job when you are in similar shoes.

11. **Be Mindful** If families will eat leftovers from Shabbos during the next few days, don't take so much food that there won't be any extra. If there are just enough servings of a dish

for the number of people at the table, don't take more than one helping. Make sure that your host family has enough.

12. **Clean-Up**   During the meal, offer once to serve and clean up and don't help if it is not wanted. Some hosts will welcome help; many will prefer that you stay out of their kitchen. More than one well-meaning guest has cleaned up when the hosts did not want them to and has *treifed* up (made non-kosher) the host's kitchen or has broken expensive china or crystal. Some guests, when told not to make the bed or strip off the sheets from a bed or sleep sofa, have torn the sheets by getting them caught on bed frames.

13. **Good Table Manners**   Use a napkin. Don't eat with your fingers, lick your fingers, or eat off your knife. Take food with a serving utensil, not with your fingers or with a utensil that you have eaten from.

14. **Compliments**   Compliment the hostess (or host, if he did the cooking).

15. **Thank-You Note**   Mail the family a thank-you note or make a follow-up phone call the next day telling them what a nice time you had. If you stay over, you can write the note before you leave after Shabbos ends and leave it on your bed.

16. **Surprises**   If you are a frequent guest at someone's house, do something special for them from time to time. Buy the hostess a large bouquet of her favorite flowers (if no one in the family is allergic to them). Offer to help clean for Passover. Notice something that the hostess is missing, or that the family likes, and surprise them with it.

Something Special   Raphael knew that a family who often hosted him liked a particular brand of chocolate. He always brought it to them when he ate there.

Two friends often ate with a family who owned an unattractive washing cup. After eating many meals with the family, the young women brought them a beautiful cup to replace the one they had.

Four yeshiva boys frequented Mimi's house for Shabbos meals. They called her three weeks before Passover and asked if they could clean her kitchen for Passover. She gladly accepted the offer. That was the best gift of all.

Michael was a great Shabbos guest. He went to a special bakery and bought the kind of chocolate cake that his hosts especially liked. He always came to the meals on time and complimented the hostess on her cooking. He left the table for 10 or 15 minutes when the young children got restless and sat on the sofa reading them stories about Amelia Bedelia. When his parents came to town, he introduced them to his hosts and told them how lucky he was to have such great friends. Years later, the host family still remembers Michael as a guest who always added to their Shabbos pleasure.

Don't's

» **Don't** accept an invitation for a meal and then cancel because you changed your mind or a better offer came up.

» **Don't** call potential hosts later than 10 pm. Call before 9 pm if people retire early.

» **Don't** invite yourself for a meal and then ask if your three friends can come, too. Be up-front when you call about how many of you want to eat together. Unless you know that someone doesn't mind, don't ask for an invitation for more than two individuals or one family at a time.

» **Don't** ask the hostess if you can talk about a complicated personal problem for a few minutes after the meal. It is sure to take far longer. Instead, ask the host or hostess if there is a time when it would be convenient to discuss some questions that have been on your mind.

» **Don't** only talk about yourself.

» **Don't** tell off-color jokes. Don't talk about sex, drugs, violence, and other topics that are not appropriate for children (even if there aren't any children present) at the meal. Such topics are not conducive to creating a spiritual Shabbos atmosphere.

» **Don't** discuss overly personal topics that will make others uncomfortable.

» **Don't** insult other groups. Don't discuss politics, unless your host brings it up.

» **Don't** dominate the conversation or interrupt others when they are speaking.

» **Don't** sing loudly if you sing off-key.

» **Don't** flirt with members of the host's family or with other guests at the table.

» **Don't** be the last person to finish eating.

» **If** you are ill and still want to come for a meal, call the hostess Friday morning and let her know that you are not feeling well. Let her decide if she wants you to come nonetheless.

» **Don't** ignore your host and her family and talk only to your friends at a meal.

» **Don't** make your hosts feel used. No one wants to feel like a meal ticket or free hotel.

» **Wait** at least a month before asking a woman who gave birth if you can come for a meal. Call during that time and ask if there is something that you can do to help.

Being a Host

One purpose of Judaism is to help us become as God-like as possible. Just as God is a giver, so are we supposed to be. One doesn't have to be married or have been raised religious to do this. Eventually, *baal teshuvas* should learn how to prepare their own Shabbos and holiday meals and become hosts themselves.

Get Recipes   After you have been a Shabbos guest a number of times, you can ask a hostess how to host others and to share recipes of foods that you like. It always makes a hostess feel good to ask for her recipes.

You can also buy or borrow one of many good kosher cookbooks or find recipes and menus on websites such as aish.com.

Plan Menu and Shopping   Next, plan a menu. Ask what foods are traditionally served on Shabbos or on various holidays. A hostess can help you make up a shopping list and recommend places to buy the kosher ingredients or the prepared foods that you will need. Ask her how long in advance you should start preparing various foods for the meals, and how long it will take to prepare the foods that you will serve.

Most people shop by Thursday night and start cooking Thursday and/or Friday for Shabbos. Kosher food stores are most crowded on Thursday nights and Fridays because that is when religious people buy most of their food for the coming week and Shabbos. The same occurs a day or two before Jewish holidays. Some women buy their meats and kosher products in a kosher store on Wednesday to avoid the crowds and then buy fresh produce a day or two ahead at a supermarket or green grocer that doesn't have long lines.

Learn To Cook   In today's world of microwave dinners and convenience foods, many people grow up never learning how to cook. You can learn how to prepare Shabbos and festival meals by watching (and helping) a hostess to do it. Ask someone whose meals you enjoy if it would be convenient to watch her prepare Shabbos or holiday meals in her home. Apprenticing can be the best way to learn how to put it all together.

Boxed to Home-Cooked   Chanie grew up in an upper-class suburb of New York. Her mother never cooked. Breakfast was boxed cereal with milk. She bought lunch in the school cafeteria and made herself a snack when she came home. Her mother's culinary repertoire included dinners that she bought at the supermarket appetizing counter, heated frozen TV dinners, warmed frozen vegetables with hamburgers or steak, or Chinese takeout. Her mother also made reservations to eat out on Friday nights.

When Chanie became a *baal teshuva*, she asked a teacher for the name of a hostess who was a good cook. She volunteered to help the hostess make Shabbos meals so that Chanie could learn to do it herself. After spending a few Fridays in the kitchen, Chanie had a good feel for how to make simple but adequate meals.

The Basics   Every Shabbos and Jewish holiday requires having wine or grape juice and bread (or matzah on Passover) for the evening and lunch meals. People who like freshly baked bread but who don't have much time can use a bread-making machine or buy frozen challah (special braided bread eaten on Shabbos and holidays) dough that is baked at home. Shabbos or holiday bread needn't be a traditional braided challah made from bleached white flour. It can be any rolls or loaves made of any of the five special grains (wheat, spelt, rye, oats, or barley) or any combination of them. Whole grains are fine. Loaves can contain herbs, fried onions, raisins, dried fruit, olives, sun-dried tomatoes, or other condiments that you like. If someone is allergic to gluten, consult a rabbi as to how to replace bread at these meals.

Freezing   Freezing foods can be a great boon. For example, many people who bake their own challah make dough using at least 4.5 pounds of flour so that they can recite a blessing over the commandment to take challah (a piece of dough that was once given to Jewish priests but is now burned) from the dough. If they eat only two or three loaves one Shabbos, they can freeze the extras for the following Shabbos.

Some women like to cook large quantities of soup, main courses, and kugels (noodle, potato, or vegetable puddings), then freeze half of what they make. They defrost those portions when they have a very hectic Friday or want to spend less time cooking another week.

Offering hospitality is not only for women. Some men are wonderful cooks and hosts.

Favorite Host   Marty became a baal teshuva in his late 20s. A few years later, he rarely went out for his Shabbos meals. He either hosted families who had hosted him or he invited other singles to his house. When he was too busy to cook, he bought kosher take-out food. When he had time, he went food shopping after work on Thursdays and cooked a gourmet meal on Thursday evenings and/or Fridays after work. He soon became a favorite host in his neighborhood.

Summary

Shabbos is a special gift that God gave the Jewish people. Eating Shabbos meals in religious Jewish homes can be a wonderful experience, both gastronomically and spiritually. It is an opportunity for many *baal teshuvas* to really experience Judaism with a Jewish family in a traditional environment and to get to know observant Jews as people, rather than as classmates or teachers. With a bit of knowledge, planning, and sensitivity on the part of *baal teshuvas*, it can be a positive experience for hosts as well.

TWENTY-THREE

Modesty

Among the most difficult issues for Jews who are becoming *baal teshuvas* to grapple with are those involving relationships between the sexes and modesty.

The Jewish laws of modesty require women to wear clothes with necklines high enough to cover the collarbone, with sleeves that reach the elbows, and whose hems cover the knee. Married women are required to cover their hair with a hat, scarf, wig, or other head covering when they are in the presence of men to whom they aren't married.[1] Many observant women also wear stockings, tights or knee-high socks. Women who do not yet dress modestly should follow the local norms when attending a synagogue or Jewish classes, or when visiting the homes or neighborhood of religious Jews.

Religious Jewish males wear a hat, cap or skullcap, a four-cornered undergarment (called an *arba kanfot* or *tzitzit,* although the latter term actually refers to the fringes) with specially knotted fringes tied through its corners. Many men wear short- or long-sleeved shirts and slacks or pants. For exercising or swimming, many wear baggy longish shorts, swim trunks, or sweat pants, rather than clothes that are tight or revealing.[2] A man should wear a head covering and pants (not shorts) when attending Jewish classes, a synagogue, or when

visiting the homes or neighborhood of religious Jews. In such mi-
lieux, neither men nor women should wear clothes that are revealing,
or that have eye-catching or offensive logos or slogans.

The Philosophy of Modesty

Eschewing modesty is a sign of modern society. Many Westerners believe that if you've got it, flaunt it. Advertisers who want to
sell anything—beer, vodka, cars, boats, vacations, or razor blades—
post a scantily clad, beautiful woman on the ad, and it works! Many
people never think twice about how this kind of bodily display de-
grades women.

Humility/Modesty   The greatest Jew who ever lived, Moses,
was not renowned because he looked like a professional bodybuilder
or great sports player. He was never voted Man-of-the-Year by *Time
Magazine*. He didn't star in any box-office hits (unless you include
his portrayal in the blockbuster movie, *The Ten Commandments*).
When the Torah gives Moses his greatest accolade, it says, "The
man Moses was the most humble of all men." He was the world's
greatest Torah teacher because he didn't let his ego get in the way of
what the Almighty wanted to transmit to him or what he transmitted to the Jewish people.

When the prophet Micah distilled the essence of Judaism into
three principles, modesty was one of them: "What does God ask of
you? Do justice, love doing kind deeds, and walk modestly (humbly)
with your God."[3]

Difficulties   Many women take issue with the Jewish laws of
modesty because they don't see value in covering one's body and
because the laws seem so extreme compared to the way of dress that
they are used to.

"After all," they ask, "what is wrong with a woman wearing sexy
clothes and getting complimented on her looks? She can be valued
for her body and for her personality and brains. What is wrong with
a woman being the center of attention on a stage or dance floor or
being applauded for being a great performer? Why should women

have to inhibit themselves because some men can't control their eyes and their thoughts?"

Vehicles for the Soul   There are many answers to these questions that are beyond the scope of this book, and they can be found in the books, tapes, and websites listed in the Appendix. The general answer to such questions is that the physical world masks a more important spiritual reality. Both men and women are responsible for trying to actualize our spiritual potentials and for helping other Jews to actualize theirs.

The Almighty intended that women should use their physical beauty and ability to attract men in the context of a marital relationship: to intensify an emotional, physical, and spiritual connection with a spouse—not simply to prove they are desirable to a multitude of men. We aren't supposed to use others to enhance our sensual pleasure. Trying to get attention simply to be noticed serves no spiritual purpose. When we look at, and interact with, others, we are supposed to discover their inner beauty—their soul—by hearing what they have to say and seeing their spiritual potential, without being overly distracted by their appearance. Women's dress and comportment should enhance the message that our bodies are vehicles to actualize the soul—a means by which we get closer to God and express the Divine image in ourselves.

Self-Esteem   There is often a relationship between a woman's self-esteem and sense of security and her need to display her body. A woman who feels good about her essence does not need to display her body in order to be noticed and admired by others. She will feel good about herself and her relationship with God regardless of whether or not others notice her and think she is beautiful. Unfortunately, far too many girls and women are raised equating their worth with how attractive they are. The media and secular society value mostly how sexy a woman is, and don't attribute much importance to women's spiritual accomplishments. Studies have shown that more than 89 percent of American women at some time are dissatisfied with their looks.[4] Western culture's emphasis on appearances results in people treating attractive people better than they treat those who are plain-looking or unattractive.[5]

Healthy self-esteem should not depend on how others "rate" our looks. It should come from valuing the Divine image and unique soul that we each have. Our bodies are important because they allow us to actualize our souls. We are not supposed to think that our contours are important in their own right.

Responding to Relatives   How can baal teshuvas respond to relatives who criticize or question their modest way of dressing and behaving? The answer depends upon whether the other person really wants to understand the baal teshuva's behavior or is simply making a statement.

When people question religious people's behavior, it is initially best not to give a lot of details. One can respond to others' feelings or give a summary answer that is sensible and to the point. If the questioner sincerely wants to understand more, a *baal teshuva* can always say more when the questioner is ready to hear it.

Seeking Understanding

Responding to Questioner's Discomfort   Validate others' feelings when they express alarm or discomfort, as long as they don't attack you. Someone may ask, "Why don't you wear normal clothes any more?" The baal teshuva must first figure out if the person is asking a real question. Often, such a "question" is simply expressing discomfort that the baal teshuva looks so different from the way she once was—and so different from the way the questioner would like her to look. Rather than explain how dressing modestly is really normal and good, the baal teshuva should first address the person's discomfort—"It does seem kind of weird that I gave up my halter tops and mini-skirts for long skirts and sleeves, doesn't it?" After getting an assenting nod or a smile from the questioner, the baal teshuva can add, "I became a more private person whom people will get to know more from the inside than from the outside."

Brief Answer   If a baal teshuva is asked why she covers so much of her body, she might say, "I realized that I wanted to be attractive without being attracting or distracting."

Making a Statement

Responding to Questioner's Discomfort   If someone asks questions that are really statements about a baal teshuva's clothes or their avoidance of mixed beaches and such, one can say, "It must seem strange to you that I now dress so differently from the way that I used to. At first, it seemed strange to me, too. It must be hard for you to imagine that any woman with my body wouldn't want to show it off."

Brief Answer   If someone asks, "So, I heard that you don't go to the beach any more. Why in the world are you depriving yourself of the fun that you used to have there?"

A possible response could be, "I can still go to some beaches. I'm just not comfortable going to beaches where I am exposed and people stare at my body.

Another frequently asked question: "Don't you think it's ridiculous to cover so much of your body when it's so hot outside?"

Response: "If I thought that it was ridiculous, I wouldn't do it, but I can certainly see why you wouldn't want to dress this way or why you think that it is ridiculous."

They say in football, "The best defense is a good offense." It is always better to be prepared with answers to potentially sticky questions before you have to respond to them rather than to have to prepare answers on the spot. As hard as it is, not getting defensive is usually the best way to handle those who question your religious practices.

Men and Women

God made men and women very different so that each would contribute something essential to each other and to the world. Men are generally challenged by the ease with which they are attracted to a woman's beauty. They can use this attraction to have inappropriate relationships with women and/or to use women as objects, or they can use this attraction to lead to, and enhance, a marriage in which they also appreciate a wife's heart, mind, and soul.

Women should not overvalue their looks and their beauty. Rather than base their worth and self-esteem on how beautiful they appear and how much attention they get, their feelings about themselves should depend upon how much they try to develop their relationship with God and do His will. A married woman should use her beauty to enhance her marriage and not allow herself to be exploited by men who view her body as an object for their pleasure. Men are helped to see the image of God in a woman and not view her as an object if she is not overly exposed.

Touching

Social Touching   Westerners take for granted that men and women have "harmless social touching." Yet Judaism prohibits people of the opposite sex from affectionately touching one another, except for close family relatives such as (grand)parents and (grand) children and husbands and wives.[6]

"Harmless" social touching tends to desensitize people to the powerful intimacy that physical connection was meant to foster. Many *baal teshuvas* find it liberating to be resensitized to the holiness of the body and to the power of touch after years of being touched, hugged, and kissed by acquaintances or relatives with whom they didn't want physical intimacy. People who reserve touching only for their intimate relationships find it jarring when strangers or distant relatives shake their hands, hug, or kiss them.

It is hard to change the *status quo* with relatives who are used to hugging and kissing us and let them know that we can no longer greet them this way. It is equally awkward for *baal teshuvas* to have to put their hands behind their backs when they are introduced to people at work or in social situations so as not to shake hands with them.

The author doesn't know how to completely resolve such dilemmas. It usually doesn't go over well for a nephew to tell his 80-year old aunt that he can no longer kiss her on the cheek because Jews reserve touching only for the most intimate of relationships. Similarly, a beautiful, 21-year-old niece is likely to offend her 60-year-old uncle if she shies away from his social kiss at her sister's wedding.

Methods of Damage Control   One way to minimize the offense and do some damage control is for baal teshuvas to explain to their relatives, "No matter what your age, Judaism always considers you to be attractive and pleasurable to touch. Judaism prohibits me from touching you, but not from loving you with my heart."

Some religious people keep a drink in one hand and a plate in the other to keep from hugging or shaking hands at social events. Some keep a crumpled tissue in their right hand, daub it at their nose, and blow a kiss into the air to avoid such touching. For those of us with year-round allergies, or who cry easily at weddings, this comes naturally.

Non-observant people who know about these issues should be sensitive to *baal teshuvas* and not embarrass them. They should understand that observing these laws is not meant to be a personal affront.

How to deal with social physical contact or shaking hands at work should be discussed with a sensitive rabbi or religious advisor. Some will advise taking a passive approach with relatives. For example, when Uncle Joe leans in to kiss his 30-year-old niece, she doesn't move away and passively allows him to kiss her. She should not take the initiative to kiss him first, though.

Summary

One aspect of observant Judaism that makes us stick out in the secular world is the emphasis on modest dress and separation of the sexes. Judaism stresses the importance of our soul more than the contours of our body; it wants us to project an image of dignity to ourselves and to the world. When we dress in a way that the Divine image shines forth, it may unsettle those who are more attuned to the superficial aspects of life. Feeling confident that we have a God-ly mission that is more important than today's fashion or the social norms of the moment can help *baal teshuvas* respond to those who are critical of their dress and to preserve their boundaries in social situations.

It's helpful to remember that when the modern world's sexual chaos seems normal, the way observant Jews dress and relate to the other sex may seem downright medieval. It is only when you step away from this chaos and try the Jewish way for a while that it makes sense. After a while—sometimes a long while—many people wouldn't have it any other way.

TWENTY-FOUR

Work and Money

Judaism has historically appreciated the importance of working for a living. For example, the Mishnah says, "Rabban Gamliel, the son of Rabbi Judah the Prince, says: 'Torah study with an occupation is beautiful, for toiling in them both makes one forget sin. And all Torah study that is not accompanied by work will be forgotten in the end and lead to sin.[1] Rashi comments on this verse, "This saves a man from sin because then he doesn't desire someone else's wealth and doesn't come to steal. Since it is impossible to live without a livelihood, one who only studies will covet and eventually come to steal."

In describing how a man should live, a code of Jewish Law[2] says, "After [praying and spending time studying Torah in the study hall], a man must go to work, for Torah study without the normal earning of a livelihood will be annulled and lead one to sin, as our Sages taught: 'A man is obligated to teach his sons a trade or profession since he otherwise teaches them to be thieves.[3]"

Baal teshuvas who study Torah exclusively for years, and/or who eschew higher secular education, may not know what is involved in earning a living and supporting a family. They may have no experience drawing up and living by a budget, nor know how much money a couple needs to earn in order to pay basic living expenses. If a woman decides to waive her husband's Torah obligation to support the family so that he can study Torah, she needs to be realistic and knowledgeable about what living this way entails. While the idea of a wife's supporting her husband's full-time Torah study is beautiful, the reality may be very challenging and overly stressful for many families.

Yeshivas and Vocations   Baal teshuvas shouldn't expect their religious teachers or rabbis to be vocational or academic counselors. Most encourage students to stay in yeshiva and learn about Judaism as long as possible, or at least long enough to become well-educated Jews who are strongly committed to staying observant. (That may minimally take several years of full-time study.) It is not their role to teach baal teshuvas job skills or to prepare them to earn a living, and few yeshivas or seminaries offer students vocational advice about how to find a career that will allow them to comfortably support a (hopefully) large family.

At the same time, some seminaries and yeshivas dissuade Jewish students from attending universities and may encourage students already in university to leave. This is because some professors espouse secular ideas and philosophies that are antithetical to Judaism and because students on most campuses act, speak, and dress in ways that are at odds with Torah values.

Nevertheless, some yeshiva students attend university at night, having been discouraged from pursuing careers that leave little time for Jewish learning, such as medicine.

Some *baal teshuvas* who need help choosing a career can benefit from professional vocational counseling. A good counselor will be knowledgeable about thousands of potential career choices and suggest those that fit with the *baal teshuva*'s aptitudes, interests, experience, financial needs, and the job market. *Baal teshuvas* can then discuss these recommendations with a religious advisor and with religious Jews who work in those fields.

Many supporters of yeshivas and seminaries, as well as some older students, work(ed) in businesses or professions. Most will be happy to advise students about their fields.

The Talmud says, *"eem ain kemach, ain Torah"*—if one doesn't have money to buy bread, one can't learn Torah. In Israel, some vocational schools, such as Machon Lev and computer institutes, were set up to equip men who have studied Torah full time with marketable job skills to support their families.

Choosing a Career   Reading books such as What Color Is My Parachute: A Practical Manual for Job-Hunters and Career-Changers (by Richard Nelson Bolles, Ten Speed Press, Berkeley, CA, 2005) can help people to narrow down their interests and focus on a specific career or field of interest.

Universities   Baal teshuvas who plan to attend university should know the challenges there and be prepared for how to avoid or respond to them. These can include teachers who espouse anti-religious and anti-Semitic ideas; classes and exams held on Jewish holidays and on Shabbos; students and teachers using foul language; a culture (especially in dormitories) that promotes drinking, drug use, partying, and sex; immodest dress; and intermingling between the sexes.

Living in apartments with observant roommates and limiting secular forms of campus socializing minimize some of these difficulties.

Jewish religious institutions such as Touro College, Stern College, Yeshiva University, and Neve Yerushalayim's Family Institute offer degrees in secular fields. Some yeshivas, such as Hebrew Theological College in Chicago and Ner Israel Rabbinical College in Baltimore, have joint programs with local universities. Many seminaries and yeshivas have arrangements with universities that allow their students to accrue college credits for their years of Jewish learning.

Many religious Jewish students attend secular universities such as Brandeis, Harvard, Columbia, University of Maryland, SUNY, CUNY, Brooklyn College, Queens College, and Barnard. These schools provide a good secular education to students who live at home, or in a dormitory room or apartment with other religious students.

The Neve Yerushalayim Family Institute has a family therapy training program with college accreditation for women who have social work degrees. Mental health training programs under Orthodox auspices that do not carry college accreditation (such as the Refuah Institute near Jerusalem), and life coach training classes offer classes for observant Jews who want to work with religious Jewish and other clients.

Jerusalem, Brooklyn, and other cities with large numbers of observant Jews have vocational training institutes for observant Jews who want to learn trades, computer, and business skills. TrainE in London (www.traine.org.uk) is a non-profit organization that offers a wide range of courses and helps place observant Jews in jobs where they can maximize their earning potential. Their branch, TraidE, offers professional services, mentoring, and financial aid to Jews who want to establish and develop new businesses.

Campus Life

Many universities have enough "Jewish life" on campus to offer kosher meal plans, social opportunities with other Jews, a daily minyan, and/or a synagogue with services at least on the Jewish holidays and on Shabbos. However, there may not be enough observant singles to provide many dating opportunities. If the school is near a large, observant Jewish community with singles, one can get an education and pursue marriage at the same time. An advisor who is familiar with various universities can help the *baal teshuva* target schools that would be optimal for him or her.

NCSY has published a booklet that describes the Jewish life on various campuses. Yeshiva University, and its sister school Stern College, were designed for, and are almost exclusively attended by, observant students. They have kosher food, daily prayer services, dormitories, and a curriculum that includes Judaica classes. (Yeshiva University offers rabbinic ordination.) Many Jews who attend Stern and YU marry each other, and many couples were introduced to their spouses by observant roommates.

Touro College and its many branches were set up to respect the needs of observant students and to create a largely Jewish social milieu, but secular Jews and non-Jews attend their classes. Many American universities, such as MIT, Harvard, Boston University, Yale, University of Maryland, and SUNY Binghamton—to name a few—have active Hillels with an Orthodox rabbi or a Chabad house onsite or nearby. They offer Jewish classes and are attended by significant numbers of Jewish students. Some commuter schools, especially in the greater New York City area, have many observant Jewish students.

Jewish Sages with Careers

Historically, many Torah scholars had illustrious secular careers. From the fifth until the 14th century, many of the greatest Jewish Sages were doctors, astronomers, financiers, government advisors, and linguists. Hundreds of Torah scholars were doctors during this period, and they wrote thousands of medical works in Hebrew. Among the Talmudic Sages, Rebbe Yochanan, Shmuel, Tuvia, and Abba Umna were expert physicians. After the Talmud was written, Assaf the Doctor authored one of the earliest medical books. At the time of Rabbi Saadya Gaon, a kabbalist and great Torah scholar named Rabbi Shabtai Donnolo was also an expert doctor. He authored a book from which *Orchos Tzaddikim* (a popular book that describes how to improve one's character) included excerpts. He also wrote a medical text that we still have today, as well as a book listing the pharmaceutical formulas for many medications. ·

It may be that a Torah scholar named Rabbi Yitzchak founded the first European medical school in Italy around the time of Rabbi Saadya Gaon. He was renowned for treating eye disorders and became the personal physician of Caliph Abdullah Mahadi of Petimi. The Ralbag, Ravad, Nachmanides, and the Ran were all famous physicians. Maimonides was the court physician for Saladin and doctors of his time came from far and wide to consult with him. His son, Rabbi Avraham, succeeded his father as leader of Egyptian Jewry and as the sultan's court physician. Ibn Ezra was a physician, linguist, poet, and author of more than 100 books. The Ibn Tibbon family had a number of physicians and linguists who translated many holy and secular books into Hebrew.

Many other Torah scholars were great ministers, diplomats, and royal advisors. Rabbi Chasdai Ibn Shaprut was a minister and advisor to the king in Cordova, Spain. Rabbi Shmuel Hanaggid was a vizier to the king of Spain. He, as well as the famous Rabbi Yehuda Halevi—renowned as a poet and author of the *Kuzari*—were also physicians.[4]

The Torah commentator Don Isaac Abarbanel was the chief financial officer for King Ferdinand and Queen Isabella. When the royal couple expelled Jews from Spain, he chose to go into exile with his people rather than keep his respected position.

In addition to being a Torah Sage, Rashi was a vintner and had a vast knowledge of medicine. During the Middle Ages, many Jews became physicians and moneylenders because Christians often barred their entry into other jobs and professions. More recently, the Chayei Adam was a businessman, and the Chofetz Chaim sold goods from the store which he and his wife ran to support themselves.

Professional Jews Today

Today, observant Jews work in a dizzying array of jobs, professions, and businesses besides those listed above. Observant Jews are comedians, architects, athletes, actors, army chaplains in Moslem countries, farmers, designers, real estate magnates, Nobel Prize winners, Attorney General of the United States, world-renowned physicists, medical researchers, veterinarians, archaeologists, journalists, inventors, and much more. The fields in which an observant Jew can work today are limited only by one's imagination.

Once *baal teshuvas* identify a field in which they would like to work, they need to decide how to get the necessary training. Later, they will need to find employment, hopefully in a setting that is conducive to observance.

Kosher Art   Ann became a baal teshuva when she was 14 years old. She had great artistic talent and wanted to attend art school. As a graphic artist, Ann could not only express herself creatively, she could also earn a living.

When she investigated schools, Ann learned that most art school students are extremely bohemian and the school environments are not conducive to religiosity. Students not only sketch nude men and women, but they cultivate a culture of disdain for conventional rules, morality, and modesty.

When Ann discussed her interest in art with the head of her seminary, the principal recommended an art institute in Jerusalem for religious, Hebrew-speaking women run by Emunah Women. Their students have won prizes for their art work and it has excellent teachers. Prior to discussing her vocational plans with the principal, Ann didn't even know that such a school existed. Ann was excited that she was accepted at a school where she didn't have to compromise either her professional or her religious goals. She took an *ulpan* (an intensive crash course in Hebrew) for a few months in Israel before school started and was delighted to both study art and live in Jerusalem.

Mentor   Herbie wanted to start a business but wasn't sure how to go about it. He went to the executive director of his yeshiva and asked to be introduced to some former yeshiva students who were now businessmen. After meeting them, one became his mentor. Mr. Fox gave Herbie advice about how to write a business plan and get financial backing for a project that Herbie was interested in pursuing. Herbie then consulted with both his mentor and his rabbi as religious questions came up about monetary issues, business ethics, and other Jewish legal questions.

Becoming a Psychologist   Rivka discussed her interest in becoming a social worker or psychologist with the principal of her seminary. The principal referred Rivka to an observant psychologist who detailed the educational process involved in becoming a social worker or psychologist, the different options available in each field, and the pros and cons of potential choices. She also apprised Rivka of the religious challenges that she would face in most "helping profession" programs because of practitioners' liberal attitudes and anti-religious biases. The psychologist helped Rivka define that she wanted to become a counselor for at-risk youth. They then planned out the steps that she would need to follow in order to do that, which included finding an observant mentor in her field and a posek who was an expert in handling Jewish legal (halachic) mental health questions.

Work Skills

Getting Your MRS   Some young women think that getting married will absolve them of the need either to choose a career or to earn a living. They go through school preparing for their MRS degree, thinking that they will never need to earn a living if they get married and raise children.

The wife of a *rosh yeshiva* warns her high school students not to think that getting married makes it unnecessary to get an education and job skills. She herself has two graduate degrees. Sometimes a male breadwinner dies, or becomes incapacitated by a medical illness or accident, and the wife needs to support the family. Some observant couples get divorced or the husband controls the family's money in a way that the wife has little financial say or access. If a woman earns her own money, it will be easier for her to take care of herself and her family if the need arises.

Many observant Jewish families need the wife to work at least part-time in order to pay for basic living expenses and the high costs of tuition for their children's Jewish education. While some women work at paid jobs primarily because they find work gratifying, other women work primarily because they or their families need the income.

God Will Provide   Studying in yeshiva or seminary should not be an excuse to avoid planning for one's financial future, even if those plans will not be implemented for a few years. Parents of baal teshuva yeshiva or seminary students who have no plans to acquire job skills (and who act as if doing so isn't important) may have legitimate worries about their children's financial futures.

Baal teshuvas need to accept responsibility for earning a living. They should not expect their parents to support them or say, "God will provide," meaning that they don't intend to work to support themselves.

The Torah obligates a man to support his family financially (and his wife emotionally as well), even if his wife is also capable of earning money.

It is a lot easier to support a family on $80,000 a year than on $18,000. With some planning and study, many young *baal teshuvas* can make career and educational choices that may, with God's help, allow them to live comfortably throughout their lives.

Marketable Profession   After learning in seminary for a year, Bina went to university and got an accounting degree. She enjoyed her work, it paid well, and it allowed her to work part-time when she had children. It made sense for her to have a marketable profession with which she could support a family, rather than scrape by on a secretary's salary.

Temp Work   Tova did not want to attend years of university and was not very intellectual. She thought that she would get an office job, but those where she could observe Shabbos and holidays in her city did not pay well. A neighbor recommended that she work for a temp agency, since Tova's husband's job provided benefits such as health insurance. That was a good option for her.

Court Steno   When Nachman helped out in the yeshiva office, people joked with him that they had never seen anyone type so fast. One day, a visitor noticed how fast he typed and suggested that he consider a career as a court stenographer. Nachman did not even know what that was. The visitor explained what a court stenographer does, adding that some earn more than $100,000 a year. When Nachman left yeshiva to work, he took a short vocational course and then got a well-paying job as a court stenographer.

Tutoring & Outreach   Ezra wanted to be an outreach rabbi, but he realized it would be difficult to do so and support a family. A counselor suggested that he consider finding an outreach job that he enjoyed and supplement his income by privately tutoring bar mitzvah boys in a suburban neighborhood where tutors made $60-100 per hour. Ezra made some inquiries and discovered that it would be easy for him to tutor bar mitzvah boys two afternoons a week. That would increase his earnings by $35,000 a year. That arrangement allowed him to work as an outreach rabbi doing what he loved most and still support his family.

Savings　Ian had a different approach. He had an MBA in finance and had worked as a stockbroker and banker for eight years. During that time, he put away a great deal of savings as a nest egg. That gave him a financial cushion to devote himself to studying in yeshiva. When he was in his 30s, he went into the rabbinate.

For those who want to live that way, there is great value, beauty, and reward for couples who are dedicated to studying and teaching Torah full time. Men can do this as pulpit or community rabbis, as outreach professionals, as teachers, as *kollel avreichim* (married men who study Torah full time), or in community kollels where the men learn during the day and teach people in the community on Sundays and at night.

Many of their wives also teach. Those who do may give private pre-marital classes to brides, teach Torah classes to women in their community, or teach children in Jewish schools. If a man truly feels that his calling is to learn in kollel, or to be a rabbi, or a woman feels that her truest calling is to be a rebbetzin or a kollel wife, he or she should do so understanding what that entails emotionally, financially, and in terms of time taken away from their family.

Baal teshuvas should not think that men who learn in kollel and whose wives support them are the only people who fulfill their Jewish potentials, and that anything else is second rate. It is wonderful for those who can, but that is not everyone's calling.

Budgets and Finances

Baal teshuvas should consider what kind of pre-tax income they will need to support a family, then plan how to get the skills and experience necessary to do so. Many of them are shocked to find out that the tuition per year for many American Jewish religious schools is $10,000 or more per child, starting in preschool! Summer camp can add another $3,000-8,000 per child to that amount. In Israel, current annual tuition costs per child range from nearly free to $2,000, plus additional costs if the child lives in a dormitory. Religious summer camp can add up to another $1,000 per child. *Baal teshuvas* may be unaware of how much pre-tax money they will need to earn in order to pay for the lifestyle that they envision having. Working out a budget while in yeshiva, seminary, or university can enlighten them about how much it costs to live and/or raise a family. This could avoid an unpleasant surprise later.

The Rabbinate as a Profession

Some people extol the virtues of being an Orthodox rabbi, and it is wonderful that many idealistic yeshiva and seminary students expect to become rabbis or teach Jewish studies. Yet, these career paths are not always easy. Many *baal teshuvas* discover, much to their chagrin, that the working conditions, job security, pay, and job benefits are poor. They may not be able to support their families. They rarely get the money or respect that they deserve. Too, there are hundreds of Orthodox shuls in the US and Canada in which only the rabbis and a few congregants are observant. It is also ironic that rabbis are observant Jews who must work almost every Shabbos and Jewish holiday!

Sadly, many non-observant Jews give huge sums of money to museums, political parties, and universities. Jews of all religious persuasions pay handsomely for vacations, eating out in restaurants, and going to entertainment. They spend tens of thousands of dollars every year on health insurance and for their children's college education. Yet, they somehow expect that Orthodox rabbis should be on call 24/7 and work for a pittance. The same applies to observant teachers in Jewish schools, whose salaries and working conditions are often pitiful.

Resistant Congregants   Shlomo was an idealistic baal teshuva who wanted nothing more than to go into the rabbinate and to influence Jews to become observant. After he married, he moved to a small Jewish community and became the rabbi of an Orthodox synagogue whose members were not observant. When he told the congregants that they must stop serving non-kosher food at their functions, they told him not to impose his standards of kashrut on them. When he urged the congregants not to talk during services, they told him not to tell them how they should behave in their synagogue. When he told the president of the congregation that he could not convert the man's future daughter-in-law to Judaism without her studying Torah and committing to observance, the president and the synagogue board decided that it was time to find a new, more flexible rabbi. Shlomo's Jewish community taught him more about politics than he taught them about Judaism.

Baal teshuvas can be blissfully unaware of the financial problems that many Jewish institutions face and how often they are unable to meet their payrolls. Some teachers wait for months to receive their meager salaries, and many schools and institutions do not offer basic health, vacation, or pension benefits that comparable secular institutions would provide. The idealism that *baal teshuvas* have while studying Torah full time on someone else's dime may be crushed when they are on the receiving end of the financial squeeze.

Financial Disaster   Mitch was a baal teshuva who lived at home. He studied in yeshiva and tutored a few students to earn some pocket money. He had no idea how much normal living costs were because his parents or the yeshiva paid for his rent, utilities, and food.

When he got married, he took a poorly paying teaching job in a Jewish day school, not realizing that his salary was woefully inadequate to support a married couple. His wife couldn't work, as she needed to complete two more years of study to become a speech therapist. They used up their wedding gift money and she took out student loans.

A year after they got married, Mitch realized that they were headed for financial disaster. He left teaching and became a real estate agent. Three years later, they had paid off all of their debts and Mitch finally had some financial breathing space. Although he became a donor to Jewish education, he felt that the financial sacrifices were too great for him to ever return to teaching.

Tutoring & Torah   Danny became a baal teshuva in Jerusalem, and he expected to learn in yeshiva for several years. Meanwhile, his father pressured him to leave and work in the family business. Danny did not want to do that. The business generated a lot of income, but it was also very stressful—especially the part about working for his father. Danny studied in yeshiva for another two years and then went back to college. He earned a bachelor's degree in math and found an enjoyable job teaching in a private school. He made extra money tutoring high school students for their SAT exams. By the time he got married, he was able to comfortably support his family on his income and his job allowed him time to learn Torah every day.

Support for Large Family   Lynn went to a state university where she majored in computers and then got an MBA. She started a home business after she got married. Working part-time, she was able to augment her husband's income. This allowed them to comfortably support the large family that they eventually had while she stayed home and took care of their children.

We can never predict when circumstances like a stock market crash, "tech wreck," or unexpected illness will wreak financial havoc on people. Still, the Almighty expects us to get job skills and work hard to earn an income and not expect financial miracles or charity to help us. People don't necessarily need a university degree to earn a good living. They do, however, need to have marketable job skills and work hard to earn a living. *Baal teshuvas* should carefully consider their financial future when making educational and job choices to avoid undue hardships later as a result of their lack of planning.

Predicting and Overcoming Challenges

Challenges   Advisors or teachers should introduce *baal teshuvas* to religious people who have jobs that interest the *baal teshuva*. Such people can describe the rewards, as well as the religious and practical challenges to be expected, in school, during training, and on the job. *Baal teshuvas* should ask such resource people the following: What are the pros and cons of your work? What practical, moral and ethical challenges have you had, and how did you overcome them? What is it like being a religious Jew in your occupation? How does your work impact your spiritual growth and your family?

Working Conditions   Such people can offer a wealth of information about practical aspects of working. For example, how much money can someone in that field earn? What are various work environments like? Is it likely that this type of work will feel fulfilling to the baal teshuva? Does the field offer job security?

Professions with a Future   Armed with this information, baal teshuvas can have a better idea as to whether a contemplated job or career will be good for them. They should also ascertain if it is likely that there will be a reasonable job market for those in that field by the time they are qualified to work in it. Many New Yorkers who got PhD degrees in subjects such as anthropology, comparative literature, and religion in the 1970s ended up being highly educated taxi drivers. Since health maintenance organizations began changing the way that doctors practice medicine and are reimbursed, many college graduates decided to get business degrees and not become physicians. Some computer technicians who trained to repair computers found that those computers were obsolete by the time they finished their courses, and computer analysts found that their knowledge of certain systems was obsolete soon after graduation.

Work Ethics

Unethical Work Practices Many workers consider it acceptable to steal an employer's time or office supplies. They do this by making personal phone calls; using work time to surf the Net and check personal e-mail; taking sick days when they are healthy; and coming in late or leaving early without deducting hours from a time sheet. They also use office supplies, copiers, and fax machines for personal matters.

Work can be a fertile ground for gossip and assassinating other peoples' character. Common unethical practices include padding clients' bills; defrauding insurance companies; billing for unnecessary or unprovided services; convincing customers that they need services or products that they don't; concealing defects or misrepresenting a product or person; and writing phony or altered reports, especially to protect someone who misbehaved. Jewish law forbids doing these things.

Work Dilemmas Judaica books and the following Internet sites discuss various topics in workplace ethics and other workplace dilemmas:

Jewish medical (such as The Schlesinger Institute for Medical-Halachic Research—www.medethics.org.il, and www.jewishvirtuallibrary.org/jsource/Judaism/medtoc.html), psychological (www.nefesh.org), and business ethics (www.besr.org; www.darchenoam.org/ethics/business/bus_home.htm has a wealth of articles on business and work ethic issues; aish.com regularly runs The Jewish Ethicist, by Asher Meir, in their weekly newsletter)].

Further, you can google Jewish medical ethics, Jewish psychological ethics, and Jewish business ethics; some resources give practical advice about how to deal with these situations.

Some dilemmas in the mental health fields include the fact that psychology and social work teachers and supervisors are often opposed to observant Judaism. They believe that adherence to Jewish values and Torah attitudes is detrimental to people's mental health, despite the preponderance of evidence that religiosity is usually associated with great emotional and physical benefits. Such supervisors and teachers of mental health professionals insist that students apply secular values in their work. This creates conflicts for observant practitioners who work with non-observant or non-Jewish patients when Judaism requires working differently than secular therapists do. These situations especially arise with Jewish couples who are living together, couples where one partner is Jewish and the other is not, and when treating some homosexuals. Observant therapists may also work differently than secular therapists do with women who have unwanted pregnancies, people who have conflicts with parents, those who have suffered tragedy and loss, and those who search for meaning in life.

A mental health supervisor or administrator who insists that staff follow politically correct treatment approaches can make it very unpleasant, or even impossible, for observant Jews to work with some patients in their facilities.

Carl Jung was sharply criticized by many therapy gurus of his day for believing that loss of faith was the main underpinning of depressed and anxious patients. Secular Jews founded other therapies that reflected their vehement opposition to observant Judaism and to religion in general.

Social Dilemmas

Some work environments have a great deal of mixing and touching between men and women, such as social kissing and hugging, men and women being secluded together, and flirting. Women may be immodestly dressed and vulgar language is part of some work cultures. Some bosses expect employees to attend the annual Xmas party, eat in non-kosher venues, and attend outings where modesty or kashrut may be compromised.

Non-Kosher Dining   Some job interviewers (such as law partners) take the potential employee to lunch at a non-kosher restaurant. Discuss with a rabbi or an observant person who has been through this how best to handle this dilemma. Some jobs require employees to wine and dine clients, and there may be no kosher restaurants in which to do this. Observant Jews in this predicament have drinks and eat a lot of fresh fruits and raw vegetables in the world's finest restaurants!

Head Covering Discuss with a rabbi or an experienced observant person whether a man should wear a head covering to an interview, or at work. Adhering to this Jewish custom sometimes means that a person won't get a job or promotions.

Shaking Hands Job interviewers are likely to shake hands with interviewees, and some employees are expected to shake hands with people they meet at work. Some poskim allow shaking a hand of someone of the opposite sex if it is preferred in such circumstances, but not initiating shaking hands with someone of the opposite sex. If your rabbi does not permit shaking hands, discuss with him how to handle such work situations.

Foiled in the Restaurant Charlene landed her dream job as a hospital administrator. To welcome her, the hospital arranged for her to meet the 20 section chiefs at a lunch in an expensive French restaurant. Charlene didn't want to lose her job before it started by telling her boss that she kept kosher. After all, her boss was very WASPy and he probably wouldn't like her making waves about some Jewish issue. She would have enough to deal with in the autumn, a few months away, when she planned to tell him that she needed to leave early on Fridays and before the Jewish holidays.

She telephoned the *maitre d'* of the restaurant as soon as she found out about the lunch and asked if he could accommodate her. Could he double wrap a potato and a whole small fish in foil, bake them for her, and serve them in the foil? Would he order a bottle of kosher French wine from the wine store down the street? Would it be okay if Charlene brought her own flatware, which she would take back with her?

Charlene was so relieved when the *maitre d'* promised to do everything that she had requested. She made sure to give him a nice tip.

The morning of the lunch, Charlene confirmed her plans with the *maitre d'* and everything seemed to be in order. After the hospital entourage arrived at the restaurant, Charlene greeted the *maitre d'* again.

When the waiter brought everyone's orders, all eyes were on Charlene as she opened her baked fish and they waited expectantly for her to start. She was devastated. Her fish had been cooked in a non-kosher wine sauce and was then wrapped in foil! She pretended to eat, everyone turned their eyes to their own plates, and she spent the rest of the meal carefully picking at her fish and then concealing it under the foil on her plate.

A frequent predicament for observant Jews is how and when to inform a boss that they will leave work early on Fridays and be absent on Jewish holidays.

Proving Oneself   When Tom interviewed for a job, he did not tell the interviewer that he was observant. When he was offered the job, he started in June right after the holiday of Shavuot. He figured that would allow him to work for several months and show that he was an asset to the company. He would soon have to take off for the Jewish New Year (Rosh Hashana) and other Jewish holidays in September, as well as leave early on Fridays when the autumn days grew short. He hoped to make up lost time on Fridays by staying late other days. He assumed that they might not have hired him if he brought up the Shabbos/holiday issue before he started working.

His judgment on all counts turned out to be correct. His boss liked him, so leaving early some days turned out not to be an issue. He was such a valued employee that he stayed at that job for many years.

Over-Shabbos Meetings   Some jobs require employees to be away from home on weekends or to attend seminars or meetings on Shabbos or Jewish holidays. Observant employees who stay in a hotel on Jewish holy days need to anticipate certain difficulties. Electronic room sensors need to be covered. Manual keys should be substituted for electronic key cards, or the room should be opened by someone who isn't Jewish. Kosher food should either be brought from home or arranged for in advance, when possible. Even when these obstacles can be overcome, many married Jews try to avoid such traveling because they miss being with their families on these special days. One should always ask about the travel expectations before taking a job that may require going out of town.

Avoiding certain work environments and challenges can be a lot easier than navigating through them. In rare cases, religious Jews may need to consult a lawyer or religious Jewish advocacy organization if they are forced to unreasonably compromise their religious convictions or are denied raises or promotions due to their religious beliefs.

Testing One's Commitment

Baal teshuvas often find that God tests their most recent commitment to observance to see if they will stick to it. After resolving to keep kosher, someone will offer to take the *baal teshuva* to the finest, non-kosher restaurant that the person yearned to eat in before becoming observant. When someone resolves to stop dating non-Jews, the gorgeous co-worker that she pined for for years suddenly asks her out. When someone resolves to keep Shabbos, the person gets the job offer of a lifetime. The catch? Never leaving work early on Fridays.

Wink from God   Charlie was a classic example of this. He didn't keep Shabbos, but he always went to synagogue on Saturdays and never worked on the High Holidays. In his late 40s, at an age when it is hard for men to find a new job, he got a lucrative job working as a manager for a major corporation. A few months later, he was invited to a meeting with all of the company's division heads to apprise them of the changes that he planned to make in the company.

Charlie was excited about meeting the company's executives until he checked his calendar. He saw that the meeting was scheduled for the Jewish New Year (Rosh Hashana). He was afraid that if he made waves, he might lose his job and never get another one. He pondered what to do and decided that he could not compromise his religious beliefs. He told the coordinator of the meeting about his dilemma.

The coordinator was very unhappy to hear this. He had spent days juggling 15 participants' schedules. After failing to convince Charlie to back down, the coordinator finally agreed to reschedule the meeting.

Charlie was so relieved. A week later, the coordinator called Charlie and told him of the painstaking efforts he had made to re-schedule the meeting. He had spent countless hours doing this. The meeting would now take place the week after the original date that was set. Charlie's heart was in his throat when he realized that the new date for the meeting was the holiest day of the year—*Yom Kippur* (the Day of Atonement)!

Charlie decided that no matter what, he wasn't going to a business meeting on Yom Kippur, despite the implied threat to his job. After much tension between the company vice president and Charlie, the meeting was cancelled. Much to his relief, Charlie didn't lose his job, and the company found alternate ways to introduce his ideas to the executives. When the company's stock reached a new high that Yom Kippur, Charlie saw it as a wink from God that he had done the right thing.

Putting it All Together

Perhaps others can benefit from the process that I underwent in formulating my career goals. I was able to identify several interests that I had, such as biology, wanting to help people, and Judaism. I also wrote down some things that I didn't like—such as the sight of blood, math, arguing, and being sleep deprived. I quickly ruled out being a doctor, nurse, teacher, lawyer, and accountant. I could not think of other professions that seemed interesting to me.

One morning, I prayed from a Sephardic prayer book and a verse from the Mishnah in the preliminary prayers spoke to me: "These are the things that a person receives interest for in this world, but the capital remains to enjoy in the World-to-Come...bringing peace between people, and between a husband and wife...." It struck me that becoming a psychologist who did couples' therapy might be a perfect option for me.

I talked to a neighbor who felt fulfilled as a psychologist and whose wife was an exhausted medical student. Both of their fields sounded interesting, yet psychology wouldn't require me to give up much sleep. I could also be a psychologist part-time and support a family on my income. Psychology would require years of study and training but I would still be young—only in my early 20s—by the time I finished.

The social atmospheres at the universities that I attended were similar to what I experienced in high school. I could choose with whom to associate and avoid people whose lifestyles and language left much to be desired. Few classes had religiously offensive books or lectures, the sole exception being the "Bible" class that I took at Tel Aviv University. I dropped it after the first session when the teacher made it clear that he was teaching "Higher Biblical Criticism," not the Jewish Bible.

My greatest religious challenges occurred during psychology internships, where the supervisors were anti-religious and believed that religion was invariably pathological. When religious issues were raised by my psychotherapy patients, I consulted a psychologically astute rabbi. He told me about what I could and could not do with patients when the standard treatments conflicted with Jewish law. He also helped me understand why God made some people mentally ill.[5]

Having a part-time private practice gave me the financial base to support a family, and also left me with enough free time to write books about Judaism and do Jewish outreach. My psychology career has given me a great deal of fulfillment and has allowed me to develop emotionally, intellectually, and spiritually. I have been fortunate to have found a career that has been so gratifying, where I have been able to actualize some of my spiritual potentials.

Giving Up Dreams—Artists and Performers

A career is often more than a way to earn money. It allows some people to express their creativity, intelligence, spirituality and/or talents, and it may give them social and emotional benefits, too. Many people get approval, esteem, a sense of competence, and respect through their work place. They develop strong friendships and have much of their social contact there.

Performers Most baal teshuva professional musicians, dancers, actors, and singers need to give up their jobs because their professions require working on Friday nights and Saturdays. Most baal teshuvas are told to give up performing in front of mixed audiences because it conflicts with Jewish laws of modesty. (There is relatively little demand for women to perform only for female audiences.) Some male musicians can still play in Jewish bands or in less prestigious venues.

It is often difficult for ex-performers to find alternate channels for the energy and passion that they can no longer express. Some will never find work that is equally gratifying. Some of these *baal teshuvas* feel that God gave them an incredible gift that they now have to bury.

Artists Fortunately, most artists such as painters, sculptors, and graphic designers can still work, although they may need to modify their style so that they don't violate Jewish laws of modesty or prohibitions against making graven images.

Identity Loss Most men and many women tend to identify with their jobs. When asked, "Who are you?" they may respond with what they do instead of with their names. Giving up a fulfilling career for religious reasons can be financially and psychologically devastating.

Some people mistakenly think that becoming a *baal teshuva* obviates the need for other identities. There are people for whom a job is simply a way of making money or a vehicle by which they serve the Almighty, but this is not the case for everyone. When someone has spent many years studying and training for a career that is emotionally satisfying, financially rewarding, and personally fulfilling, what happens when he or she gives it all up to become observant? With what do they replace it?

Response from FFBs   Many FFBs consider the performing arts silly and nothing to regret giving up. They may not relate to the losses that baal teshuvas experience. They can't understand that an actor/dancer/singer/performer who gives it all up to serve God may feel depressed. When they tell baal teshuvas that they shouldn't want or need these things in the first place, it only pours salt into the baal teshuva's wounds.

It is hard for others to know how it feels to lose the heady feeling of performing and being admired by thousands of people every night. They may not appreciate what it means to earn a good living doing what one loves and then to be indefinitely unemployed with no saleable job skills. The out-of-work performer may mourn losing the intense feelings when the music, singing, and/or dancing come together and create a joyful experience every day.

It is very painful when well-meaning FFBs tell *baal teshuva* dancers that they can always dance at weddings, or that women singers can sing with other ladies at the third Shabbos meal to make up for the professional careers they gave up. These "alternatives" are not substitutes for people who were serious performers or artists. Such "advice" trivializes their talents.

Opera   Goldie was a child with an extraordinary voice. Her voice teacher told her mother that Goldie's voice was so incredible that she should study locally until she turned 18, then study with a world-class opera teacher in Europe. As a teen, Goldie couldn't wait to be an opera singer and spent countless hours practicing and performing. When she was 17, she became a baal teshuva and was told that she shouldn't sing in front of men. She was devastated, and reluctantly gave up her dream of becoming an opera singer. She never found another outlet for her musical talent.

Ballet   Suzanne was a dancer with a renowned ballet company who became a baal teshuva at the height of her career. Apart from the fact that the company had its most important performances on Friday nights and Saturdays, the dancers' costumes weren't modest, the women had to dance with men, and there were men in the audience. She gave up her career, yet dancing solo in her living room was a poor substitute for the professional classes and public performances that had been a mainstay of her life for nearly a decade.

From a spiritual point of view, giving up a career that involves religious infractions is unequivocally good. From an emotional perspective, it can take years for *baal teshuva* artists, singers, dancers, musicians, and actors to come to terms with their losses. Rabbis and advisors need to be very careful about the way that they tell *baal teshuvas* that they need to give up their performing careers, and make sure before doing so that it is necessary. It needs to be done with great sensitivity, support and compassion.

Remedies & Outlets   In recent years, some baal teshuvas in Brooklyn created a support group for performers. Baal teshuva actresses, singers, musicians, and writers in Israel have written and performed musicals that have played for months to sold-out women-only audiences. Makor, on Manhattan's Upper West Side, had a Girls' Night On every few months where female performers (mostly singers or musicians) played to women-only audiences. Harmony is a concert given over three nights by more than 125 girls and women performers in the Five Towns of Long Island, NY, every other year. Atara, a group of women performers from Stern College, had its debut in 2007. Ayelet HaShachar of Baltimore and other women's singing groups write music with Jewish lyrics and perform it to female audiences and on CDs.

Some religious girls' high schools have produced and performed full-length musicals. Linda Zulberg's production of *The Sound of Torah* in Johannesburg is one such example. For the past several years, Rebbetzin Devorah Green in Jerusalem has produced a full-length play every year that is performed by, and for, girls and women.

Baal teshuva singer Julia Blum has produced CDs and travels several times a year performing concerts for women. Roger Mehl, a *baal teshuva* actor/singer/dancer and star in *Starlight Express* produced and performed a one-man show about his journey to become observant. Rachel Factor, a former Rockette, also produced and performed a one-woman show about her life story. She currently has a performing arts school for girls in Jerusalem.

How wonderful it would be if more observant Jews would create opportunities for religious performers to use their talents!

When Jewish law allows people to continue in their careers, *baal teshuvas* should find out about them by contacting rabbis who deal with these issues. They should also try to meet others who can advise them of substitute ways to express their creativity as religious Jews.

Summary

Baal teshuvas may benefit from vocational guidance that informs them about the education, training, work conditions, and income that different jobs entail. Doing so can help them to earn a living and find fulfilling work while maintaining their spiritual integrity. Fortunately, observant Jews now work in a myriad of fields. They have paved the way for others to follow in their footsteps without compromising their religious ideals.

Once someone has narrowed down potential career choices, they should meet observant Jews who work in those fields and find out what their challenges have been and how they have overcome them. Some of these people can mentor *baal teshuvas* as they get a secular education and enter the work place.

Some *baal teshuvas* will give up their chosen vocation in order to live as observant Jews, and they will need to fill that void. It is my hope that we will see more *baal teshuvas* creating ways to channel their amazing talents to benefit other Jews and the world.

Epilogue

Becoming observant is fraught with challenges. We cannot even imagine the paths that some Jews take in order to become observant. I am often humbled by *baal teshuvas*' sacrifices and inspired by their convictions.

We live in a world where so many people want only to be comfortable. They don't do much with their lives because they try to avoid having challenges. Yet seeking comfort, material success, or hedonistic pleasure doesn't quell a Jewish soul's yearning for so much more. It knows that we were put here to rectify ourselves and to spiritually fix the world. Without confronting and overcoming challenges, we could never develop our spirituality. Lacking that, there is no purpose to life.

When *baal teshuvas* confront difficulties, they sometimes feel defeated and wish to stop struggling. If we were training for a very important competition and knew we were contenders for first prize, we would welcome every opportunity to train and prepare for the "big event." We can welcome our continual spiritual challenges as building blocks to an everlasting relationship with our Creator. They are the keys to indescribable pleasure in our afterlife.

When we study Torah, read books or hear lectures, and get advice from rabbis, friends, and advisors, we should use this information to charge our spiritual batteries and give us the fortitude to deal with our challenges. Yet we need also to have faith that the One Above has a plan for us and that every challenge and hardship that we face is necessary and valuable.

Our positive attitudes and faith will enable us to scale our personal mountain until we reach its peak. No two of us will travel exactly the same path because no two of us were meant to have the same journey. Yet, appreciating how far we have travelled can give us the strength to continue on the road to becoming the person that God wants us to be.

The Talmud says, "In the world to come, the evil person and the righteous person will each be shown his evil inclination. The evil person will see that it was nothing more than a thread, while the righteous one will see that his was as high as a mountain. The evil person will say, 'How was it possible that I didn't overcome this tiny thread?'

"The righteous person will say, 'How could I possibly have conquered that mountain?'"

The Talmud also says about the soul in the next world, "In the place that a *baal teshuva* stands, a person who was always totally righteous cannot stand." (*Brachot* 34a)

Every Jew is supposed to be a *baal teshuva*. We should always have the enthusiasm that *baal teshuvas* bring to observance, their thirst for knowledge, and their love of God and Judaism. We should all aspire to take the journey necessary to actualize our spiritual potentials and to be the best Jews that we can.

We are privileged to live in a time when we see the words of the prophet coming to fruition, "And behold, days are coming when I will send a famine in the land. Not a famine for bread, and not a thirst for water, but to listen to the words of the Lord." At that time, before the Messiah comes, "the hearts of the sons will be turned to the fathers and the hearts of the fathers will be turned to the sons."

May it happen soon and in our days.

Appendix A:
Finding a Seminary
or Yeshiva

This appendix was designed to help *baal teshuvas* (and other Jews) who want to learn more about Judaism find suitable programs. The majority of such programs are in New York or Jerusalem, but there are other schools world-wide. The following list can help people select a program that suits them, and learn more about programs that others recommend.

Seminaries

When observant Jews refer to a seminary, they mean a post-high school institution where women study Torah Judaism full time. Some seminaries, such as Bais Yaakov in New York or Jerusalem, Breuer's Teacher's Seminary in Manhattan, or Bais Rivkah (Chabad) in Crown Heights, are geared toward teaching religious women with strong Jewish backgrounds how to teach Jewish topics. After two years of study, students earn a teacher's certificate, which gives them the credentials they need to teach in Jewish schools.

Some of the better-known *baal teshuva* seminaries are listed below in alphabetical order. This list was not meant to be all-inclusive. For more information, visit their websites or google *baal teshuva yeshivas* or seminaries. The website www.seminarycentral.com claims to offer "a complete listing of English post-high school Jewish programs." At the time of this writing, a few of the coed and non-seminary programs mentioned on their site are not under Orthodox auspices. However, they do have an excellent listing of seminaries as well as many touring, study, and vocational programs that are suitable for observant Jews.

Note: Unless otherwise specified, classes mentioned below are taught in English. The ages listed are general student population ages, often times institutions will have older or younger students as well.

Jerusalem

» **EYAHT** is under the auspices of Rebbetzin Denah Weinberg. It has small classes, with mostly North American women in their 20s and older. It has a chareidi orientation and stresses strict adherence to Jewish law, service of God, and personal self-improvement. www.eyaht.org

» **Maayanot** has a program under Chabad auspices for women aged 20-29. Students learn an academic curriculum in a warm environment with small classes that also emphasize personal growth. www.maayanot.edu

» **Machon Roni** in the Old City is the women's division of the Diaspora Yeshiva. It emphasizes Torah study and personal growth. www.diaspora.org.il

» **Michlala** is a religious women's university in Jerusalem that trains students from religious backgrounds to be teachers. It stresses academic excellence and covers subjects that include language and science, plus a broader range of Jewish topics than are taught in Bais Yaakov schools. Classes are in Hebrew.

» **Midreshet HaRova** is a religious Zionist seminary located in the Old City. It has an intense learning program with classes from 8:30am until 10pm. It attracts North Americans, South Africans, Europeans, and Israelis in their late teens and early 20s. Classes are in Hebrew and English. There are also advanced classes in Hebrew for Israeli and Hebrew-speaking Anglo women one day a week. www.midreshetharova.org.il

» **Midreshet** Lindenbaum has a religious Zionist orientation, and is headed by Rabbis Chaim Brovender and Shlomo Riskin. It is a one-year study program for more than 200 post-high school women from English-speaking countries and Israel, mostly from modern Orthodox backgrounds. It has a variety of programs, some of which offer college credit. www.lind.org.il

» **Midreshet Rachel V'Chaya,** run by Rabbi Yitzchak Shurin and Rebbetzin Lynn Finson, is the women's division of Darche Noam. It offers a range of small classes for women in their 20s and early 30s who have some Jewish knowledge and background. Diverse teachers educate students to become religiously and emotionally well balanced. www.darchenoam.org

» **Neve Yerushalayim** is the oldest and largest (currently, more than 800 students attend its various programs) of the *baal teshuva* seminaries. It has a chareidi orientation with classes from beginner to advanced levels. It offers a variety of programs, with classes in English, French, and Hebrew. It also has an affiliated Family Institute where female social workers train to become family therapists. www.nevey.org

» **Nishmat**, run by Rebbetzin Chana Henkin, has a religious Zionist orientation and emphasizes Torah scholarship and development of textual skills. Its programs are for beginners to advanced students, including a unique *yeotzet rabbinit* track. www.nishmat.net

» **Shearim,** run by Rebbetzin Holly Pavlov, offers small classes with a chareidi orientation. It stresses developing textual skills and is mostly attended by college graduates and by women who work outside the home. www.shearim.com

Tzfat

» **Machon Alte Seminary** is a small, warm school run by Chabad Lubavitch for women ages 18-32 with little or no Jewish background. They offer a full-time curriculum that includes classes on Chassidic thought, mysticism, meditation, Jewish law, Torah and Prophets, and more. www.machonalte.com

» **Ascent**, run by Chabad, has a retreat/study center that offers coed classes to beginners on topics of basic Judaism and mysticism. www.ascent.org.il

Bat Ayin (Gush Etzion area)

» **Midreshet Be'erot Bat Ayin** combines nature, spirituality, and hands-on learning (baking bread, gardening, etc.) with Torah study. www.berotbatayin.org

New York City

» **Drisha** on the Upper West Side of Manhattan, is run by Rabbi David Silber. Its intellectual program for women stresses textual study and in-depth understanding of topics in Tanach, Talmud, Jewish philosophy, and more. Classes range from beginner to advanced. Students can take individual classes or enroll for multi-year, full-time study. Fellowship programs are available. www.drisha.org

» **The Jewish Renaissance Center,** on the Upper West Side of Manhattan, is run by Rebbetzin Leah Kohn. It has a chareidi orientation covering a range of topics. There are small classes and one-on-one learning at all levels. Students are in their early 20s and older, mostly with little or no Jewish background. There are day and evening classes, summer and winter weeks of learning, and Sunday and pre-holiday seminars. They also offer lectures in Brooklyn and Englewood (NJ) and summer seminars in the Catskills. Individual counseling and Shabbos and Yom Tov (Jewish holiday) hospitality are available on request. www.jrcny.org

» **Stern College** is a women's college located near mid-town Manhattan. One can earn a college degree while taking Judaism classes in a Torah environment. It is the sister school of Yeshiva University. www.yu.edu/stern

» **Touro College** has many branches in New York, in other American cities, and in Jerusalem. It offers a variety of secular and Jewish classes leading to a college degree. Classes are coed. www.touro.edu

St. Paul, MN

» **Bais Chana,** run by Manis Friedman, is one of the oldest *baal teshuva* seminaries in the US. Classes include Chassidic philosophy and it has a Chabad-Chassidic orientation. www. baischana.org.

For more Chabad schools, see their seminary directory at www. chinuchoffice.org

Yeshivas

In or near Jerusalem

» **Aish Hatorah,** started by Rabbi Noach Weinberg, is in the Old City. It offers a six-week Essentials program to men and women with little or no Jewish background. It also has short-term programs in basic Judaism for men in their 20s and older, as well as fellowships in Jewish leadership, public relations, and more. Its full-time chareidi, intellectually focused (they don't have much emotional/spiritual focus as a Chassidic program would) program trains many students to be outreach rabbis. www.aish.com

» **Bircas Hatorah,** run by Rabbi Shimon Green, is in the Old City. It has a unique chareidi orientation with beginner-to-advanced Jewish learning. The school emphasizes textual learning and self-improvement (*mussar*). Small classes, mostly mature students, ages 20 and older. www.bircas.org

» **Darche Noam/Shapell's** Run by Rabbis Shaya Karlinsky and Yitzchak Hirschfeld, is the men's counterpart of Midreshet Rachel V'Chaya. They teach textual skills while nurturing personal and ethical development. Classes are small, with teachers from diverse backgrounds across the observant spectrum. www.darchenoam.org

» **Diaspora Yeshiva** on Mt. Zion (next to the Old City) is known for its open atmosphere and small classes. Classes are basic to advanced for men who don't want a rigid, structured yeshiva environment. www.diaspora.org.il

» **Yeshivat Dvar Yerushalayim** has a chareidi orientation. It teaches basic principles of Judaism and Torah in English, French, and Hebrew and also offers advanced courses. Classes are small with students from many countries. www.dvar.co.il

» **Machon Meir** Religious Zionist atmosphere with beginner to advanced classes in English and other languages. It attracts international students, including Israelis who participate in *hesder* yeshiva and national service. www.machonmeir.net

» **Mayanot Institute** of Jewish Studies has a Chabad-Chassidic flavor. It is run by Rabbi Shlomo Gestetner. It offers basic to advanced Judaism classes with personalized studies. There are small classes with men in their 20s and older. www.mayanot.edu

» **Yeshivat Ohr Somayach,** Chareidi orientation. Run by Rabbi Nota Schiller. Several programs offer basic to advanced classes. It is geared toward helping *baal teshuvas* integrate into the religious world. www.ohr.org.il

Other Parts of Israel

» **Lev Yisrael,** located in Bet Shemesh, has a Chassidic orientation. Its goal is to help *baal teshuva* males integrate into the religious Jewish world without losing their individuality and their enthusiasm for Judaism. www.levyisrael.com

» **Yeshivas Ohr Avraham,** located in Beit Shemesh, teaches *baal teshuvas* who have some basic textual skills and a commitment to Judaism. It stresses developing knowledge and textual skills in learning Torah, integration of Torah into one's life (including marriage), and developing a sense of responsibility for the Jewish people. www.ohravraham.com.

» **Yeshiva Ohr Torah Stone (Yeshivat Hamivtar)** was founded by Rabbi Shlomo Riskin and is in Efrat. The current Rosh Yeshiva is Rabbi Joel Zeff. It emphasizes textual study of Talmud and has a religious Zionist orientation. Several programs offer classes from beginner to advanced, including a rabbinical ordination track. Students are mostly in their 20s and 30s. www.yhol.org.il

New York

» **James Striar School of General Jewish Studies** is for young men with little or no religious background. It is part of Yeshiva University and is located in upper Manhattan. www.yu.edu

» **Kol Yaakov Torah Center** is run by Rabbi Leibel Tropper in Monsey, NY. It attracts post-college *baal teshuva* men, many of whom work or have advanced degrees. It has a chareidi orientation and an accredited college program as well as a rabbinical training program. It offers a full-time program with introductory to advanced studies in Torah and Talmud study. www.horizons.edu

» **Yeshiva Ohr Somayach** has a chareidi orientation. It is located in Monsey, NY, and is similar to Yeshiva Ohr Somayach in Jerusalem. www.ohr.org.il

» **Yeshiva Shor Yoshuv** has a chareidi orientation. It is located in Far Rockaway, NY. Telephone: (718) 327-9158.

» **Yeshiva Tiferes Bachurim** is a Chabad Rabbinical College, located in Morristown, NJ. www.rca.edu

Los Angeles

» **Yeshiva University of Los Angeles** is a high school whose orientation is similar to Yeshiva University's in New York. www.yula.org.

Coed Studies in Jerusalem

» **Pardes Institute,** emphasizes intellectual openness and textual study. Offers several programs from beginner to advanced. Students are mostly ages 20 and older. www.pardes.org.il

Worldwide Studies

Below are a few educational organizations that offer classes appropriate for non-observant Jews and for *baal teshuvas*. Also check your local Orthodox synagogues for Judaism classes.

» **Aish HaTorah** has 26 branches worldwide. Branches in North America: Austin,Texas, Boston, Cleveland, Denver, Detroit, Lakewood, NJ, Livingston, NJ, Los Angeles, Minnesota, New York City, Passaic, NJ, Philadelphia, South Florida, St. Louis, Toronto, Washington, DC. Their international branches are in Jerusalem, Australia, Brazil, Chile, England, the Ukraine, Belarus, and South Africa. www.aish.com.

» **Chabad-Lubavitch** has branches in cities all over the United States, as well as worldwide—from Argentina to Vietnam. There are many Chabad houses on college campuses. www.chabad.org.

» **Chicago Torah Network** offers classes, workshops, and singles events for Jewish men and women in Chicago and its suburbs. www.torahnetwork.org

» **Community kollels** are in many cities around the world. Google "community kollel" for an up-to-date listing.

» **DATA (Dallas Area Torah Association)** has amazing rabbis and rebbetzins, plus a very special educational center in Dallas with branches in other parts of Texas. www.datanet.org

» **Hillels** exist at some universities and have Orthodox rabbis who teach Judaica classes or who invite observant speakers to give talks on campus. www.hillel.org.

» **The Jewish Learning Exchange (JLE)** in Golders Green, London, offers classes and social events for Jews ages 17 to 35. They hold more than 80 weekly classes all over London for singles, couples, and professionals, as well as annual educational tours to Eastern Europe and Israel. www.jle.org.uk

» **The Jewish Learning Exchange** in Los Angeles offers weekly classes, user-friendly synagogue services, and home hospitality for Shabbos and Jewish holidays. www.jlela.com

» **Maimonides Leaders Fellowships** has programs at more than 20 college campuses in North America. The program lasts 10 weeks, during which students attend a weekly 2.5 hour seminar, covering diverse leadership topics, general understanding of the Torah, and practical applications of leadership in society. Students receive a stipend. www.maimonidesfellowships.com

» **Ohr Samayach International** has a number of branches around the world, including in New York, Philadelphia, Detroit, Chicago, South Florida, Los Angeles, Toronto, Thornhill, Ontario, London, England, Johannesburg, Cape Town, and Sydney. www.ohr.edu. The Jewish Learning Exchange is an affiliate of theirs.

» **Torah Mitzion** offers community classes and has a religious Zionist orientation. At present, they have more than 25 branches on several continents. www.torahmitzion.org

Appendix B:
Resources and Bibliography

Baal Teshuva Issues
Becher, Mordechai and Newman, Moshe. *After the Return*. Feldheim, New York, 1995.

Basic Judaism
Blech, Benjamin, *Understanding Judaism: the Basics of Deed and Creed*. Rowman and Littlefield, Baltimore, 1991.

Blech, Benjamin, *The Complete Idiot's Guide to Understanding Judaism*. Alpha Books, New York, 1999.

Donin, Hayim Halevy, *To Be a Jew*. Basic Books, New York, 1972.

Kornbluth, Doron, *Jewish Matters*. Targum Press, Southfield, MI, 1999.

Children
Donin, Hayim Halevy, *To Raise a Jewish Child*. Basic Books, New York, 1991.

Orlowek, Noach, *Raising Roses Among the Thorns*. Feldheim, Jerusalem, 2003.

Radcliff, Chana Sara, *Raise Your Kids Without Raising Your Voice*. Harper Collins, Canada, 2006.

Dating and Marriage

Aiken, Lisa, *Guide for the Romantically Perplexed*. Devora Publishing, Jerusalem, 2003.

Einhorn, Rosie and Zimmerman, Sherry, *Talking Tachlis*. Targum Press, Southfield, MI, 1998.

Kaplan, Aryeh, *Made in Heaven: A Jewish Wedding Guide*. Moznaim Publishing, New York, 1983.

Manolson, Gila, *Head to Heart: What To Know Before Dating and Marriage*. Targum Press, Southfield, MI, 2002.

Manolson, Gila, *The Magic Touch: A Jewish Approach to Relationships*. Feldheim, New York, 1992.

English Translations

The Five Books of Moses with Commentary

The Artscroll Chumash, Stone Edition. Mesorah Publications, Brooklyn, 1993. Artscroll also has Schottenstein linear editions of the Chumash with Rashi's commentary.

The Gutnick Edition of the Chumash. Kol Menachem, Brooklyn, 2004.

The Prophets and Scriptures with Commentary

Artscroll series

Judaica Press series

Family Holiness

Kaplan, Aryeh, *Waters of Eden: The Mystery of the Mikvah*. NCSY/Union of Orthodox Jewish Congregations of America, New York, 1976.

Slonim, Rivkah (ed.), *Total Immersion: A Mikvah Anthology*. Urim Publications, Jerusalem, 2005.

Holidays

Apisdorf, Shimon, *The Rosh Hashanah Survival Kit*. Leviathan Press, Baltimore, 2003.

Apisdorf, Shimon, *The Yom Kippur Survival Kit*. Leviathan Press, Baltimore, 2003.

Apisdorf, Shimon, *The Passover Survival Kit*. Leviathan Press, Baltimore, 1997.

Kitov, Eliyahu, *The Book of Our Heritage*. Feldheim, New York, 1973.

Intermarriage

Kornbluth, Doron, *Why Marry Jewish?* Targum Press, Southfield, MI, 2003.

Jewish History

Ganz, Yaffa, *Sand and Stars* (vols 1, 2): *The Jewish Journey Through Time*. Shaar Press, Brooklyn, 1995.

Wein, Berel, *Echoes of Glory*. Shaar Press, Brooklyn, 1995.

Wein, Berel, *Herald of Destiny*. Shaar Press, Brooklyn, 1993.

Wein, Berel, *Triumph of Survival*. Shaar Press, Brooklyn, 1990.

Kashrut (Keeping Kosher)

Apisdorf, Shimon, *Kosher for the Clueless but Curious*. Leviathan Press, Baltimore, 2005.

Jaffe, Azriela, *What Do You Mean You Can't Eat in My House Any More?* Schocken Books, New York, 2005.

There are many reliable kashrut organizations. Below are three of the largest national kashrut supervisory agencies whose kashrut certification appears on products sold throughout the US:

Orthodox Union (www.oukosher.org) Lists thousands of products under the Orthodox Union's kosher supervision. You can also ask questions about kashrut or about specific products: Kosher hotline: 212-613-8241, or fax your question to 212-613-0752.

Kof-K (www.kof-k.org) Questions can be telephoned to 201-837-0500 or faxed to 201-837-0126.

Star-K (www.star-k.org) under the administration of Rabbi Moshe Heinemann of Baltimore, lists helpful information for consumers, including keeping kosher, keeping kosher when traveling, Passover, and other informative articles, updates, and alerts. Questions can be asked by telephoning the Hotline, 410-484-4110, by faxing 410-653-9294, or by email: info@star-k.org.

Kosher Information Bureau (www.kosherquest.org) The most comprehensive Web site regarding Kashrus in the world. KosherQuest provides an outstanding resource for the Kosher consumer listing over 30,000 products that are reliably certified as Kosher in a database that can be accessed by product type or by manufacturer. The search can be further customized by the consumer to meet any specification that he or she may choose, including limiting the search to products with a specific certification, products that are specifically Cholov Yisroel, etc. Product search is only one of many features of this site. The Web site is designed with a magazine format, and has articles that are updated regularly. Besides feature articles, KosherQuest has a Kosher update/alert section, listing new products and changes in Kashrus status of products; a recipe section; an ask the Rabbi section, listing questions answered by Rabbi Eliezer Eidlitz: Rabbi Eliezer Eidlitz's book "Is It Kosher?" is online in its entirety, providing yet another valuable tool for our visitors; and an e-mail: Kosher Hotline" where questions regarding Kashrus can be sent directly to Rabbi Eliezer Eidlitz for a personal and timely response.

Meditation
Kaplan, Aryeh, *Jewish Meditation*. Schocken Books, New York, 1982.

Svirsky, Efim, *Connection*. Institute of Psycho-spiritual Therapy. Jerusalem, 2004.

Modesty

Manolson, Gila, *Outside, Inside: A Fresh Look at Tzniut.* Targum Press, Southfield, MI, 1997.

Mourning

Lamm, Maurice, *The Jewish Way in Death and Mourning.* Jonathan David, New York, 1969.

Mysticism

Tatz, Akiva, *Living Inspired.* Targum Press, Southfield, MI, 1993.

Tatz, Akiva, *Worldmask.* Targum Press. Southfield, MI, 1995.

Prayer

Donin, Hayim Halevy, *To Pray as a Jew.* Basic Books, New York, 1980.

Iskowitz, Yaakov Yosef (ed.), *Aneni: Special Prayers for Special Occasions.* Feldheim, New York, 2001.

Kirzner, Yitzchak, and Aiken, Lisa, *The Art of Jewish Prayer.* Judaica Press, New York, 2002.

Munk, Elie, *The World of Prayer.* Feldheim, New York, 1988.

Zakutinsky, Rivka (ed), *Techinas: A Voice From the Heart, As Only A Woman Can Pray.* Aura Press, Brooklyn, 1992.

Shabbos/Shabbat

Palatnik, Lori, *Turn Friday Night into Shabbos: The Shabbat Experience Step-By-Step. Jason A*ronson, Northfield (NJ), 1999.

Grunfeld, Dayan, *The Shabbos.* Feldheim, New York, 2003.

Ribiat, David, *The 39 Melochos: An Elucidation of the 39 Melochos from Concept to Practical Application* (vols 1-4). Misrad Hasefer, Lakewood, NJ, 2004.

Science

Aviezer, Nathan, *In the Beginning: Biblical Creation and Science.* Ktav, Hoboken (NJ), 1990.

Aviezer, Nathan, *Fossils and Faith.* Ktav, Hoboken (NJ), 2001.

Schroeder, Gerald, *The Science of God.* Broadway Books, New York, l998.

Schroeder, Gerald, *The Hidden Face of God.* Touchstone, New York, 2001.

Speech

Pliskin, Zelig, *Chafetz Chaim: Guard Your Tongue.* Ahavas Chesed, Inc., Brooklyn, 1977.

There is a Shmiras Halashon Hotline, where callers can ask questions about what is permitted to say about others. The hotline is open Monday through Thursday and Saturday nights from 9-10:30 pm, EST. For more information about books, daily emails, and lectures regarding guarding the tongue, see www.chofetzchaimusa.org.

Teenagers

Tatz, Akiva. *The Thinking Teenager's Guide to Life.* Targum, Southfield, MI, l999.

Torah

Aiken, Lisa and Michaels, Ira. *Genesis: The Untold Story.* Rossi Publications, Los Angeles, 2007.

Why Bad Things Happen

Aiken, Lisa. *Why Me, God?* Rowman and Littlefield, Baltimore, 1996.

Blech, Benjamin. *If God Is So Good, Why Is the World So Bad?* Simcha Press, Deerfield Beach (FL), 2003.

Women's Issues

Aiken, Lisa. *To Be a Jewish Woman.* Jerusalem, 1992.

Heller, Tzippora. *Our Bodies, Our Souls.* Targum Press, Southfield, MI, 2004.

Kornbluth, Doron, and Sarah Tikvah (eds), *Jewish Women Speak about Jewish Matters.* Targum, Southfield, MI, 2002.

Miscellaneous

Kaplan, Aryeh, *Handbook of Jewish Thought* (vols 1, 2). Moznaim, Brooklyn, 1992.

Kaplan, Aryeh, *Resurrection, Immortality and the Age of the Universe*. Ktav, Hoboken (NJ), 1993.

Kornbluth, Doron (ed.), *Jewish Matters: A Pocketbook of Knowledge and Inspiration*. Targum, Jerusalem, 1999.

Twerski, Abraham. Author of 53 titles on a variety of topics!

Internet Sites

www.aish.com
www.asktherabbi.org
www.beingjewish.com
www.beyondbt.com
www.chabad.org
www.innernet.org.il
www.jewishanswers.org (can ask questions)
www.jle.org.uk (Jewish Learning Exchange, England)
www.jwisdom.com
www.NCSY.org (for teens)
www.nerleelef.com
www.ohr.edu (Ohr Samayach)
www.simpletoremember.com
www.torah.org
www.613.org

Beware—some proselytizing Christian organizations hide their real intentions by posting websites with the name baal teshuvah or Judaism in them!

Books

www.aryehkaplan.com—a one-stop store of his prolific and amazing books.

www.judaicapress.com
www.rabbiwein.com

Downloadable classes
www.teachittome.com
www.mp3shiur.com
www.learntorah.com
www.yadavraham.org
Many of the above Internet sites also have downloadable classes.

Get a free Jewish studies partner
www.partnersintorah.com
www.gottorah.com

Weekend Retreats/Events
www.gatewaysonline.com
www.discoveryproduction.com
www.njop.org

Resource Organizations
Association of Jewish Outreach Programs (AJOP)—www.ajop.org

Aish HaTorah—www.aish.com

Chabad Lubavitch—www.chabad.org

Jewish Learning Exchange—www.jle.org, www.jle.org.uk (England)

National Jewish Outreach Program (NJOP)—www.njop.org. Their website lists crash courses in basic Judaism or Hebrew offered throughout the United States.

National Conference of Synagogue Youth (NCSY)—www.ncsy.org

Outreach Judaism (anti-missionary)—www.outreachjudaism.org

Matchmaking Services
www.jdate.com
www.sassonvsimcha.org
www.jewishdatingandmarriage.com
www.sawyouatsinai.com

www.sagewannabe@aol.com. Run by Rabbi Benzion Klatzko and Dr. Goldwasser.

www.seeyouonshabbos.com. For baal teshuvas ages 22-35.

Vocational Resources

www.seminarycentral.com offers a list of English post-high school Jewish degree and

vocational programs. At this time, most, but not all, are suitable for observant Jews.

Resource People

Rabbi Dovid Cohen, *shlita*, is a world-renowned halachic authority and posek based in Brooklyn. He generously makes himself available at no charge to anyone who calls with halachic questions. From around Labor Day until mid-June, he takes calls Sundays, Mondays, Wednesdays, and Thursdays from 3-4 pm and 10-11 pm Eastern time, and Tuesdays from 10-11 pm. (718) 376-7388, or (718) 376-7423. If you get a busy signal, keep trying. Do not call earlier or later than these times as no one will answer the phone.

Appendix C:
History of the Baal
Teshuva Movement

This following can help readers understand why so many Jews have returned to observant Judaism in recent years.

Egypt, Israel and the First Exile Judaism teaches that God took the Jewish people out of Egypt more than 3,300 years ago. Seven weeks later, He gave them the Torah and its oral explanation (later written down as the Talmud). A generation later, two-and-one-half to three million Jews entered the land of Israel and began to settle it. Four hundred and forty years after entering the Holy Land, King Solomon built the First Temple in Jerusalem. The Jews eventually worshiped idols and did not properly observe the Torah. As a result, the Assyrians conquered most of Israel and exiled the Ten Tribes. After idolatry became rampant in southern Israel, the Babylonians in 422 BCE destroyed Solomon's Temple and Jerusalem and exiled most of the remaining Jews from our land.[1]

Israel and the Second Exile About 42,000 Jews returned to Israel 70 years later, while most Jews remained in the Diaspora. During the majority of the Second Temple era, Jews in Israel were almost universally knowledgeable of Judaism and it was mostly practiced according to the rabbinic interpretation of the Oral Law. This Oral Law was given to the Jews at Mount Sinai along with the Written Law, also known as the Five Books of Moses, or "Torah." In time, the Jews in Israel fought with, and hated each other. As a result, in the year 70 CE, the Romans destroyed the Second Temple and Jerusalem, ending the Jewish commonwealth. The Romans exiled and enslaved the vast majority of Jewish survivors. In 132 CE, Hadrian decided to make Jerusalem into a pagan city and he outlawed various Jewish practices and teaching Torah. The Jews responded with the Bar Kochba Revolt. By the year 135 CE, when the Romans finally succeeded in putting down their rebellion, the Romans had either starved to death or killed most of the Jews in Israel.[2]

Diaspora/Christian Persecution   For the most part, Diaspora Jews then lived in Jewish communities until the Emancipation brought about by Napoleon in the early 19th century. They observed Jewish laws and customs and did not settle in non-Jewish neighborhoods unless they converted out. Only a minority of Jews during those thousands of years ever denied that God gave Jews the Torah and that Jews were supposed to observe it, although many assimilated or converted out in order to have easier lives socially and financially. Christian persecution of Jews in Europe often included barring Jews from trades, professions, and universities, in addition to public humiliation, pogroms, staging forced theological debates and exposure to Christian evangelism, confiscating Jewish property and wealth, and expelling them.

Diaspora/Emancipation & Enlightenment   After the Emancipation and "Enlightenment" (Haskalah movement) in Europe, hundreds of thousands of Jews raced to abandon Jewish observance. German Jews began the first Jewish movement in history that insisted that the Torah was not Divinely given.

The "Reform movement" changed the *status quo* that had existed for more than three millennia. Reform leaders taught that Jews should only observe those rituals that made sense according to modern, human reasoning. They dispensed with Jewish dietary laws, holidays, and Shabbos. They changed the prayers to reflect their belief that Jews would never return to the land of Israel nor have another Temple. They taught that Berlin should be the Jews' Jerusalem. They did away with a God-centered religion and instead made man the center of daily life. They dispensed with a religious system that was concerned with spiritually refining ourselves and sanctifying our interactions with the physical world and with people. They took Judaism from a full-time way of life that made daily activities holy and converted it into a part-time intellectual or cultural pursuit whose practice took place but a few times a year in the synagogue and home.

Massive Assimilation One rapid consequence of the conditions that led to the Reform movement was that Jews became ignorant, and intolerant of, Torah Judaism and observant Jews. The lack of Jewish knowledge by "emancipated Jews" was paralleled by a rush for social acceptance, secular education, and financial opportunities in the Christian world. Within one or two generations, there was massive assimilation of Reform Jews and Jews who wanted to modify traditional Judaism. Moses Mendelssohn was an observant Jew who taught that one must be a Jew in one's home and a man in the street. This adoption of non-Jewish values led to the inevitable assimilation of his descendants. None of his grandchildren—including Felix Mendelssohn, the greatest composer of church music of his time—remained Jewish. Jews thronged to attend secular schools and universities that attacked Judaism. European Jews quickly lost their holy knowledge and traditions. Western European Jews were so at risk of disappearing that Rabbi Samson Raphael Hirsch had to find a way to bring them back from the brink of total assimilation. (He succeeded to some extent by teaching Torah concepts in a way that appealed to modern Jews, and integrated Judaism with knowledge of the secular world.) By the advent of World War II, 40% of Polish Jews no longer kept Shabbos, despite the fact that they had formerly been among the most religious of the Eastern European Jews. The repudiation of Shabbos observance and other Jewish traditions by Western European Jews was far greater.

Reform Judaism negated Jewish traditions and authenticity, while keeping its members uneducated about the Torah, Jewish beliefs, and practices. The tragic result was that Reform Jews almost invariably had no Jewish descendants within two to three generations. Reform Judaism has lost so many adherents to assimilation and intermarriage that they redefined who is a Jew (inventing the concept that patrilineal descent allows one to be Jewish) in order to keep themselves alive.

American Jewry's Death and Rebirth   Almost all non-German Jews who immigrated to America from the late 1700s and onward came from observant families. Most wanted to escape anti-Semitic persecution or wanted better financial opportunities. Many believed that both goals would be facilitated by assimilating into American society. Several decades after emigrating to America, the descendants of most Jews from Europe had either intermarried or were only culturally Jewish. A hundred years after their forebears landed on the shores of the United States, only a tiny fraction of Americans with Jewish ancestors were either born Jewish or still identified as Jews.

In six years' time, Hitler succeeded in annihilating six to seven million Jews.[3] Before the Holocaust, there were at least 18 million Jews world-wide. After the Holocaust, there were 12 million. In the 1960s, there were six million American Jews. Forty years later, normal population growth would have resulted in at least 24 million American Jews. Instead, by the year 2000, only 4.3 million American Jews considered themselves Jewish, and only half of them connected with Judaism enough to affiliate with a synagogue of any denomination. Why? Lack of Jewish education and an intermarriage rate of 40% or more.

Turning the Tide   In the 1950s and 1960s, three organizations in America tried to turn the tide of assimilation:

1. **Rabbi Menachem Mendel Schneerson, z"tl,** trained and encouraged more than 5,000 Lubavitch emissaries to reach out to assimilated Jews around the world.

2. **NCSY,** the youth movement of the Orthodox Union (OU), under the guidance of Rabbi Pinchas Stolper, brought American high-school students back to Torah Judaism.

3. **Yeshiva University's Torah Leadership Seminar,** along with Yeshiva University graduates such as Rabbi Shlomo Riskin, also reached out to unaffiliated and non-observant American Jews.

In time, Rabbi Ephraim Buchwald started a beginner's minyan at Lincoln Square Synagogue in Manhattan. Over the next two decades, these rabbis and teachers taught uneducated Jews about traditional Jewish rituals and showed them the beauty of Torah.

Six-Day War In 1967, the lightning victory of Israeli Jews against Arabs who tried to annihilate them in the Six-Day War suddenly ignited feelings of Jewish pride across the world. This made many Jews more open to learning about their heritage and willing to adopt Jewish rituals. During the next few years, the first baal teshuva yeshivas and seminaries opened in New York (Shor Yashuv Yeshiva and Bais Chana) and in Jerusalem (Aish HaTorah and Ohr Samayach for men, Neve Yerushalayim for women). Around this time, Rabbi Shlomo Carlebach brought his charisma, warmth, and Chassidic music to Jews around the world and opened their hearts to Judaism. Rebbetzin Esther Jungreis did the same through her emotionally stirring talks and her organization, Hineni.

NJOP In 1987, Rabbi Ephraim Buchwald started the National Jewish Outreach Program (NJOP). He advertised its free crash courses in Hebrew and basic Judaism on radio, in the New York subways, and in the mass media. Over the past two decades, tens of thousands of adult Jews have attended these classes, taught by thousands of volunteer teachers.

In 1988, the Association for Jewish Outreach Professionals (AJOP) started as a forum where hundreds of outreach professionals could share ideas and support one another in this burgeoning field.[4]

Discovery Seminars   In time, Aish HaTorah developed its Discovery seminar, which has been attended by more than 100,000 Jews. Its website, featuring interesting articles about a variety of Jewish topics, gets more than two million hits every month.

Today   Today, SEED (yeshiva students teaching in various Jewish communities) programs and community kollels teach Jews about Judaism through classes, Shabbatons, retreats, and lectures. Partners in Torah offers every Jew the opportunity to be paired with someone who will teach them Jewish studies in-person or over the phone. Kiruv, or Jewish outreach, workers are now everywhere that Jews can be found. Chabad-Lubavitch outreach rabbis and their wives are on countless college campuses, making Passover seders in Nepal, and lighting Chanukah menorahs in shopping malls and town centers around the world.

Some outreach teachers learn Torah with Jews one-on-one or in small classes in work places. They run lunch-and-learn programs in law and banking offices, teach Jewish medical and business ethics, run singles' events, teach courses in marriage preparation and enrichment, and offer community programs, summer camps, educational travel programs, retreats, and more.

The strength of the *baal teshuva* movement is felt by the burgeoning number of men and women learning in yeshivas and seminaries. There are now more Jews learning in yeshivas in Israel than at any other time in history. There are also many synagogues and Jewish schools whose members or students are mostly *baal teshuvas*. It is my hope that this phenomenon will only grow.

May we soon see the fulfillment of the Biblical verse that after the Jews are dispersed to the four corners of the earth, and have suffered through their exiles, we will finally return to God and to observance of His Torah. May we soon become the light unto the nations that was the Almighty's hope for us all along.

Glossary

Many religious Jews speak a mixture of their native language and Hebrew and/or Yiddish terms. Here is a glossary of some common words to help *baal teshuvas* and their relatives to understand what others are saying.

Note: Many "s" sounds become "t" sounds when spoken in a Sephardic/Israeli dialect.

Aibishter
The One Above, i.e., God.

Al Hamichyah
A prayer thanking God after eating grain-based foods such as cookies, cake, crackers, or pasta.

Aliyah
Literally, "going up." When a Jewish man is called up to the Torah in the synagogue, he gets the honor of giving honor to the Torah. This is called "getting an aliyah." Making *aliyah* means immigrating to Israel.

Aravos/Aravot
The two willow branches that are part of the Four Species used on the holiday of Tabernacles. Five aravot are taken together on the last day of the holiday.

Asher Yatzar
A prayer thanking God that our bodies function properly. It is said after using the bathroom.

Ashkenazic
Jews whose ancestors came from non-Mediterranean European countries.

Assarah B'Teves/Tevet
A minor fast day in December that commemorates Jewish national tragedies that led to the Jewish exile and destruction of Jerusalem.

Assur
Forbidden.

Aufruf
A celebration where a groom is called to the Torah on Shabbos before his wedding. People throw candies at him afterward, and his parents usually sponsor a light meal, known as a *kiddush*, afterward.

Avel
Someone who is mourning a deceased close relative.

Aveilus/aveilut
The period of mourning for a close relative. It lasts a year for a parent. During this time, a mourner may not attend public or most happy celebrations.

Avraham (Avinu)
(Our Patriarch) Abraham.

Baal Teshuva
A previously non-observant Jew who became observant.

Badeken
Ceremony prior to the wedding, when the groom veils the bride.

Bais Din/Bet Din
A Jewish court of law.

Bais Medrash/Bet Midrash

The study hall of a yeshiva or synagogue where men study religious texts. Can also be the chapel in a synagogue.

Bamidbar

The Biblical book of Numbers.

Bar Mitzvah

When a Jewish boy becomes a Jewish adult at the age of 13. He is usually called up to the Torah, and the prayer service is followed by a celebratory meal.

Bas Mitzvah/Bat Mitzvah

When a Jewish girl becomes a Jewish adult at the age of 12. It is often marked by celebrating with a modest party or a celebratory meal.

Beemah

The elevated part of a synagogue from which the Torah is read.

Bekeshe

A silk (usually black) caftan worn by men in honor of Shabbos and Jewish holidays.

Bentching

Reciting the grace after meals.

Bentching Licht

Lighting the Shabbos or holiday candles and saying a blessing over them.

Beraishis/Beraisheet

The Biblical book of Genesis.

Bochur

An unmarried Jewish male (plural, *bochurim*).

Boreh Nefashos/Boreh Nefashot

A short prayer said after eating foods such as meat, dairy, vegetables, most fruits, or most beverages when they are not eaten with bread.

Bracha
A blessing.

Bris/Brit Milah
A ritual circumcision. Healthy Jewish boys are ritually circumcised on their eighth day of life and are given their Hebrew name at this time. If a child is sick, the procedure is postponed until he is healthy.

B'sha'ah Tovah
Literally, "at a good time." The Jewish way of congratulating a woman when we hear that she is pregnant. This wishes her a healthy delivery.

Chalav Akum
Milk from kosher animals to which no non-kosher ingredients were added. The milking itself was not supervised by a religious Jew.

Chalav Yisrael
Kosher milk that was produced under the supervision of a religious Jew from the time the animal was milked until the milk was packaged.

Challah
A whole loaf of (braided) bread eaten on Shabbos and Jewish holidays.

Chametz
Foods containing leavened grain products. It is forbidden to eat such food on Passover.

Chanukah
Eight-day rabbinic holiday in December. It commemorates the Jews' spiritual victory over Greek ideas and their ousting of Greek military rule.

Chanukiya
The eight-branched candelabrum that Jews light on *Chanukah*.

Chassan/Chattan
A Jewish man from the time that he is engaged until shortly after he is married.

Chasunah/Chatunah
A Jewish wedding.

Cholent
A long-cooking stew typically made out of meat or chicken, potatoes, barley, beans, onions, and seasonings. It starts cooking Friday afternoon and is left on a warmer until it is served for Saturday lunch.

Chrain
Horseradish, often eaten with gefilte fish.

Chumash
The Five Books of Moses.

Chumrah
Religious stringency.

Chupah
The wedding canopy.

Cohen
A Jewish man who is a descendant of the first Jewish priest, Aaron, and certain of Aaron's relatives.

Dovid (Hamelech)
(King) David.

Devarim
The Biblical book of Deuteronomy.

Eliyahu (Hanavi)
Elijah (the prophet).

Esrog/Etrog
Fragrant citron that Jews take along with branches of three other species during the holiday of Tabernacles.

Fleishig
Meat.

Frum
An observant Jew.

Gadol
A spiritually great Jew, often a rabbinic leader and expert in Jewish law.

Gefilte fish
A food made out of ground fish, onions, eggs, and seasonings that is customarily eaten on Shabbos and Jewish holidays.

Halacha
Literally "the way to go." A Hebrew term for Jewish law.

Hallel
Praises of God (psalms) that are recited on Jewish holidays and on the New Moon.

Hashem
"The Name." A way of referring to God.

Hashkafa
Jewish philosophical outlook.

Hashkama
Prayer service that begins early in the morning.

Havdala
The beautiful ceremony that marks the end of Shabbos or Jewish holidays. It is usually said over a cup of wine or grape juice, using a braided candle and fragrant spices on Saturday night. One uses only the cup of wine when *havdala* is said after Jewish holidays.

Hetter
A rabbinically approved leniency.

Hoshana Rabbah
The last day of the holiday of Tabernacles. People say many prayers in the synagogue while the men walk around inside

carrying their Four Species. We strike a bundle of five willow branches on the floor at the end of the morning service.

Kabbalah

The mystical explanations of the Torah.

Kabbalas Shabbos/Kabbalat Shabbat

Songs (prayers) that welcome Shabbos on Friday night.

Kaddish

"Sanctification." A public prayer that sanctifies God's Name.
It may be said by a prayer leader or by mourners when a quorum of Jewish men is present.

Kallah

A Jewish woman from the time that she is engaged until
shortly after she gets married.

Kavanah

Intention to perform a religious commandment, or concentration when praying.

Ketubah

Jewish wedding contract that protects the bride's financial interests and spells out her husband's obligations to her. Some
couples frame and display a decorated one in their home.

Kiddush

Prayer in which we sanctify Shabbos or Jewish holidays over
a cup of grape juice or wine. Also, a meal that is sanctified
with a cup of wine or grape juice at the synagogue after Saturday services.

Kipah

A skull cap worn by Jewish males. Also known as a yarmulke.

Kollel

A post-graduate yeshiva where married men study Judaism
(usually Talmud) full time, often for many years.

Kosher
Ritually fit or permitted to eat.

Kulah
Religious leniency.

K'zayis/k'zayit
Literally, "like an olive." A quantity of food equal to about an ounce. After eating at least this amount of a food, one must say a prayer thanking God. It is the minimum that a Jew must eat of certain foods to fulfill certain religious obligations.

Layah
The fourth Matriarch of the Jewish people. Also, a common Hebrew name for Jewish girls. Usually spelled Leah.

Levayah
A funeral.

Loshon hara
Speaking negatively about someone, even when what is said is true.

Lulav
Palm branches that are taken together with myrtle, willows, and a citron on the holiday of *Succot* (Tabernacles).

Maariv
The evening prayer service.

Machatanim
The parents of your son- or daughter-in-law.

Machmir
Religiously stringent.

Machzor
Prayer book for Jewish holidays.

Maikel
Someone who is religiously lenient.

Mattan Torah

The giving of the Torah on Mt. Sinai to the Jewish people more than 3,300 years ago.

Matzah

Square or round sheets of unleavened crackers that Jews eat during the holiday of Passover.

Mashgiach

A supervisor. Someone who ensures that a restaurant or company's products are kosher. Also, someone who helps yeshiva students to achieve their spiritual potential.

Mashiach

The Messiah.

Mazal Tov

Literally, "good luck," or "congratulations."

Mechitzah

Divider between the men's and women's sections in a synagogue or at religious affairs.

Megillah

Literally, "scroll." Usually refers to the book of Esther, which is read on the holiday of Purim. Can also refer to books in the Jewish canon written on scrolls, such as the books of Lamentations or Ruth.

Menorah

The seven-branched candelabra that was lit in the Jewish Temples. Often (inaccurately) used to refer to lamps with eight branches that Jews kindle on the holiday of Chanukah.

Mevushal

Literally, "cooked." Refers to dry foods that are cooked enough to reheat on a warmer on Shabbos. Also, refers to kosher wine that was cooked so that Jews can drink it if it is subsequently handled by a non-Jew.

Mezuman
Three or more Jewish men who ate a meal together and who say an introduction to the Grace after Meals.

Mezuzah
A parchment with a portion of the Shema prayer written on it. It is placed on the doorposts of one's house, often in pretty casings.

Midrash
Homiletical stories that explain deeper meanings of the Torah.

Mikvah
A ritual bath where women immerse before they get married and after their monthly periods. Some men immerse there to elevate themselves before Shabbos and Jewish holidays. Also, metal and glass utensils previously owned by a non-Jew are immersed in a mikvah (with the recitation of a blessing) before use; vessels used in food preparation made from some other materials may be immersed without saying a blessing.

Milchig
Dairy.

Minchah
The afternoon prayer service.

Minyan
A quorum of 10 adult males—the minimum needed to say communal Jewish prayers.

Mishnah
The Oral Law written down in Hebrew around the year 200CE.

Mishnayos/Mishnayot
Sections of the Mishnah.

Moshe (Rabeinu)
(Our teacher) Moses.

Motzi
The blessing said over bread.

Muktzah
An item that may not be moved on Shabbos or Jewish holidays.

Mutar
Permitted.

Nach
Acronym for "Nevi'im Ketuvim," the 19 books of the Prophets and Jewish Scriptures.

Navi
A Jewish prophet.

Negel Vasser
Ritual hand washing that Jews perform when they wake up in the morning. Water is poured from a cup alternately over each hand three times.

Negiah
Forbidden touching between a man and woman who are not married to each other. *Shomer negiah* means someone who does not touch the person he or she dates until they are married.

Netilas/Netilat Yadayim
The ritual washing of hands before eating bread. Water is poured from a cup two or three times onto the right hand, then two or three times over the left hand. The person says a blessing over washing their hands, and then dries them.

Netz
Literally, "sunrise." Refers to morning prayers that begin before sunrise so that the main prayers are said at sunrise.

Pareve
Neither dairy nor meat. Also, something that is neutral or not exciting.

Pas/Pat Akum
Bread baked with only kosher ingredients without a Jew being involved in the baking process.

Pas Yisroel/Pat Yisrael
Bread that was baked with the involvement of a Jew using only kosher ingredients.

Pas Nicht
Yiddish for "it doesn't go." Doing something that is improper.

Payos/Payot
Sidelocks worn to fulfill the Biblical commandment not to round the corners of a man's head with a razor blade.

Pesach
The holiday of Passover. During these seven days (in Israel) or eight days in the Diaspora, Jews don't eat foods containing leavened grain. They eat using special dishes and utensils that are not used the rest of the year.

Pidyon Ha'ben
A ceremony in which one-month-old first-born boys are redeemed by the father's giving a small amount of money to a Jewish priest.

Pirkei Avos/Avot
Talmudic selection known as "Ethics of the Fathers." Jews read one of these chapters each Shabbos afternoon between Passover and the Jewish New Year and study these ideas at other times.

Posek
A rabbi who renders decisions about Jewish law.

Poskin (shailas)
Rendering decisions when questions are asked about Jewish law.

Pshat

The simple (plain) meaning of a Torah verse.

Purim

A joyful rabbinic holiday when Jews celebrate being saved from annihilation by the Persians. It is customary for people to drink a lot of alcoholic beverages, to eat a festive meal, to hear the reading of the Scroll of Esther (*Megillah*), and to give gifts to the poor and delicious foods to their friends.

Pushke

Charity box at home or in the synagogue.

Rachel

The third Matriarch of the Jewish people. Also, a common Hebrew girl's name.

Rambam

Acronym for Rabbi Moshe ben Maimon. Maimonides was a great Jewish scholar, author, and physician in the 11th century. He lived mostly in Egypt during his adult life.

Ramban

Acronym for Rabbi Moshe ben Nachman, also known as Nachmanides. He was a great Jewish scholar, commentator, and physician in the 12th century. He lived in Spain until the Christians exiled him. He spent the last years of his life revitalizing Jewish communities in Israel.

Rashi

Acronym for Rabbeinu Shlomo Yitzchaki, a great French Jewish scholar. He lived in the 12th century and wrote important commentaries on the Torah and Talmud.

Rav

A rabbi. A Judaica teacher and/or the person to whom one asks religious questions.

Rebbe

A boys' teacher of religious studies. Also, a leader of a Chassidic group.

Ribbono shel Ha'Olam
Master of the World. Another name for God.

Rivka
Rebecca, the second Matriarch of the Jewish people. Also a common Hebrew girls' name.

Rosh Chodesh
The New Moon. The first day of every Jewish month. When there are two days of *Rosh Chodesh*, they include the last day of the prior Jewish month.

Rosh Hashanah
The Jewish New Year. Two days, usually in September.

Rosh Kollel
The head of an institution of higher studies where married men study Judaism full time.

Rosh Yeshiva
The head of a men's institute of Jewish studies.

Sarah
The first Matriarch.

Seder
A special meal on the first night (in Israel) or first two nights (in the Diaspora) of Passover that commemorates the Jews' Exodus from Egypt.

Sefardic/Sephardic
Jews or traditions from Mediterranean or Arab countries.

Sefer Torah
Torah scroll.

Selichos/Selichot
Penitential prayers usually said by Ashkenazic Jews at midnight on Saturday night before the Jewish New Year and continuing early every weekday morning until the eve of the Day of Atonement. Sephardic Jews start saying these prayers

40 days before the Day of Atonement and continue until the eve of the Day of Atonement.

Shabbos/Shabbat
The Sabbath. Begins Friday afternoon before sunset and ends at nightfall Saturday evening. On Shabbos, we spend extra time praying and studying Torah, eating special meals, and singing special songs. Many weekday activities (including 39 categories of creative work) are forbidden in order to help us to focus on spiritual pursuits and to crown God as the ultimate Creator.

Shacharis/Shacharit
The morning prayer service.

Shalosh seudos or seudah shleesheet
The third meal eaten on Shabbos, usually in the late afternoon.

Shatnez
A garment that the Torah prohibits wearing because it contains both linen and wool.

Shavuos/Shavuot
The holiday commemorating the Jews' receiving the Torah on Mt. Sinai. It is a two-day holiday outside of Israel, one day in Israel. It is customary to stay up all (the first) night learning Torah and to pray the morning service before sunrise the next morning.

Sheitl
A wig worn by married Jewish women to fulfill the obligation to cover their hair in the presence of men besides their husbands.

Shekiya
Sunset.

Shema
The prayer declaring the Jews' belief in one God. It is recited in the morning and evening prayers, as well as before going to sleep.

Shema al hameetah
The *Shema* prayer that one says before going to sleep.

Shemini Atzeres/Atzeret
The holiday immediately following the seventh day of *Succot* (holiday of Tabernacles). It is observed for two days outside of Israel; one day in Israel.

Shemoneh Esrai
The central Jewish prayer, said three times every weekday and four times on Shabbos and most Jewish holidays.

Shemot
The book of Exodus.

Sheva Brachas/Brachot
6-day post-wedding celebrations in which the seven blessings said under the wedding canopy are recited at a meal with the bride, groom, and at least nine other men present.

Shiur
A class about a Jewish topic. Also, a sufficient measure of something needed to fulfill a religious obligation, or enough food or drink consumed to require saying a blessing afterward.

Shivah Assar B'Tammuz
The fast day of the Tenth of Tammuz. It begins the Three Weeks of Jewish mourning that occur during the summer and which culminate in the fast day of the Ninth of Av.

Shtreimel
A fur hat worn by some Chassidic men in honor of Shabbos or Jewish holidays.

Siddur
Prayer book.

Simcha
A happy occasion, such as a baby naming, ritual circumcision, bar or bat mitzvah, or wedding.

Simchas/Simchat Torah
The holiday of Rejoicing with the Torah. In Israel, it is the same day as *Shemini Atzeret* (the day after *Succot* ends); outside of Israel, it is the second day of *Shemini Atzeret*.

Succah
Temporary booth that Jews eat and live in during the holiday of Tabernacles.

Succos/Succot
The holiday of Tabernacles, when Jews take the Four Species and sit or live in a temporary booth.

Taanis/Taanit Ester
The minor fast day that precedes the holiday of Purim.

Taharas/Taharat Hamishpacha
The laws of family holiness that require a married couple to refrain from physical intimacy periodically and that require the wife to immerse in a ritual bath before resuming marital relations.

Tallis/Tallit
A prayer shawl worn by men. It has special fringes on its four corners.

Tallis/Tallit Katan
A garment with special strings in its four corners. Also called *arba kanfot*. Men usually wear it under their clothes.

Talmud
The Oral Jewish Law. It contains the Mishnah, plus stories and explanations that elaborate on the Mishnah. Also called

the Gemara, it was written in Aramaic, by Babylonian Jewish scholars, around 500 CE.

Tanach

Acronym for "*Torah, Nevi'im, Ketuvim.*" The 24 books of the Jewish Bible.

Tefillin

Boxes attached to leather straps that Jewish men place on their head and arm when praying on weekdays. The boxes contain four Scriptural paragraphs written on parchment.

Tehillim

Psalms written by King David and other spiritual greats. Some or all of the 150 tehillim are recited to help Jews who need extra Divine assistance, in addition to being included in daily prayers.

Three Weeks

A period of national Jewish mourning. It starts on the fast day of the 17th of Tammuz and ends on the fast day of Tisha B'Av. Weddings and celebrations are not held during this time.

Tichel

A scarf worn by married Jewish women to fulfill the obligation to cover their hair.

Tisha B'Av

The Ninth of Av. A sad, 25-hour fast day that commemorates the destructions of both Jewish Temples and the Jews' exile from Israel. It usually occurs in August.

Torah

Literally, "Teaching." It usually refers to the Five Books of Moses.

Tovel or toyvel

Immersing dishes or cooking utensils made by non-Jews in a ritual bath or natural body of water. This spiritually elevates them before a Jew uses them.

Treif
Not kosher (i.e. not permitted to be eaten or not ritually fit.)

Tzaddik
A righteous person.

Tzais/Tzait (Hacochavim)
Nightfall, when stars appear signalling the time when Shabbos or Jewish holidays end.

Tzedakah
Charity.

Tzitzit
The fringes on a Jewish male's four-cornered garment.

Tznius/Tzniut
Jewish laws of modesty. A modest woman is *tzanuah/tznuah*.

Tzom Gedalya
The minor fast day that follows the Jewish New Year. The fast is held on the third day of the month of Tishrei and is named after the last Jewish governor of Israel. His assassination by a Jew led to the Babylonian exile of the Jews from Israel.

Ulpan
An intensive crash course in modern Hebrew, designed to promote proficiency with the language after a few months of study.

Upsheirin/Upsheirnish
A boy's first haircut at the age of three.

Ushpizin
The Jews' seven spiritual forefathers who are invited to the *succah* each night of *Succot*.

Vayikra
The Biblical book of Leviticus.

Yaakov
Jacob, the third Patriarch of the Jews. Also, a common Hebrew boy's name. It is sometimes pronounced Yankov.

Yarmulke
A skull cap whose purpose is to show respect for God and a
man's humility.

Yeshiva
An institution where boys or men study Judaism.

Yid
A Jew.

Yiddishkeit
Observant Judaism.

Yitzchak
Isaac, the second Patriarch of the Jews. Also, a common Hebrew boy's name.

Yom Kippur
The Day of Atonement, when Jews fast for 25 hours and
spend most of the day introspecting, repenting, and praying
in the synagogue.

Yom Tov
A Jewish holiday. We wish Jews *"a gut Yom Tov"* on Jewish
holidays.

Yoseph
Joseph, a son of the Patriarch Jacob, and progenitor of two
Jewish tribes. Also, a common Hebrew boy's name.

Z"l
"Zichrono (zichrona) l'vracha" "May his (her) memory be for a
blessing." Said after mentioning the name of a deceased Jew.

Z"tl, pronounced Zatzal
It means *"zeicher tzaddik l'vracha"* "May the memory of a
righteous person be a blessing." We say this after mentioning
the name of a righteous deceased Jew, especially rabbis.

Notes

Why Jews Become Baal Teshuvas

1. http://en.wikipedia.org/wiki/Eugenics

2. FBI Uniform Crime Reports.

3. www.disastercenter.com/crime/uscrime.htm

4. Overall, the Seventh United Nations Survey of Crime Trends and Operations of Criminal Justice Systems, covering the period of 1998-2000,   reported 23,677,8000 a s - saults, car thefts, murders, rapes, and drug offenses in the US. (United Nations Office on Drugs and Crime, Centre for International Crime Prevention). See United States Uniform Crime Report, www.disastercenter.com/crime/uscrime.htm.

5. Quoted on http://query.nytimes.com/gst/fullpage.html?r es=9B0DE0D9163EF93AA35750C0A961948260   6. http://marriage.rutgers.edu/Publications/SOOU/TEXT-SOOU2007.htm

7. Reported by the Children's Fund, citing 2004 Key Facts about American Children. Published by http://blogcritics.

org/archives/2005/10/15/222604.php. See also www.cdc.gov/
mmwr/previewe/mmwrhtml/00001702htm. The deleterious
effects of divorce and growing up without a father are docu-
mented on http://www.photius.com/feminocracy/facts_on_
fatherless_kids.html

8. "The number of children living with both parents declined
from 85 to 68 percent between 1970 and 1996. The
proportion of children living with one parent has grown
from 12 percent to 28 percent during this same time
span." Quoted from the Census Bureau's release about its
report on "Marital Status and Living Arrangements," cited
on http://www.divorcereform.org/chilrate.html. The State of
Our Unions 2005, a report issued by the National
Marriage Project at Rutgers University, reported that only
63% of American children grow up with both biological parents—the lowest figure in the Western world.

9. According to a survey conducted by the National Opinion Research Center at the University of Chicago, cited on
http://www.divorcereform.org/mel/a2parentscarce.html.

10. For example, the National Center for Health Statistics
(NCHS) projects a divorce rate approximating this amount.
Their conclusions are based on a 1995 federal study of
nearly 11,000 women ages 15-44. It predicted that
one-third of new marriages among younger people will end
in divorce within 10 years and 43 percent will end
within 15 years. Cited on http://www.truthorfiction.com/
rumors/d/divorce.htm.

11. US Census Bureau statistics, quoted on www.clasp.org/pub-
lications/Marriage_Brief3.pdf

12. According to divorcemagazine.com, cited by http://blogcrit-
ics.org/archives/2005/10/15/222604.php

13. Furstenberg, Peterson, Nord, and Zill, "Life Course," 656ff. Cited on page 76 of The Abolition of Marriage, by Maggie Gallagher. Cited on http://www.divorcereform.org/chilrate. html.

14. These statistics are cited by http://www.divorcereform.org/ chilrate.html. Ten percent of children of divorce will go on to witness three or more family breakups. Cited on page 76 of The Abolition of Marriage, by Maggie Gallagher.

15. CBS news poll, late October-early November, 2005.   Cited on http://www.aei.org/publications/pubID.23539/pub_detail.asp. Another 18   percent of families eat together only three or four nights a week. Research has shown that children who eat dinners with their families on a regular basis generally have less drug and alcohol use and greater psychological health than those who don't.

16. Ibid.

17. The 2004 National Survey on Drug Use and Health, Department of Health and Human Services reported that 8%   of Americans ages 12 (!) and older were current illicit drug users. The 2001-2002 National   Epidemiological Survey on Alcohol and Related Conditions, directed by the National Institute on Alcohol Abuse and Alcoholism, determined that 8.5%   of Americans are alcoholics or alcohol dependent. This seems to be a rather low estimate. In 2004,   about 45%   of Americans who drink alcohol reported that they binged on drinking alcohol in the month prior to the survey. This data is cited on http://www.oas. sambsa.gov/nsduh.htm#NSDUHinfo.

18. http://www.pbs.org/fmc/book/pdf/ch4.pdf

19. Public Health Reports, cited in http://www.usatoday.com/ news/health/2006-12-19-premarital-sex_x.htm.

20. Edward O. Laumann, John H. Gagnon, Robert T. Michael, and Stuart Michaels, The Social Organization of Sexuality: Sexual Practices in the United States. Chicago. 1994.   21. Ibid.

22. Ibid.

23. http://www.pbs.org/fmc/book/pdf/ch4.pdf

24. Orthodox psychologist David Pelcovitz, quoted on http://www.eppc.org/publications/programID.5,pubID.2307/pub_detail.asp. When I wrote my doctoral dissertation on the topic of drug and alcohol use by Orthodox Jews and other high school students in 1978, the strongest factor in many prior studies had shown that religious involvement was the single best predictor of non-use of drugs. My study showed that that was still the case, but that Jewish high school students were beginning to drink socially in ways that were unprecedented. Arnie Goldfein, the president of Jewish Alcoholics, Chemically Dependent Persons and Significant Others, was quoted in this 2005   article as saying that he believed that the rates of substance abuse among Jews in general had recently risen to those of population at large, "around 8 to 10 percent."

Emotional aspects of becoming

1. "Faith in Figures," Nov. 6, 2006, p. 31.

2. Yoma, 86:2

Choosing a Rabbi

1. Theodore I. Lenin and Associates, "Rabbi and Synagogue in Reform Judaism." West Hartford: Central Conference of American Rabbis, 1972, pp. 98-99.   Footnotes on Modesty

1. Jewish law does not require married women to cover their hair in the presence of other women, their sons, father or grandfather. Nonetheless, many women cover their hair in the presence of all males, and some even do so when they are alone.

2. Although not due to the laws of modesty, most yeshivish males tend to wear white shirts and black slacks during the week. They wear white shirts, black suits, and black hats to celebrations, on Shabbos and Jewish holidays. On Shabbos and Jewish holidays, many Chassidic (as well as some other) men wear black silk caftans and fur hats.

3. Micah 6:8.

4. To appreciate how maladaptively Americans relate to their appearances, consider the following: Forty percent of women and 33% of men are generally dissatisfied with their overall looks. Eighty-nine percent of women are dissatisfied with their body at some time. Ninety-one percent of American female college students diet, and 22% diet "often" or always. Twenty-five percent of college-age women have an eating disorder. Fifty-one percent of nine- and 10-year-old girls feel better if they are on a diet. Forty-two percent of first- through third-grade girls want to be thinner. Referenced in www.sandiego.edu/sli/documents/YouandYourBody.pdf.

5. Studies have shown that people who are rated as being very attractive are treated better than plainer or unattractive people. The former get better grades in school, earn more, and get better jobs. www.sciencenetlinks.com/sci_update.cfm?DocID=299. See also www.findarticles.com/p/articles/mi_m1355/is_12_100/ai_77931216.   6.   Non-affectionate touching between men and women that occurs in a professional setting, such as a male doctor examining a female patient, or a female physical therapist supporting a

man who is learning to walk, is permitted. Some rabbis also permit men and women shaking hands for social purposes.

Work and Money

1. Avot 2:2.

2. Orach Hashulchan 156.

3. Kiddushin 29a.

4. The prior three paragraphs are summarized from Mishpacha Magazine, Succot 5768.

5. The answer to this question is discussed at length in my book, Why Me, God—A Jewish Approach to Coping with Suffering.

Appendix C: History of the Baal Teshuva Movement

1. Secular historians date the destruction of the First Temple to 586 BCE. Jewish and secular sources differ on dates during this millennium, sometimes by as much as 167 years.

2. The Talmud recounts how Bar Kochba and the Jews he led were initially victorious against the Roman legions. Unfortunately, he came to believe that his cunning and might, and not miraculous Divine assistance, were responsible for his victories. When he became arrogant and told God, "You don't have to make me victorious. Just don't get in my way," God withdrew His Divine assistance with catastrophic consequences. According to Josephus, the Roman legions sent to put down the Revolt starved to death or murdered 580,000 Jews by the time they ended the Revolt in 135 CE.

3. Documents released by the Former Soviet Union around the
   year 2000 indicated that about a million Jews were murdered
   in the FSU during World War II. These Jews were not known
   to have been murdered when statistics of deceased Jews were
   originally compiled. Thus, the actual number of Jews who
   were killed during the Holocaust was closer to seven million.

4. AJOP now stands for the "Association of Jewish Outreach
   Programs," reflecting the fact that Jews do not need to be
   professionals in order to do outreach.

THE AUTHOR

Lisa Aiken was born in Baltimore, MD. She received her MA and PhD in clinical psychology from Loyola University of Chicago. Dr. Aiken was the chief psychologist at Lenox Hill Hospital in New York City in the l980s and had a private psychotherapy practice in New York City for 20 years.

Dr. Aiken is listed in 13 *Who's Who* books, including *Foremost Women of the Twentieth Century*, *Who's Who in the East*, and *Who's Who in Business and Professional Women*. She has also given talks to diverse Jewish audiences in nearly 200 cities worldwide.

Dr. Aiken is a psychologist, author, public speaker, and licensed Israeli tour guide. To order her books, tapes, CDs, or to book her as a tour guide or speaker, contact her at lisaaiken@ymail.com.

OTHER BOOKS AUTHORED OR CO-AUTHORED BY LISA AIKEN:
THE ART OF JEWISH PRAYER
TO BE A JEWISH WOMAN
WHY ME, GOD? A JEWISH GUIDE TO COPING WITH SUFFERING
BEYOND BASHERT: A GUIDE TO DATING AND MARRIAGE ENRICHMENT
THE HIDDEN BEAUTY OF THE SHEMA
WHAT YOUR UNBORN BABY WANTS YOU TO KNOW
GUIDE FOR THE ROMANTICALLY PERPLEXED
TUNING IN
GENESIS: THE UNTOLD STORY